B-1 LANCER

Volumes 1–4
Now Available in the
Walter J. Boyne Military Aircraft Series

F-22 Raptor
America's Next Lethal War Machine
STEVE PACE

B-1 Lancer
The Most Complicated Warplane Ever Developed
DENNIS R. JENKINS

B-24 Liberator
Rugged but Right
FREDERICK A. JOHNSEN

B-2 Spirit
The Most Capable War Machine on the Planet
STEVE PACE

Volumes 5–8 to publish in 2000!

B-1 LANCER

The Most Complicated Warplane
Ever Developed

Dennis R. Jenkins

McGraw-Hill

New York   San Francisco   Washington, D.C.   Auckland   Bogotá
Caracas   Lisbon   London   Madrid   Mexico City   Milan
Montreal   New Delhi   San Juan   Singapore
Sydney   Tokyo   Toronto

Library of Congress Cataloging-in-Publication Data

Jenkins, Dennis R.
    B-1 Lancer : the most complicated warplane ever developed / Dennis
R. Jenkins.
        p.   cm.
    Includes index.
    ISBN 0-07-134694-5
    1. B-1 bomber.   I. Title.
UG1242.B6J46   1999
623.7'463—dc21   99-30207
                                                                        CIP

McGraw-Hill
A Division of The McGraw·Hill Companies

1 2 3 4 5 6 7 8 9 0   KGP/KGP   9 0 4 3 2 1 0 9

ISBN 0-07-134694-5

*The sponsoring editor for this book was Shelley Ingram Carr, the editing
supervisor was Stephen M. Smith, and the production supervisor was Sherri
Souffrance. It was set in Utopia by North Market Street Graphics.*

Printed and bound by Quebecor/Kingsport.

McGraw-Hill books are available at special quantity discounts to use as
premiums and sales promotions, or for use in corporate training programs.
For more information, please write to the Director of Special Sales,
McGraw-Hill, 11 West 19 Street, New York, NY 10011. Or contact your local
bookstore.

This book is printed on acid-free paper.

CONTENTS

FOREWORD	ix
PREFACE	xiii

1. Prehistory: The Genesis of Strategic Bombing — 1

Heir-Apparent: The B-70 Valkyrie	10
XB-70A Flight Testing	16

2. B-1A: The Advanced Manned Strategic Aircraft — 21

Joint Strategic Bomber Study	38
B-1A Flight Testing	42
B-1A Description	47

3. From the Ashes: The B-1B — 57

Cruise Missile Carrier Development	59
Long-Range Combat Aircraft (LRCA)	59
B-1B Flight Testing	63
B-1B Production	65
Test Programs	67
Electromagnetic Pulse	69
B-1B Antenna Measurements	70
Y2K Testing	74
Support Aircraft	75
Operational Service	82
First Combat	87

4. The Science: Construction, Systems, and Weapons — 91

Fuselage	91
Crew Compartment	93
Wings	94
Structural Mode Control System	98

Tail Surfaces   99
Engines   99
Secondary Power System   100
Fuel System   101
Landing Gear System   101
Hydraulic System   102
Central Integrated Test System   103
Automatic Flight Control System   103
Offensive Avionics System   103
Communications and Navigation Equipment   105
Defensive Avionics System   105
Expendable Countermeasures System   110
Color Schemes   110

5. Rethinking the Mission: More Acronyms   **113**

Incidents and Accidents   113
Defensive Avionics System Problems   116
The Air Force and GAO Battle It Out   118
Conventional Mission Upgrade Program   120
Defensive Systems Upgrade Program   132
Summary   133

6. Weapons: Nuclear and Conventional Armament   **135**

Nuclear Rotary Launchers   136
Conventional Weapon Modules   139
External Pylons   139
Nuclear Weapons   140
Cruise Missile Testing   148
Conventional Bombs   151
AGM-154 Joint Standoff Weapon   157
AGM-137 Tri-Service Standoff Attack Missile   158
AGM-158 Joint Air-to-Surface Standoff Missile   159
Mines   159
Practice Bombs   159
Weapons Bay Auxiliary Fuel Tank   160
AGM-86C CALCM   160

Appendix A: B-1A Serial Numbers   **163**
Appendix B: B-1B Production Serial Numbers   **165**
Appendix C: Chronology   **169**
Appendix D: Acronyms and Abbreviations   **173**
Appendix E: World Records   **179**

INDEX   **185**

The McGraw-Hill Companies is pleased to present the **Walter J. Boyne Military Aircraft Series.** The series will feature comprehensive coverage, in words and photos, of the most important military aircraft of our time.

Profiles of aircraft critical to defense superiority in World War II, Korea, Vietnam, the Cold War, the Gulf War, and future theaters detail the technology, engineering, design, missions, and people that give these aircraft their edge. Their origins, the competitions between manufacturers, the glitches and failures, and type modifications are presented along with performance data, specifications, and inside stories.

To ensure that quality standards set for this series are met volume after volume, McGraw-Hill is immensely pleased to have Walter J. Boyne on board. In addition to his overall supervision of the series, Walter is contributing a Foreword to each volume that provides the scope and dimension of the featured aircraft.

Walter was selected as editor because of his international preeminence in the field of military aviation and particularly in aviation history. His consuming, lifelong interest in aerospace subjects is combined with an amazing memory for facts and a passion for research. His knowledge is enhanced by his personal acquaintance with many of the great pilots, designers, and business managers of the aviation industry.

As a Command Pilot in the United States Air Force, Colonel Boyne flew more than 5000 hours in a score of different military and civil aircraft. After his retirement from the Air Force in 1974, he joined the Smithsonian Institution's National Air & Space Museum, where he became Acting Director in 1981 and Director in 1986. Among his accomplishments at the Museum were the conversion of Silver Hill from total disarray to the popular and well-maintained Paul Garber Facility, and the founding of the very successful *Air&Space/ Smithsonian* magazine. He was also responsible for the creation of NASM's large, glass-enclosed restaurant facility. After obtaining permission to install IMAX cameras on the Space Shuttle, he supervised the production of two IMAX films. In 1985, he began the formal process that will lead ultimately to the creation of a NASM restoration facility at Dulles Airport in Virginia.

Boyne's professional writing career began in 1962; since that time he has written more than 500 articles and 28 books, primarily on aviation subjects. He is one of the few authors to have had both fiction and nonfiction books on *The New York Times* best seller lists. His books include four novels, two books on the Gulf War, one book on art, and one on automobiles. His books have been published in Canada, Czechoslovakia, England, Germany, Italy, Japan, and Poland. Several have been made into documentary videos, with Boyne acting as host and narrator.

Boyne has acted as consultant to dozens of museums around the world. His clients also include aerospace firms, publishing houses, and television companies. Widely recognized as an expert on aviation and military subjects, he is frequently interviewed on major broadcast and cable networks, and is often asked by publishers to review manuscripts and recommend for or against publication.

Colonel Boyne will bring his expertise to bear on this series of books by selecting authors and titles, and working closely with the authors during the writing process. He will review completed manuscripts for content, context, and accuracy. His desire is to present well-written, accurate books that will come to be regarded as definitive in their field.

Under normal circumstances, any aircraft with the beauty, performance, and sophistication of the Rockwell B-1B would have been instantly acclaimed by the public, and become, like the Lockheed SR-71, a highly recognized and applauded demonstration of American capability.

Unfortunately, this is not the case with the "Bone," as it is known to its crewmembers. The B-1B, like its predecessor the B-1A, has been subjected to a media roast throughout its career, criticized because it was expensive and with every mishap seized upon with glee. The major difficulty the media had was their inability to grasp just how sophisticated and versatile the B-1B was. The most obvious clue—that 100 B-1Bs were intended to do the task that once required 2000 B-47s or 600 B-52s—was never commented on. Nor was it mentioned that the hostile environment in which the B-1B was intended to operate was vastly more effective (read: dangerous) than any in history.

The aircraft is now proving itself, just as its Rockwell and USAF proponents knew it would. It will, within a few years, have convinced even the most ardent scoffers that, as expensive as it seems, it is still a bargain, for it does what no other bomber can do, and it will do it for decades.

There is no denying that because of changing budgets and normal bureaucratic indecision, the Rockwell B-1B endured a prolonged conception and a protracted gestation. Fortunately, it also experienced an extraordinarily expeditious birth, for the production of 100 B-1Bs was done with speed and style, running ahead of schedule and below cost projections. Because of its sophistication and the high performance demanded of it, the B-1B then had to face a very long development period and a series of organizational and mission changes before it finally engaged in combat.

All during this extended period, which began in 1961, the aircraft was under siege politically. President Jimmy Carter thought so little of it that he cancelled the B-1A program in 1977. Fortunately, President Ronald Reagan saw things differently and ordered the production of 100 aircraft, with a contract signed in January 1982.

No aircraft in history was ever subjected to such an agonizing series of appraisals and reappraisals, and many experts in the industry did not expect the final product to be a worthwhile addition to our bomber fleet. The consensus was that it was simply too much to expect Rockwell to be able to convert the original design into a successful aircraft with a completely different mission profile. Such an undertaking is a prescription for disaster in almost any industry, especially aviation, in which changes come so swiftly. Indeed, the very length of the program presented an unusual handicap. Over time, many of the designers and engineers who had started the project had retired or moved on to other companies. It seemed to many that if ever an aircraft was destined by fate to be turkey, it was the B-1B.

Fortunately, the Bone proved itself in combat, debuting in Operation Desert Fox in December 1998. Its mission there—dropping 500-pound conventional bombs—was far different from the devastating nuclear strike for which it was designed, but it performed well. It did equally well in the difficult air operations against Yugoslavia. However, it is not an exaggeration to say that at least a portion of the media would have been delighted if the B-1B had failed in combat and thus proved all the many charges that had been leveled against it. It is also absolutely accurate to say that the B-1B's successful operation has not received proper notice from the media that have been so critical for so many years.

A long career for the B-1B has just begun. It will be retained as the heart of the American bomber force well into the twenty-first century, and it is entirely possible that it will serve as long or even longer than its predecessor, the Boeing B-52.

As author Dennis R. Jenkins recounts in a brief but comprehensive survey of strategic bombing, the B-52 first flew in 1952 and is programmed to be in service for many years to come. Its longevity stems from its being treated, correctly, as a platform for new weapon systems. The new weapon systems, combined with excellent maintenance programs, have given U. S. taxpayers a rare military bargain in the B-52, although it, too, was long vilified in the media as being a billion-dollar blunder.

Jenkins has done a magnificent job of explaining why the B-1B will be an equivalent bargain over its own long lifespan, for it also has proved itself as a platform, adaptable to virtually every weapon system. He has captured the full story of the Bone, recounting with equal skill all of the many engineering, political, and piloting dramas that have distinguished its career.

The average reader will be startled by the level of detail given by Jenkins in his study of the aircraft. He covers every facet of the B-1B as a machine, describing its structure, aerodynamics, and equipment. He also covers every facet of the B-1B as a weapon, including its ordnance, defensive and offensive systems, and flying characteristics. Further, the author provides this flood of facts in a highly readable, well-illustrated narrative.

I was particularly impressed by Jenkins's work because I have been fascinated by the aircraft for years and thought that I knew quite a bit about it. After finishing the first quarter of the manuscript, I realized this was a mistake, for Jenkins was presenting ideas and details far beyond my knowledge, but essential to a true appreciation of the plane.

In the 1960s, I had worked with the System Program Officers responsible for the Advanced Manned Precision Strike System (AMPSS), and had followed the program over the years. I recall vividly the general indignation felt within the USAF when the B-1A was arbitrarily cancelled, for there was a valid concern that the B-52 might prove to be the last manned bomber.

Perhaps more importantly, I feel close to the aircraft because I have flown it. In November 1989 I was fortunate enough to be allowed to go to Ellsworth Air Force Base, South Dakota, for indoctrination and an introductory flight. My expectations were not high, for the B-1Bs were in an intensive training program, and I would have been grateful if my hosts just put me in the jump seat for most of the mission, with perhaps a little stick time in the right seat at some point.

Instead they rolled out the red carpet and, after some simulator training (during which I crashed on virtually every takeoff), put me in the left seat. Almost immediately after takeoff a fire-warning light came on, and we aborted. I was depressed—some flight, only 10 minutes—until they rolled out a second B-1B for another takeoff and a 4-hour low-level mission that included an aerial refueling. It was a spectacular flight and the aircraft performed beautifully. The crew was brave enough to let me have the controls most of the mission.

However, even more important than the aircraft's performance was that of the flight crew. They were absolutely superb, and, even though I was not allowed to see all of the defensive systems, because of their classification, it was evident that the crew's capability was multiplying the effectiveness of the aircraft's equipment by a factor of three or more. This was an important revelation to me, for at the time the B-1B was taking heavy criticism over the state of its defensive systems. The crew was candid—the installed equipment was not performing to contractual requirements. But they also were forthright in stating—without any braggadocio—that their experience and expertise enabled them to use terrain masking and other techniques to bring their equipment up to standard. They had absolute confidence that they could penetrate to their target, deliver their nuclear weapon accurately, and fly home safely.

The flight was in 1989. In the intervening years, as author Jenkins points out, equipment has been continually modified and upgraded. So have the Air Combat Command crews, who have kept abreast of the changes and bring to the airplane the absolute professionalism that makes the B-1B the backbone of the American bomber fleet.

—Walter J. Boyne

In early December 1998, tensions between the United Nations' weapons inspection teams and Saddam Hussein became unbearable, so on 17 December the United States and Great Britain launched raids against selected military targets in Iraq. On the second night of the raids, two Boeing North American B-1B Lancers were part of a joint service package that attacked a Republican Guard barracks. Thirteen years after the first operational B-1B had been delivered to the Air Force, the aircraft made its combat debut. The B-1B had sat out Operation Desert Storm in 1991 because it was still dedicated to the nuclear deterrent mission. But many things had changed in the intervening 7 years.

The B-1B had always seemed to be an aircraft in search of a mission. For almost 20 years the U.S. Air Force had been trying to find a replacement for the Boeing B-52 Stratofortress. The first serious attempt resulted in the North American B-70 Valkyrie. It was perhaps the most technologically advanced aircraft of its era, but the mission for which it had been designed fell out of favor and the project was largely reduced to a technology demonstration for the stillborn American SST. The next B-52 replacement was the B-1A. This program never managed to gather much political support, even within the Air Force, and was cancelled before the last prototype had flown. The B-52 soldiered on.

In 1980 Ronald Reagan won the presidential election based partially on a platform of rebuilding the American military. When Reagan asked what should finally replace the B-52, visions of an Advanced Technology Bomber equipped with the latest stealth technology was at the top of the Air Force's list. This would entail an extensive design and development program that would last many years. The Air Force knew, however, that the newfound wealth finally finding its way to the military would not last long—maybe not even until the ATB could be fielded.

In an effort to hedge its bet, the Air Force also asked Reagan to fund a production run of 100 "stripped" versions of the cancelled B-1A. The rationale was that most of the development costs, and indeed a great deal of the production tooling, had already been paid for. This was a brilliant ploy, for it would bring about a limited-capability bomber intended to bridge the interim period until the ATB could be fielded.

Reagan approved the idea, and the resulting B-1B development and production program was a model of efficiency. In an era when the F-22 has taken almost 20 years to develop, the entire B-1B effort took only 6 years from the signing of the fist contract to the delivery of the 100th and last aircraft.

But the resulting aircraft was never truly embraced by the Air Force. A less-than-thorough test program resulted in an aircraft with some lingering problems. After standing nuclear alert for 10 years, the B-1B became a dedicated conventional bomber, even though it could not carry precision-guided weapons—or, actually, any nonnuclear weapons other than a large load of Mk 82 "dumb" bombs.

However, the Conventional Munitions Upgrade Program, along with an entire new generation of "smart" weapons, is giving the B-1B a new lease on life. In effect the aircraft has become a very large fighter-bomber. Luckily, at least in lightly loaded configurations, the B-1B has the performance to go with the new mission. According to its pilots, including many who have previously flown F-16s, the B-1B performs much like a large fighter, with plenty of power provided by its four afterburning turbofan engines.

As it enters the new millennium, the B-1B's position in the U.S. bomber force is secure. The production of the Northrop B-2A Spirit ended at 21 aircraft, ensuring that the Advanced Technology Bomber will never be more than an expensive "silver bullet" to be kept in reserve for only the most important missions. And the retirement of all the B-52Gs in the early 1990s has left only 94 B-52Hs in service—although the Air Force has recently predicted they will remain in the active forces until at least the year 2020. This force is bolstered by the 93 remaining B-1Bs, now dedicated to the conventional war-fighting mission.

I would like to thank all the individuals and organizations that have graciously given their time and energy to help with this book. As always, my good friends Mick Roth, Terry Panopalis, Tony Landis, and Erik Simonsen contributed greatly. Another long-time friend, Don Logan, also provided invaluable assistance. Those seeking further information on the B-1 should pick up a copy of Don's excellent book, *Rockwell B-1B: SAC's Last Bomber* (Schiffer Publishing, Ltd., Atglen, Pa., 1994). Douglas Thar, SAF/PAN, Lieutenant Don Kerr at the 7th BW/PA, Major Linda Hutchins at ASC/PA, Alfredia McGill at OC-ALC/PA, and Jake Swinson at Eglin AFB all provided tremendous assistance. Pete Sfameni at AIL provided insight into the trials and tribulations of the ALQ-161 system. Mike Mathews and Mike Lombardy at Boeing provided great support. Sig Grudzinski at Rome Laboratories supplied some great photos of the "upside down Air Force." Dennis Taylor at the Defense Visual Information Center (DVIC) found all the B-1 photos I asked for. Wes Henry and Dave Menard at the Air Force Museum provided their usual exemplary support during my research. Shelley Carr at McGraw-Hill made the entire Walter J. Boyne series possible, and Steve Pace introduced me to Shelley. Cynthia J. Thomas helped distract me periodically, allowing me to keep what small amount of sanity that may remain. And many thanks go to Mary E. Jenkins, my mother, for always encouraging me to try new things.

—DENNIS R. JENKINS

Prehistory: The Genesis of Strategic Bombing

During World War I, the airplane was a relatively new invention that many militaries were unsure what to do with, and its continued development after the War to End All Wars followed a somewhat haphazard course around the world. History has shown that military leaders often seek the weapons that might have won the previous war—it is rare that they envision weapons that might be useful in the next war. One of the exceptions was William Lendrum "Billy" Mitchell, who was an early advocate of air power and of a strong, independent air force. Mitchell commanded the U.S. Army Air Corps during World War I, rising to the rank of Brigadier General.

There were other proponents of air power, including British General Hugh Montague Trenchard and Italian General Giulio Douhet, whose *Command of the Air* (1921) set forth theories that were to form the basis for the future development of military air power. Essentially, these theorists believed that the first function of an air force was to carry the attack beyond the battlefield into the heart of enemy country, destroy the industries that support the opposing armies, and sap the will of the civilian population.

In 1919 Mitchell became assistant chief of the Army Air Service, and in that capacity organized a series of tests to demonstrate the effective use of strategic air power. During 13–21 July 1921, Mitchell's Martin MB-2s performed a series of bombing tests against captured German warships off the Virginia coast. Although conducted against nonmaneuvering ships that were not returning fire, Mitchell nonetheless managed to sink a major warship—a feat previously believed impossible.

The biplane remained dominant for military use until the 1930s. Government sponsorship of monoplane designs, however, exerted such a great influence on airframe design and related engine, propeller, and fuel developments that the monoplane eventually became the only type able to meet the incessant demand for increased aircraft performance. Significant innovations adopted during this period included retractable landing gear, flaps, variable-pitch propellers, and the supercharger. Wars in Ethiopia, Spain, and China during the 1930s enabled the Germans, Italians, Russians, and Japanese to evaluate their new warplanes under battle conditions.

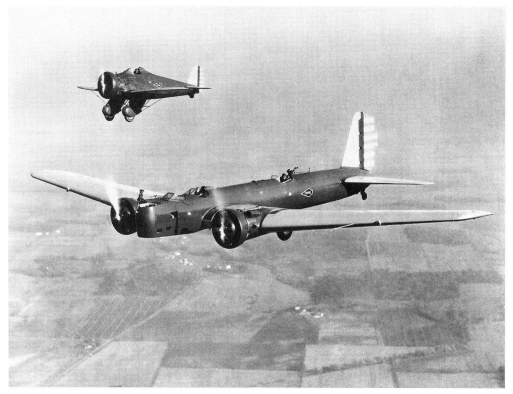

The Boeing Y1B-9A was a major step forward in 1931. Two Pratt & Whitney R-1860 engines developed 600 horsepower each and allowed a top speed of 190 mph—almost 50 mph higher than most contemporary bombers, and equal to many pursuit aircraft of the time (such as the Y1P-26 seen here). This greatly complicated defensive tactics, and gave a very fuzzy look at the future of strategic bombardment. *(Boeing)*

Unconvinced, the conservative American armed forces continued their reliance on more conventional weapons, especially battleships and other sea power. But Mitchell would not be put aside, and his constant criticism of his superiors led to a court-martial in 1925 where he was stripped of his command and reduced in rank. Sentenced to 5 years' suspension from active service, he resigned his commission. As a civilian he continued to lobby for a strong air force, and many of his ideas were accepted and implemented by the outbreak of World War II. Mitchell died on 19 February 1936 at the age of 57. He was posthumously reinstated to the rank of Brigadier General, and today is regarded as one of the principal architects of American air power.

Other armed forces were more farsighted, a fact demonstrated by Germany during the Spanish Civil War of 1936, in which bombers were employed as an integrated element of the blitzkrieg. Fortunately, this German head start was short lived. In anticipation of the upcoming war, the U.S. Army Air Corps was authorized to expand from a peacetime force of 2300 aircraft to 5500. But only a few hundred of these were bombers, mainly older Martin B-10s and Douglas B-18s. However, once World War II began, American industry came up to speed rapidly, and by the end of the war almost 14,000 Boeing B-17 Flying Fortress and 18,000 Consolidated B-24 Liberator heavy bombers had been produced. The Americans and British proved decisively that heavy bombers could take the battle into the heart of the enemy's territory and destroy both its ability and its will to fight.

World War II ended when two Boeing B-29 Superfortresses dropped atomic bombs on Japan. The United States had produced almost 4000 of these heavy bombers, although there were only a handful of atomic bombs in the U.S. arsenal. In this moment, the bomber

The Boeing B-17 Flying Fortress was arguably the most modern bomber available at the beginning of World War II. This restored B-17G shows the extensive defensive armament added to the aircraft during the war. Together with tight formations that allowed cooperative fire from many bombers, the B-17 proved bombers could attack high-value, heavily defended targets—although many times the price was very high. *(Boeing)*

The B-29 could carry 16,000 pounds of bombs over 3500 miles, along with twelve .50-caliber machine guns for defense. A top speed of over 350 mph could be attained at 25,000 feet. The B-29 was the first operational bomber with a pressurized fuselage, allowing combat missions to be flown above the effective range of most antiaircraft artillery. *(Boeing)*

Originally the B-32 had been ordered as "insurance against failure of the B-29," but was not needed in the end. The B-32 entered production without the pressurized cabin and sophisticated defensive armament of the B-29, greatly limiting its effectiveness. The few production examples were scrapped quickly after the end of the war, and none survive today. *(Lockheed Martin)*

had become the single most powerful weapon the world had ever seen. Perhaps Mitchell had been right.

Postwar bomber design was maintained at a surprisingly high level, but production funding was constrained in order to accommodate the rather severe postwar economic slump. Serious interservice rivalry, the end product of these funding constraints, developed between the Air Force and Navy, mostly centering on which service had responsibility for strategic deterrence. Navy arguments stemmed from its firm belief that carrier-borne bombers strategically placed on the world's oceans could more quickly deliver atomic weapons to target areas than conventional bombers based in the continental United States. The Air Force countered that aircraft carriers were exceptionally vulnerable to attack, and carrier-borne bombers were too small to carry the rather large "Fat Man" style atomic weapons then being produced.

General Curtis E. LeMay, a bomber pilot during World War II, became the next champion of American air power when he was appointed commander in chief of the Air Force's Strategic Air Command in 1948. By the mid-1950s neither service had emerged from the strategic weapons delivery argument unquestionably victorious. However, the funding emphasis had shifted in favor of Air Force medium and heavy bombers, underscoring the fact that the responsibility for strategic nuclear weapons delivery had quietly fallen on the Air Force side of the fence.

But things did not always work as planned. The protracted development of the Convair B-36 very-heavy bomber, caused by funding and priority considerations during the last years of World War II, resulted in an aircraft that was largely obsolete by the time it entered operational service. Although the B-36 undoubtedly played a large part in deterrence during the 1950s, it is questionable how effective it would have been in combat. It was, how-

The possibility existed during the early years of World War II that the United States would need to attack Europe or Japan directly from North America. This would require an extremely long-range bomber, and Convair was awarded a contract to develop the B-36. Although the course of the war would eliminate much of the need for the aircraft, development continued at a very slow pace. At the end of the war a new reason had been found for the aircraft—delivering the new, and very heavy, atomic bombs. *(Convair via Don Pyeatt)*

The end, and the beginning. The B-36 was the last piston-powered heavy bomber; the Boeing B-52 was the first all-jet heavy bomber. *(Via the Tony Landis Collection)*

The medium bomber force received a significant boost in performance with the introduction of the Boeing B-47 Stratojet. With a top speed of over 600 mph, the B-47 was effectively as fast as many contemporary fighters, and was capable of carrying most of the smaller nuclear weapons in the inventory. *(Boeing)*

The Boeing B-50 was a development of the World War II B-29 using more powerful engines and improved systems. A large body of opinion within the Air Force considered it superior to the B-36, but it could not fly as far or carry as heavy a load. *(Boeing)*

Unlike the B-36, the B-50 was adapted for aerial refueling, shown here with a KC-97. Interestingly, both aircraft were derivatives of the B-29 and shared many common systems. In-flight refueling overcame many of the handicaps associated with the B-50, and would also allow a different approach for future all-jet aircraft. *(Boeing)*

ever, the only platform capable of carrying the newly developed hydrogen bombs. Continued debate between the Air Force and Navy over the B-36's role largely overshadowed its contribution as a deterrent.

The B-36 clearly demonstrated the factor that had often made the bomber vulnerable to the fighter-interceptor—a large disparity in performance. Even 1950-era radar had no trouble detecting a high-flying bomber at ranges in excess of 50 miles. This gave the defending fighters 10 to 15 minutes to launch and climb to an appropriate intercept altitude. It should be noted that, as well proven in World War II, finding the bombers was one thing—shooting them down was something else altogether. But as the probability of the bomber completing its mission was eroded, so too was its credibility.

In August 1953, when the Soviet Union exploded its first hydrogen bomb, it was LeMay who oversaw the swift introduction of new jet bombers to replace the propeller-driven B-29s, B-36s, and B-50s (an improved B-29) that still equipped the Strategic Air Command (SAC). Rising world tensions prompted the hurried introduction of the jet-powered Boeing B-47 Stratojet medium bomber, resulting in an aircraft that had many flaws and was largely unsuited to the role forced upon it. Later modifications resulted in extremely capable versions of the B-47, but a great deal of time and money was wasted in the process. Nevertheless, just over 2000 B-47s were produced between 1947 and 1957, although most had been removed from front-line service by mid-1960s.

The replacement for the B-47 did not fare much better. The 116 Convair B-58 Hustlers were a technological triumph—a supersonic bomber that was as fast as any contemporary fighter. But it had pushed the state of the art a little too far, and was a maintenance nightmare. A short 10 years after its introduction it was removed from service and unceremoniously scrapped.

But for all the missteps taken, one aircraft was developed that will forever be linked to strategic bombardment. The Boeing B-52 Stratofortress was the first all-jet heavy bomber

The world's first supersonic bomber was the Convair B-58 Hustler. Although it was a stellar performer, the aircraft pushed the state of the art a little too far and was a maintenance nightmare. This resulted in a short 10 years of operational service before the aircraft were retired and quickly scrapped. *(U.S. Air Force)*

to become operational with the Air Force. Essentially a design derivative of the B-47 begun during the late 1940s, the XB-52 (49-230) was rolled out in great secrecy during the night of 29 November 1951, although the YB-52 beat it into the air, making its first flight on 15 April 1952. Offering the Air Force high performance at altitude, true intercontinental range, inflight refueling, and large payload capacity, it was the first heavy bomber design truly to exploit LeMay's vision of strategic air power.

Given that the B-52 has seemingly been around forever and is always present during world crises, it seems hard to believe that only 744 B-52s were manufactured in Seattle and Wichita, and all except the 295 "short tail" B-52G/H models were removed from service by the mid-1970s. The B-52G/H proved remarkably adaptable to changing tactics and missions. Originally designed to fly high-altitude missions with free-fall nuclear bombs, the B-52 was soon adapted to an early standoff (cruise) missile—the North American GAM-77 (later AGM-28) Hound Dog. The B-52H was designed to carry the stillborn Douglas GAM-87 Skybolt ballistic missile, although it too ended up carrying Hound Dogs. When high-altitude tactics lost favor after the Soviets developed an effective defense system, the B-52G/H was adapted to low-level "oil burner" missions. Later enhancements included low-light television and forward-looking infrared systems to help pilots fly at extremely low altitudes. The aircraft were constantly updated with new electronic countermeasures equipment and radios. When a new generation of air-launch cruise missiles was developed in the mid-1970s, the B-52G/H became the launch platform of choice. The aircraft were later adapted to carry precision-guided munitions and antiship missiles.

The B-52's operational career has exceeded, by far, anything envisioned when the aircraft was designed. At the time, the Air Force anticipated retiring the bombers around 1965

The aircraft that will forever be linked to the strategic bombardment mission is the Boeing B-52 Stratofortress. First flown in 1952, the B-52 is currently projected to remain in first-line service until the year 2020—almost 70 years. This B-52H shows the 1998 configuration of the aircraft. *(U.S. Air Force)*

The B-52 has proven remarkably adaptable to weapons that were not even on the drawing board when the aircraft was designed. A variety of standoff missiles, cruise missiles, and precision-guided munitions have been carried by the B-52 over the years, in addition to a full range of nuclear and conventional bombs. This early configuration B-52H is shown with a load of AGM-69A SRAMs under the wing. *(U.S. Air Force)*

An early standoff missile was the AGM-28 Hound Dog. The inability of the B-70 to carry this and similar weapons played a part in the aircraft's cancellation. The B-52 made extensive use of aerial refueling, and stood nuclear alert for almost 40 years as part of the American strategic triad of deterrent forces. *(U.S. Air Force)*

as newer designs became available. This was in keeping with the average replacement cycle that had been observed for the previous couple of decades. But political, economic, and technological considerations would cause the B-52 to remain in frontline service for nearly half a century. During an October 1998 rapid deployment to the Persian Gulf in response to a new Iraqi crisis, cruise-missile-equipped B-52Hs were the only aircraft ready to press the attack upon arrival. Two months later they were instrumental in a series of raids on Iraq. Although the last B-52H was accepted by the Air Force in 1962, recent plans show 50 to 90 aircraft remaining in service until well after the turn of the millennium.

The B-52, of course, was not the only bomber developed during the three decades from 1950 to 1980. In fact, a significant number were designed, especially during the 1950s, and on several occasions production contracts were awarded and executed. One example was the General Dynamics FB-111A, which started out as a large interdiction fighter (hence its rather odd designation). Although they would remain in service for 20 years, the 76 FB-111As were never truly embraced by SAC, and were immediately sold to Australia (as F-111Gs) upon their retirement. Other examples include the Martin B-57 Canberra and Douglas B-66 Destroyer, medium bombers that proved remarkably adaptable to a variety of missions.

Heir-Apparent: The B-70 Valkyrie

In October 1954, LeMay put forth a mission requirement for an advanced jet heavy bomber to replace the upcoming B-52 and B-58 beginning in 1965. LeMay wanted a bomber that had the range and payload-carrying capability of the B-52, combined with the supersonic speed of the B-58. The Air Research and Development Command (ARDC) responded by issuing weapon system requirements WS-110A and WS-125A during February 1955. These called for advanced bombers that would have a Mach 0.9 cruise speed to an area some 1150 miles from their target, then "dash" at Mach 2-plus to the target at high altitude, slowing again to Mach 0.9 for the trip home. The WS-110A was to use conventional jet fuel, while the WS-125A was to be nuclear powered. SAC wanted one, or both, of these advanced bombers to be operational by 1963.

On 16 July 1955 Boeing, Convair, Douglas, Lockheed, Martin, and North American were awarded preliminary study contracts. Based on the results of these preliminary studies, Convair and Lockheed were selected to pursue the WS-125A nuclear-powered bomber. Since Martin and Douglas were busy developing new intercontinental ballistic missiles (ICBM), on 11 November 1955 two WS-110A study contracts were issued to Boeing and North American. On 9 December 1955, these contracts were expanded to include the construction of full-scale engineering mock-ups and additional wind tunnel studies. Curtiss-Wright, General Electric, Pratt & Whitney, and Rolls-Royce began studying suitable power plants.

Boeing and North American presented their initial WS-110A designs to the ARDC during October 1956. In order to meet the range and supersonic dash requirements, both designs were large, even by heavy bomber standards. Boeing's design had a gross takeoff weight of 610,000 pounds, while North American's weighed nearly 750,000 pounds. Each design featured "floating wingtips," a term originally coined by Boeing to describe winged fuel tanks about the size of a B-47's fuselage and weighing 190,000 pounds each. They were attached to the bomber's wingtips for the early subsonic cruise portion of the mission, and were jettisoned just prior to commencing the supersonic run to the target. Each of these three-part aircraft was 150 feet long, spanned about 260 feet, and stood approximately 40 feet high. Boeing's design used four General Electric X275 turbojet engines, while North American opted for six of the same engine.

It took four months for the Air Force to evaluate the two WS-110A designs, and, on 11 March 1957, both were rejected as too large and complex. Both study contracts were extended and the contractors went back to the drawing boards. During mid-1957, both contractors elected to use a high-energy chemical "zip" fuel that contained boron. Adding boron to a conventional petroleum-based fuel increased both speed and range, and brought the new title "chemically powered bomber (CPB)" to the competition. With six GE X279E engines using the new boron fuel, Mach 3 cruise at 70,000 feet became possible, and unrefueled range increased to 8750 miles.

The original North American WS-110 concept was a three-part aircraft. Each of the "wingtips" was essentially a flying fuel tank that would be jettisoned from the main aircraft prior to penetrating enemy airspace. The large canard caused concern because it seriously blocked the pilots' forward vision. *(North American Aviation)*

North American's design now featured a large delta wing with wingtips that could be folded downward during flight to capture the shock wave generated by the forebody, creating additional "compression lift" at supersonic speeds. A large forward canard helped trim the aircraft in flight and lowered landing speed, while a two-position windscreen could be lowered to improve visibility during takeoff and landing. Gross takeoff weight was estimated at 500,000 pounds.

Boeing proposed a 200-foot-long delta-winged design with retractable canards that resembled the Bomarc surface-to-air missile. Gross takeoff weight had dropped to a more reasonable 499,500 pounds. Boeing was also aware of NACA's work on compression lift, but was highly skeptical of the theoretical figures generated by NACA and elected not to use the concept in its design.

Boeing and North American resubmitted their proposals in August 1957, and, on 23 December 1957, North American was selected as the winner of the WS-110A competition. Boeing protested the decision, but a congressional inquiry determined that the competition had been fairly conducted, and the Air Force's decision was upheld. On 2 January 1958 North American received a full-scale development contract (AF-36599). In a departure from past practice, North American was made the prime contractor for the entire WS-110A program, except for the engines, which were separately contracted to General Electric.

At the end of 1957, the WS-125A nuclear-powered bomber program was cancelled. The technical challenges were tremendous and would cost an inordinate amount of money to solve—money the Air Force believed could be better spent on the WS-110A and ICBMs. At the same time the Air Force announced an 18-month acceleration in the WS-110A program and moved the first flight up from December 1963 to December 1961. SAC was to receive its first aircraft in December 1963, and its first combat-ready wing would be available by August 1964. On 6 February 1958, the new aircraft was officially designated XB-70, and on

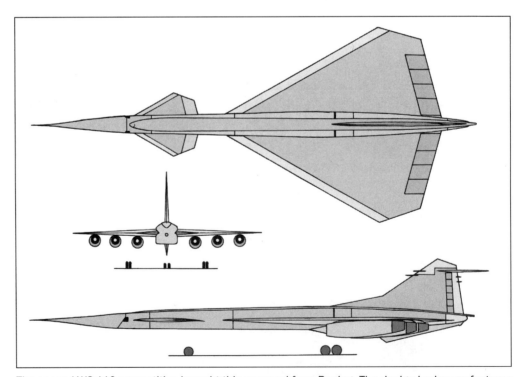

The second WS-110 competition brought this proposal from Boeing. The design had many features that would later show up on the Boeing 773 SST, particularly the wing and engine nacelle shapes. Since Boeing had been the Air Force's primary supplier of heavy bombers for nearly three decades, it was somewhat surprising that they lost the B-70 competition. *(Boeing)*

The North American XB-70A Valkyrie was the fastest, highest-flying bomber ever built. The aircraft's Mach 3 performance was faster than any other aircraft in the U.S. inventory except the Lockheed Blackbirds. The test pad the aircraft is sitting on at Edwards AFB would later be used by the B-1 during its test program. *(NASA via the Tony Landis Collection)*

3 July SAC officially named the new bomber "Valkyrie." On 31 December 1958, North American was issued a contract (AF-38669) to construct a single XB-70 flight test aircraft.

By midsummer 1959, GE had successfully flight tested the first YJ93-GE-5 engine using the new boron-laced fuel. But on 10 August 1959 the boron chemical fuel program, along with the YJ93-GE-5, was cancelled, largely because of technical difficulties encountered during development, and the fact that the engine was not proving as powerful or economical as predicted. Various environmental concerns and difficulties handling the toxic fuel also contributed to the decision. However, GE had also developed a YJ93-GE-3 version that burned conventional JP-4 fuel. Without the boron additive, the B-70's range would be reduced by 10 percent, but a single in-flight refueling by a KC-135 still allowed the bomber to meet its 8078-mile mission requirement.

In Washington, budgetary and political considerations were forcing a general reexamination of U.S. defense spending. During the late 1950s and early 1960s, ICBMs began to emerge as reliable weapons that were much less expensive than manned bombers to build (however, their development costs are now acknowledged to be the single most expensive project in U.S. military history). Their perceived lower cost, coupled with the fact that pilots would not be placed in harm's way, strongly enticed civilian planners. On 3 December 1959, the results of a year-long task force study were released that cast serious doubts on the manned bomber program. Budget director Maurice Stans was searching for a way of balancing the budget during Eisenhower's last year in office. He seized upon the task force study to show the manned bomber could no longer compete with the ICBM as an offensive weapons system. The missile-versus-bomber debates were born.

Pro-missile advocates argued that their lower cost, pinpoint accuracy, intercontinental range, and rapid reaction time made ICBMs superior to manned bombers. Pro-bomber advocates countered with the fact that manned bombers could be recalled; they submitted that once an ICBM was launched it was committed to strike its programmed target. Moreover, they argued that since an ICBM required a mere 30 minutes to reach its target, there wouldn't be time for negotiations, and an all-out nuclear confrontation could ensue. Bombers could also be deployed as a "show of force," much like battleships of a previous era, and were useful in conventional conflicts in which an ICBM was worthless. These arguments grew heated and resulted in a serious division of opinion within the military and Department of Defense (DoD).

The end result of this round of missile-versus-bomber debates was that the B-70 program was cancelled. Only the single XB-70 prototype under construction, GE's work on the YJ93-GE-3 engine, and IBM's preliminary work on the AN/ASQ-28 bombing-navigation system would continue, albeit at a very reduced level. All other subcontracts were terminated. The single XB-70 was rescheduled to fly in December 1962, a one-year delay. Various modifications for the B-52 force were also approved.

However, persuasive arguments from Air Force Chief of Staff Thomas White and Deputy Chief of Development Roscoe C. Wilson led Congress to authorize additional funding for the B-70 program. On 31 July 1960, Congress approved an additional $75 million, increasing total FY61 appropriations to $365 million. This made it possible to complete the XB-70 prototype, provide a static test airframe, reinstate most subcontractor work, and build 12 operational B-70s. General Wilson, who hoped for possible "squadron strength" by 1966, said, "While we need the brute power of ICBMs, they lack the flexibility essential to winning a military victory. We will continue to need manned aircraft to seek out hidden and mobile targets, to restrike residual targets, and perform a variety of other tasks. We look forward to the B-70, which is now under development, as the essential partner of the ICBMs." On 21 September 1960, North American received a contract (AF-42058) to build a single preproduction YB-70 to supplement the prototype XB-70. The second aircraft would feature a complete avionics and weapons system, and include provisions for an operational four-man crew. Overall B-70 costs had increased to a projected $1300 million.

But the reprieve was short-lived. Soon after President John F. Kennedy took office, he followed the recommendation of his Secretary of Defense, Robert S. McNamara, and again cancelled the B-70 program. Kennedy released an official statement in March 1961 that said, in part, that America's forthcoming missile capabilities ". . . makes unnecessary and economically unjustifiable the development of the B-70 as a full weapons system at this time." The President further recommended that the B-70 program ". . . be carried forward, essentially to explore the problems of flying at three times the speed of sound with an airframe potentially useful as a bomber, through the development of a small number of prototype aircraft and related bombing and navigation systems."

Thus, on 10 April 1961, the B-70 program was reduced to two XB-70A aircraft (62-0001 and 62-0207). On 31 July 1961, the $365 million amount already allocated was trimmed to $75 million, and the XB-70A's first flight was delayed again, this time to December 1963. The meager $75-million budget covered only a single XB-70A, and the second aircraft was on hold pending additional funding.

In January 1962, McNamara defined the government's position when he said, "Considering the increasing capabilities of surface-to-air interceptor missiles, the speed and altitude of the B-70 would no longer be a very significant advantage. Furthermore, it has been designed without the adaptive capabilities of using air-to-surface missiles such as the Hound Dog and Skybolt, and in a low-altitude attack it must fly at subsonic speeds. In addition, the B-70 is not well suited to an era in which both sides have large numbers of ICBMs.

It would be more vulnerable on the ground than hardened missiles, and it does not lend itself to airborne alert measures."

These points were largely valid, if somewhat overemphasized. It was true the B-70 could not easily be adapted to the two air-to-ground missiles then in development to equip the B-52 and RAF V-bombers. Due to its speed, carrying external missiles on the B-70 was not feasible, and the missiles were too large for the weapons bay. And although the XB-70A would later prove to be capable of low-level flight, the airframe was not designed to endure it frequently (but then, neither was the B-52's), and the lack of terrain-following radar meant the pilot had to fly manually—a difficult task under the best conditions. But even though the mission the B-70 had been designed for had gone out of favor, the aircraft still represented a potent weapons system. The later development of smaller standoff missiles that could be carried internally might have produced a truly awesome combination. In any event, it was not to be.

A last ditch effort to rescue the program was made when the Air Force changed the aircraft's designation to "reconnaissance-strike," creating the RS-70. Using the ruse of a new mission, the Air Force proposed acquiring 60 operational RS-70s by 1969, at an estimated cost of $50 million each. Another 150 were to be delivered during the 1970s. Other than the addition of a limited reconnaissance capability, these aircraft were essentially identical to the already cancelled B-70.

In July 1963, the House Armed Services Committee requested $491 million for three RS-70 prototypes. Congress, however, only authorized $275.9 million. The "RS" classification was subsequently dropped, and the funds were used to complete the two XB-70As previously ordered. By the end of the year it was clear there was no chance the B-70 would enter production and that the only function of the two XB-70As would be to serve as development platforms for the American Supersonic Transport (SST). The B-70 had become a sheep in wolf's clothing.

On 11 May 1964, the first XB-70 was rolled out at North American's facility (Site 3) at Air Force Plant 42 in Palmdale, California. Even on the ground, the futuristic-looking aircraft appeared to be traveling 2000 mph. Yet what had started as an advanced SAC bomber some 10 years earlier was already considered obsolete—and it hadn't even flown.

The XB-70A used a 6297-square-foot delta-shaped wing equipped with large folding wingtips. As speed increased, the wingtips were lowered to 65° anhedral to capture the shock wave under the wing and generate additional lift. This configuration also improved directional stability and allowed the twin vertical stabilizers to be smaller than otherwise required. A large canard was used to counteract trim changes occurring between stall (150 knots) and Mach 3 cruise. Six General Electric YJ93-GE-3 afterburning turbojet engines were mounted side by side in the aft section of a 35-foot-wide fuselage bay. Two variable-geometry air intake inlets located under the wing just behind the leading edge provided air for the engines. The under-wing fuselage contained fuel, landing gear, and a large weapons bay. A slim upper fuselage extended from the top of the delta wing and contained the cockpit, avionics, more fuel, and provided the mounting location for the canard.

Approximately 68 percent of each XB-70A's structural weight consisted of stainless steel, and the brazed stainless-steel honeycomb-sandwich-panel skin construction was probably one of the aircraft's most controversial features. North American believed these panels were light, strong, and had excellent insulation qualities, but flight testing revealed that the panels suffered from skin detachment at high speed. Both XB-70As experienced this several times, the worst incident occurring when the first aircraft lost a triangular section of its wing apex forward of its splitter plate and air inlets, causing severe engine damage. The aircraft later lost a 40- by 36-inch piece of skin from the underside of its left wing, and an 8- by 38-inch strip from its right fuselage section later still. Loss of these skin panels occurred

Six General Electric J-93 engines provided the power to propel the XB-70 to over 2000 mph, at least for short periods of time. North American elected to use a stainless steel honeycomb construction instead of the titanium used by Lockheed in their Blackbirds. This resulted in some problems during the flight test program when sections of the skin delaminated and separated at high speed. *(Tony Landis Collection)*

when thermal expansion during supersonic flight weakened the metallic bond between the panel's face sheet where the brazing was too thin or poorly formed, which led to the skin cover separating from the core.

North American engineers traced the immediate problem to insufficient quality control during the fabrication process. Earlier test samples of the material had not demonstrated the problem, probably because they had been manufactured in small batches under almost laboratory conditions. Translating these manufacturing processes into the large-scale production necessary to build an aircraft the size of the XB-70A had been more difficult than expected. Improved fabrication techniques coupled with rigid quality control measures significantly reduced the problem on the second XB-70A. Nevertheless, at least one large piece did separate from the upper surface of the second aircraft's right wing during high-speed flight. This construction technique would have required more experience to perfect, and it is likely a different material would have been found if the Valkyrie had entered production.

Several other problems were encountered during construction of the XB-70As, including difficulties sealing the fuel tanks. The fuel tank ullage was purged with gaseous nitrogen to reduce the possibility of fire or explosion. But North American could not find a sealant that resisted both JP-4 and high heat to use around the hydraulic lines and electrical wires, which ran through fuel tanks. After 18 months of experimentation, Viton B sealant was found to resist the leaks. It is interesting to note that Lockheed experienced similar problems with the A-12/SR-71, but since the low-vapor-pressure JP-7 fuel was fairly immune to fire, Lockheed simply let the Blackbirds leak.

XB-70A Flight Testing

Originally intended to fly in 1961, then 1962, then 1963, the first XB-70A finally made its maiden flight on 21 September 1964. To enable North American to collect a $250,000 bonus, the aircraft had to meet certain milestones during this flight, including a Mach 1 dash at 35,000 feet. At the controls were North American's chief engineering test pilot Alvin S. White and Air Force project pilot Colonel Joseph F. Cotton. Following rotation, the canard flaps and nose landing gear retracted as expected.

However, the main gear refused to retract, and the nose gear was eventually reextended with all three landing gear remaining down for the rest of the flight. It was decided to proceed on a preplanned low-speed test flight, but the No. 3 engine soon experienced problems that required it to be shut down. Following a 1-hour, 7-minute flight on five engines, White landed the aircraft at nearby Edwards AFB. As the aircraft rolled out, the two rear wheels on the left main bogie refused to rotate, blowing the tires and starting a small fire. The fire department quickly extinguished the fire, and repairs were accomplished with minimal delay to the test program. Needless to say, North American did not collect the bonus money.

On 17 July 1965, the second XB-70A joined the flight test program. On its maiden flight, the aircraft achieved Mach 1.41 at 42,000 feet; by its eighth test flight it had attained Mach 2.34 at 57,500 feet. The second aircraft differed from the first in several important respects. The wing was mounted at a 3° dihedral, eliminating a slight instability suffered by the first aircraft. The fuel tanks were better sealed, the honeycomb skin had fewer flaws in it, and a complete set of avionics was included, evidenced from the outside by a large dielectric panel under the extreme nose. A sophisticated automatic air inlet control system was also provided in place of the manual system used on the first aircraft.

Finally, on 14 October 1965, the first XB-70A achieved its design speed of Mach 3.02 (2000 mph) at 70,000 feet. Then, on 3 January 1966, the second XB-70A reached Mach 3.05 at 72,000 feet. Interestingly, both aircraft had reached their Mach 3 goal on their 17th flights. On 19 May 1966, demonstrating its high-speed capabilities, the second XB-70A cruised at Mach 3 for 32 minutes, covering eight states in the process.

The National Sonic Boom Program (NSBP) was set up to measure the effects of controlled sonic booms, along with other tests such as maneuvers associated with anticipated SST flight envelopes. Government and private researchers would evaluate the psychological reaction and structural damage associated with sonic booms from large supersonic aircraft. The test series was directed by NASA, managed by the Air Force, and used Air Force facilities at Edwards. The second XB-70A was selected to perform sonic boom tests because it more nearly approximated the Boeing 773 SST's size than smaller aircraft such as the B-58 or F-104 that were used earlier.

The NSBP had begun on 6 June 1966 with the second XB-70A performing the initial sonic boom test at Mach 3.05 and 72,000 feet. On 8 June 1966, the No. 2 XB-70A was making the second NSBP test flight, the 95th of the B-70 program. Al White was in the pilot seat for his

Like all delta-wing aircraft, the XB-70 landed very nose-high. The program used a B-58 as a chase aircraft, but even the Mach 2+ Hustler was quickly left behind as the XB-70 streaked towards its maximum speed. *(NASA via the Tony Landis Collection)*

The six large elevons on each wing provided control during all flight regimes. Unusually, the canards had trailing edge flaps to lower landing speeds. The XB-70 was a large aircraft, with a take-off weight of over 500,000 pounds—almost five times the weight of a Blackbird. *(NASA via the Tony Landis Collection)*

49th time, while Major Carl S. Cross was making his first XB-70A flight. The flight test objectives consisted of 12 subsonic airspeed calibration runs and a single supersonic test run, after which White and Cross were to rendezvous with a contingent of GE-powered aircraft for a publicity photo shoot. General Electric had obtained Air Force approval to organize the formation of aircraft around the XB-70A on a noninterference basis. A Northrop F-5A and T-38A, a McDonnell F-4B, and a Lockheed F-104N were to form up with the XB-70A while a Learjet loaded with photographers recorded the event.

Cameras began clicking at 08:45 a.m. and the photo session was over at 09:25. But at 09:26, aircraft radios crackled frantically "mid-air . . . mid-air . . . mid-air." Somehow, the F-104N had hit the XB-70A, and neither would recover from the collision. NASA's Joseph A. Walker, in the F-104N, and Cross, in the XB-70A, were killed. Al White managed to eject from the XB-70A, but his escape capsule partially malfunctioned, leaving him seriously injured. The loss of the pilots dealt a severe blow to the flight test community at Edwards, and the loss of the more-capable of the Valkyries adversely affected the continuation of the test program.

The first XB-70A had been undergoing refurbishment and upgrading when the accident occurred. During this downtime, the aircraft received a $2 million improvement to its escape capsules and an automated inlet control system similar to the one installed in the second aircraft. But nothing could be done about its fragile wing skins, or the slight instability caused by its wing placement. Although there were some doubts that the aircraft could achieve all of the goals previously established for the NSBP, there was no other suit-

The Valkyrie used an aerodynamic phenomenon known as "compression lift" to achieve its performance. A shock wave generated by the forward fuselage was captured under the folding wingtips, increasing the available lift at high altitudes and high speeds. The second aircraft is shown here, discernable by the black dielectric panel under the nose for the offensive avionics system. *(NASA via the Tony Landis Collection)*

able aircraft and the first XB-70A made its first flight of the program on 3 November 1966. Eleven flight tests were flown before the Air Force announced they were withdrawing from the program and NASA took over as the sole sponsor.

Between the end of January and early April 1967, additional instrumentation designed to measure structural response to gusts, stability and control, and boundary layer noise was installed on the remaining XB-70A. The first NASA flight occurred on 25 April 1967 with Joe Cotton and Fitz Fulton at the controls. Twenty-three test flights were carried out by NASA, and the highest speed attained during this phase was Mach 2.55 at 67,000 feet. Earlier, NASA had hoped for SST flight research at Mach 3.0, but continued problems with skin losses during high Mach flight placed a Mach 2.5 limit on the first XB-70A. Research continued until the end of 1968.

On 4 February 1969, the first XB-70A was ferried to the Air Force Museum at Wright-Patterson AFB, Ohio. Prior to its final landing, pilots Fitz Fulton and Ted Sturmthal made a farewell pass over the field. The log book showed 83 flights totaling 160 hours, 18 minutes when Fulton turned the aircraft over to the museum curator.

The total cost of the B-70 program has been reported as $1500 million, averaging approximately $11.6 million for each of the 129 flight tests made by the two aircraft. It was this staggering fact that may have prompted Sturmthal to comment, "I'd do anything to keep the B-70 in the air, except pay for it myself."

B-1A: The Advanced Manned Strategic Aircraft

Budgetary restrictions and the Eisenhower and Kennedy Administrations' clear belief that ICBMs were the strategic weapons of the future partially explained why the B-70 did not go to production. Interestingly, although the cost of developing the Atlas and Titan ICBMs was orders of magnitude greater than any proposed manned bomber program, the missile was perceived as a less costly deterrent. General Thomas S. Power, Commander-in-Chief of SAC, offered another reason: the B-70 was designed for flight at very high altitudes—an advantage when the aircraft was first conceived, but which had lost favor when the Soviet Union developed effective high-altitude antiaircraft missiles. This change in attitude had begun shortly after Gary Powers's U-2 was shot down in May 1960, although it is arguable that an "effective" missile defense was responsible for downing the aircraft. The Air Force nevertheless continued to insist that manned bombers would continue as a necessary part of the United States' "strategic triad" deterrent capability, and several studies were undertaken to investigate the B-70's perceived deficiencies. The Air Force still needed to find a replacement for the B-52.

The first of the post-B-70 studies was completed in 1961. Known as the Subsonic Low Altitude Bomber (SLAB), the study determined that a fixed-wing aircraft with a gross take-off weight of 500,000 pounds and a 12,500-mile range, including 5000 miles at low altitude, was needed. A useful payload of only 12,000 pounds was found necessary, underscoring accomplishments in reducing the weight of thermonuclear weapons. The mission profile for SLAB was decidedly different than the one for the B-70 had been. Instead of trying to fly over defenses, which was proving to be harder than expected, the bomber would fly *under* defenses. By flying fast and low, it was unlikely that radar would detect the aircraft until it was too late to do much about it. And most surface-to-air missiles of the period were basically worthless at low altitudes, leaving only antiaircraft artillery to worry about.

Next came the Extended Range Strike Aircraft (ERSA), a 1963 study that determined that a 600,000-pound aircraft using a variable-geometry wing was necessary. Although the aircraft gross weight had increased, both the payload (10,000 pounds) and range (10,000 miles, with 3000 miles at 500-foot altitude) had decreased. In August 1963, the Low Altitude

Manned Penetrator (LAMP) study was completed, recommending a 350,000-pound aircraft with a 7100-mile range, including 2300 miles at low altitude. The payload of LAMP increased to 20,000 pounds, an acknowledgment that the aircraft might have to carry conventional weapons at some point. Although all of these concepts included a low-level interdiction capability, they also continued the high-speed, high-altitude capability that had traditionally defined the strategic bomber.

During mid-1963, a Manned Aircraft Studies Steering Group headed by Lieutenant General James Ferguson (Deputy Chief of Staff, Research and Development) examined various possibilities for a B-52 replacement. These included long-endurance subsonic aircraft, supersonic reconnaissance aircraft, and eventually LAMP, which the steering group somewhat belatedly recognized as a promising concept.

In the meantime, another major Air Force effort to determine its future needs was making progress. Project Forecast had been initiated in 1963 under the direction of General Bernard A. Schriever, Commander of the Air Force Systems Command and an advocate of acquiring an advanced manned bomber.

In October 1963, Ferguson, Schriever, and Lieutenant General William H. Blanchard (Deputy Chief of Staff, Programs and Requirements) met with other members of Project Forecast and the Manned Aircraft Studies Steering Group. The two organizations, after debating such factors as size and payload, eventually reached conclusions that were to provide the foundation for a new bomber, now termed the Advanced Manned Precision Strike System (AMPSS).

During November 1963, the Air Force released requests for proposals (RFPs) to Boeing, General Dynamics, and North American Aviation. However, Secretary of Defense Robert S. McNamara questioned the validity of the assumptions used by the Air Force to justify the AMPSS procurement, and only $5 million was made available. Because of this, the three contractors were limited to preliminary conceptual studies. Nevertheless, AMPSS became the first study to define the elements that would eventually dictate the design and mission objectives of any future bomber. The AMPSS study called for an evaluation of the technical feasibility of four aircraft concepts: (1) all subsonic low-altitude; (2) subsonic low-altitude with a medium-supersonic (Mach ~ 1.5) high-altitude capability; (3) subsonic low-altitude with a high-supersonic (Mach > 2.0) high-altitude capability; and (4) subsonic with a vertical/short takeoff and landing (V/STOL) capability. All of the concepts had to be capable of being based at relatively austere, dispersed sites and had to have a rapid reaction time to eliminate the airborne alerts being flown by the B-52.

Some of the tentative requirements outlined by the Air Force were quickly questioned by all of the contractors. The V/STOL concept in particular was not deemed feasible for an aircraft with the heavy gross weight required for an intercontinental bomber, and was eliminated from further consideration. The need to further study any high-speed high-altitude designs was also questioned, based on the B-70 experience. In any case, the industry's negative comments proved academic—by the time the results of the three studies had been received in mid-1964, the requirements had changed, yet again.

Although the bomber concept remained essentially unchanged, some of the requirements had been substantially redefined, resulting in the Advanced Manned Strategic Aircraft (AMSA). The Air Force had already decided that AMSA should be capable of high-subsonic, low-altitude penetration, and also be capable of Mach 2+ at higher altitudes. Ideally, a way would be found to allow supersonic speeds at low altitudes, further enhancing the aircraft's survivability. The original requirements to operate from austere dispersal sites and rapid reaction times remained unchanged, but a new emphasis on "hardening" the aircraft against the effects of electromagnetic pulse (EMP) was added.

The original AMPSS contracts were modified to include studies by all three contractors into the AMSA concept. The AMSA program called for five concurrent studies, each with a

This was one of the North American designs for the Advanced Manned Penetrating Strategic System (AMPSS) during the early 1960s. The extreme sweep on the wings and the unusual "sideways" box air inlets are noteworthy. *(Boeing North American via Steve Pace)*

long list of separate criteria, such as crew factors, maintainability, reliability, survivability, vulnerability, limited war analysis, design trade studies, titanium cost versus benefits analysis, alternate armament loading, and a bomber decoy missile analysis. The sheer number of studies, plus the aircraft's long gestation period, caused some pundits to redefine the AMSA acronym as "America's Most Studied Aircraft."

As a result of these studies, and numerous peripheral studies that took place under their auspices, several high-risk areas were identified and potential mitigation actions planned. Additionally, essential development was accomplished in some areas including developing "brass board" versions of some of the advanced avionics and testing them aboard a modified C-135. In July 1964, in order to provide a basis for further study, the Air Force set AMSA's gross weight at 375,000 pounds, with a range of 7250 miles, including 2250 miles at very low altitudes (~500 feet).

Political reaction to the AMSA at first appeared highly favorable, and, in December 1963, General LeMay, then the Air Force Chief of Staff, briefed President Lyndon B. Johnson on AMSA's importance to the strategic triad. During 1964, the Joint Chiefs of Staff approved the Air Force's plans for AMSA, and Congress approved funding for program definition and the advanced development of engines and avionics. Secretary McNamara, however, again refused to commit any DoD funds unless he was given a better justification for developing any new manned bomber. The Secretary simply did not believe the manned bomber was a viable strategic weapon.

Attempts to change McNamara's opinion of AMSA were unsuccessful. The Secretary believed ballistic missiles could perform the "assured destruction" strategic mission better

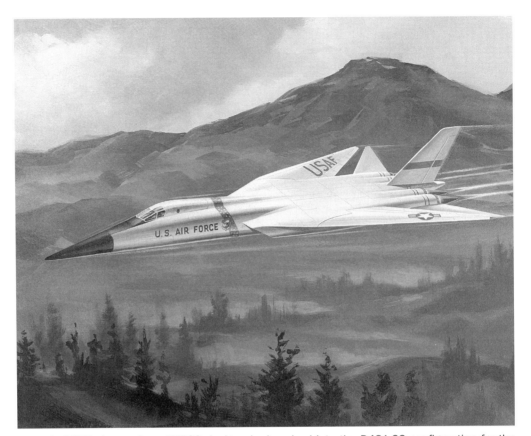

By early 1967, the previous AMPSS designs had evolved into the D481-33 configuration for the Advanced Manned Strategic Aircraft (AMSA). The basic planform is similar to the earlier AMPSS design, but the inlets are more conventional. Many design features are similar to the North American A-5 Vigilante navy strike aircraft. *(Boeing North American)*

than manned bombers and insisted that development of a new manned system was unnecessary. On the other hand, he believed that propulsion and avionics research and development should continue to produce advances in the state of the art applicable to existing or future manned systems. Thus, while only limited funding would be released for AMSA program definition studies, larger amounts would be allocated for subsystem and component research.

In late 1964 Boeing, General Dynamics, and North American submitted their initial AMSA study results. Concurrently, propulsion reports were received from Curtiss-Wright, General Electric, and Pratt & Whitney, while IBM and Hughes reported on their avionics studies. In 1965, General Electric and Pratt & Whitney were selected to construct demonstrator engines, and IBM was funded to continue conceptual work on an avionics architecture. A total of $25 million was made available for the AMSA efforts. While this seemed encouraging, a great deal of uncertainty still surrounded the AMSA project.

In December 1965, the DoD selected the General Dynamics FB-111A to replace the SAC's early model B-52s and all B-58s by the end of fiscal year 1972 (FY72). The Air Force had not requested the development of a bomber version of the controversial F-111, and opinion varied widely on its likely value. Still, the acquisition of a comparatively low-cost interim bomber had some merit, and the Air Force endorsed production of the aircraft as long as it did not jeopardize the eventual development of a new strategic bomber (AMSA). As General Ferguson stated in 1966, the FB-111 was and would remain a "stopgap airplane," an assessment shared by the entire Air Staff, even if Secretary McNamara continued to think otherwise.

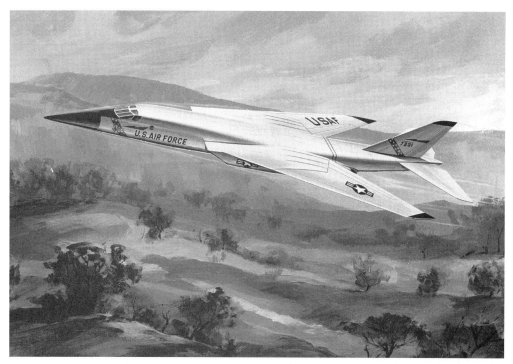

The AMSA design continued to evolve into 1968, with the engines being moved forward and the horizontal stabilizer being moved aft. The wing sweep is becoming less extreme, partially due to an emphasis on increased low-level performance at the expense of absolute high-altitude speed. *(Boeing North American)*

A collection of models shows some of the concepts developed for the SLAB, ERSA, LAMP, AMP, and AMPSS studies throughout the 1960s. The D481-39 model in the center foreground is very similar to the eventual D481-55B design for the B-1A. The placement and shape of the horizontal stabilizer is noteworthy. *(Boeing North American via Steve Pace)*

On 22 September 1967, North American Aviation, Inc., and Rockwell Standard Corporation merged to form the North American Rockwell Corporation.

During the first part of 1968, IBM and the Autonetics Division of North American Rockwell were selected to conduct more studies on the AMSA's advanced avionics. The contractors were to determine if various concepts were achievable within the projected schedule and funding constraints. To this end, 10 subcontractors, selected by the two firms, studied a wide range of components including forward-looking radar, Doppler radar, and forward-looking infrared equipment.

In early 1968, the Joint Chiefs of Staff again recommended the immediate development of AMSA. Secretary McNamara once more rejected the idea, preferring instead to continue the development of new technology subsystems and components for upgrading the performance of the FB-111A and the remaining B-52s.

The election of President Richard M. Nixon in 1968 brought about a fundamental transition in strategic thinking, particularly with regard to the manned bomber. In March 1969 Melvin R. Laird, the new Secretary of Defense, announced that only 76 of the projected 253 FB-111As would be procured, mainly because the aircraft lacked the range and payload for strategic operations. Secretary Laird also directed the acceleration of the AMSA design studies, noting that despite the improvements earmarked for the B-52G/Hs, a new strategic bomber was ". . . a more appropriate solution for a longer term bomber program."

In April 1969, Secretary of the Air Force Robert C. Seamans, Jr., formally designated the AMSA aircraft as the B-1A. The AMSA program office that had been established on 13 March 1964 within the Aeronautical Systems Division was redesignated the B-1 System Program Office (SPO) and assigned overall responsibility for the airframe, engine, and avionics development efforts.

New airframe RFPs released on 3 November 1969 were meant to lead to the prompt award of a final development and production contract. Although numerous companies had originally expressed interest, only three proposals were received, from Boeing, General Dynamics, and North American Rockwell. Also in November, engine RFPs were released to General Electric and Pratt & Whitney, and the avionics RFP was released to 15 avionics companies, although only five of them chose to submit proposals by the December 1969 deadline.

The avionics proposals were quickly evaluated, and the Autonetics Division of North American Rockwell and the Federal Systems Division of IBM were selected on 19 December. In a departure from the recent past, these two contracts no longer centered on feasibility or conceptual studies, but specified advanced development and design. A single contractor would be selected later to conduct detailed design and to manufacture the avionics. Unfortunately, the overall avionics program would soon experience serious setbacks.

The airframe and engine proposals were received in January and February 1970, respectively, but selection of the winners progressed slowly due to congressional funding reductions in FY70-71, which forced the Air Force to replan the entire B-1 program.

The Source Selection Evaluation Board assembled for the first time on 8 December 1969, and seriously began evaluating the revised airframe and engine proposals during the spring of 1970. On 5 June, following a presentation to the Defense Systems Acquisition Review Council, Deputy Secretary of Defense David Packard endorsed the Air Force's contractor selections. Later that day, Secretary of the Air Force Seamans announced that North American Rockwell and General Electric had been selected as the B-1A airframe and engine contractors, respectively. The selections were based on superior technical proposals and lower estimated total costs. Production was expected to include 240 operational aircraft, and the Air Force estimated that the $2000-million B-1A program would generate 192,000 jobs nationwide.

The Air Force negotiated separate cost-plus-incentive-fee development contracts with North American Rockwell and General Electric. In theory, this type of contract provided better incentives for technical innovations, but had been largely banned by McNamara during his reign as Secretary of Defense due to serious cost overruns on the F-111 and C-5A programs. Secretary Laird believed that, if properly managed, the contracts would ultimately produce better products for less money.

The North American Rockwell contract (F33657-70-C-0800) had a target ceiling of $1350 million. If performance, cost, and schedule commitments were met, the contractor's incentive fee would amount to $115.75 million. The contract's 90/10 sharing arrangement meant that 10 percent of any amount over the target ceiling would be deducted from the contractor's incentive fee, but if the contractor fulfilled his commitments for less than targeted, 10 percent of the difference would be added to the incentive fee. The contract called for the delivery of five test aircraft, two structural test airframes, and overall system integration, which meant that North American Rockwell would not only be responsible for the B-1A airframe, but for the complete weapons system, including the avionics, ground support equipment, training, and the like. The only items specifically excluded from the arrangement were the engines, which would be government-furnished equipment (GFE).

The General Electric contract (F33657-70-C-0801) had a target price of $406.7 million and a potential incentive fee of $30.2 million. It covered the design, fabrication, and qualification testing of 40 engines. The cost-sharing basis for the GE contract was similar to that used for the airframe, except the percentages were different—80/20, instead of 90/10.

The B-1A differed radically from the B-52, which had been the Air Force's primary bomber for almost 20 years. The variable-geometry wing and high thrust-to-weight ratio

By the time this sketch was released by Rockwell International, the final B-1A design was essentially finalized. Note that the stabilizing fins for the crew escape module are missing—in fact, there is no evidence of the module at all. This may have been during one of the periods that the Air Force was studying alternate escape methods. *(Boeing North American via the Terry Panopalis Collection)*

would enable it to use short runways, and new methods for rapidly checking out and verifying subsystems would theoretically result in a low maintenance repair rate and fast turnaround. Although only two-thirds the size of the B-52, with aerial refueling the B-1A would be able to carry twice the weapons load over the same intercontinental distances. New hardening techniques would enable the B-1A to withstand greater overpressures and thermal radiation from nuclear weapons. Self starting and a quick navigation alignment capability would allow the B-1A to get airborne more quickly, enabling it to stand alert on the ground rather than in the air. An automatic terrain-following radar and supersonic speed capability at low altitudes would permit the new bomber to penetrate sophisticated defenses. Moreover, the new bomber's small radar cross section and low altitude would minimize its detection by enemy radars.

A decision was made to minimize management costs within the government and contractor organizations, hopefully without compromising effectiveness. To assist in defining how to accomplish this goal, a special study was conducted under Project Focus. Sponsored by the B-1 SPO and actively supported by the two major contractors, Project Focus eventually satisfied some of the Air Force's money-saving objectives.

Most of the Project Focus recommendations were approved by Secretary Seamans before the end of 1970. One of them dealt with minimizing the number of B-1 SPO personnel in close proximity to the principal contractors and subcontractors. This arrangement had been successful on smaller projects in reducing the amount of paperwork that routinely plagued development programs, but it potentially limited the government's ability to detect routine problems before they could affect cost, schedule, or performance. The Air Force believed a savings of about $60 million might ensue, but the concept had never been applied to such a large program before. Many other Project Focus recommendations were also endorsed, but some of them, particularly those with long-range impact, were of questionable value.

The emerging B-1A was intended to be a production program, not another in a long series of studies. However, without definitive financial support from Congress, the Air Force did not know how many B-1As would ultimately be ordered. The program was further constrained because Deputy Secretary of Defense Packard's "fly-before-you-buy" concept emphasized hardware demonstrations at predetermined project milestones prior to making full-scale production decisions. In addition, approval from the Department of Defense Systems Acquisition Review Council would be needed before the B-1A could enter full-scale production. At times it seemed that for every process the Air Force attempted to streamline, the Department of Defense added yet another new layer of bureaucracy.

Perhaps Project Focus's most important recommendation was that efforts not directly contributing to the production decision should be deferred until after the go-ahead decision had been made. Project Focus also suggested that B-1A flight test hours could be reduced by combining the development, test, and evaluation (DT&E) with the initial operational test and evaluation (IOT&E). This was a fairly drastic departure from the established Air Force testing cycle in which the contractor was responsible for all "development" testing (Category I), and the Air Force began participating during Category II "operational" testing. The new concept of having Air Force and contractor personnel fly together was intended to eliminate the duplication that usually occurred during Category I and II flights under the traditional test program without in any way compromising the flight test program's thoroughness. Based on this new philosophy, the flight test program was scheduled for 1060 hours, 100 of which were to be completed prior to the production decision.

Project Focus did not overlook wind-tunnel testing, and recommended that the government facilities at Arnold Engineering Development Center (AEDC) in Tullahoma, Tennessee, be used to the maximum extent possible in order to minimize costs. Officials from the B-1 SPO met with AEDC personnel and estimated that the airframe would require

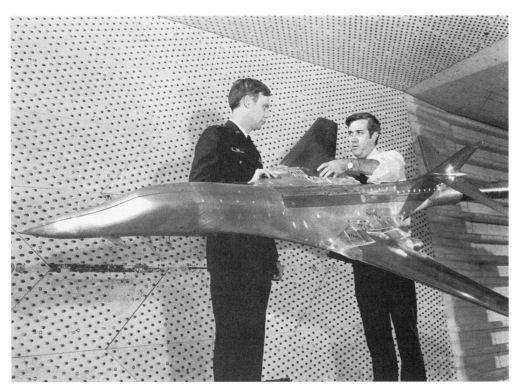

North American also used the wind tunnels at the Air Force's Arnold Engineering Development Center in Tullahoma, Tennessee. This model was used for tests to determine the ability of various fairings to improve the quality of airflow over the wing where it joins the fuselage. *(U.S. Air Force/DVIC DF-SN-84-01714)*

18,000 hours of wind-tunnel testing while the engine and intake would require an additional 12,000 hours. The contractors generally concurred with these estimates.

By late summer 1970, Congress had restricted B-1A funding to levels below $500 million for several fiscal years to come. While Project Focus and other management initiatives helped to save money, they could not totally prevent some undesirable delays. This prompted a review of operational requirements in an attempt to lower costs. Originally it had been desired for the B-1A to sustain at least Mach 1.2 during low-level penetration. This produced a heating rate that was at the outer edge of what an aluminum structure could withstand, so in some areas the use of other materials, primarily titanium alloys, was specified. Titanium is significantly more expensive than aluminum, both to procure and to work with during fabrication. In addition, the stresses imposed by encountering low-level turbulence at supersonic speeds dictated a generally more robust structure. Various human factors studies, ignoring the apparent success of the F-111 during low-level supersonic interdictions, suggested that penetration speeds should be lowered to Mach 0.85 (~650 mph) to allow the crew more time to identify and attack targets. Since accepting a lower penetration speed looked like it would allow Rockwell to significantly lower the cost of the airframe, the Air Force conceded and changed the requirements. This enabled a greater percentage of the airframe to be manufactured from conventional aluminum alloys. Titanium would be needed mainly for the highly stressed wing carry-through structure, the inboard portions of the outer wing panels around the pivot points, and for some skin panels around the engine exhausts and lower rear fuselage. Still, 21 percent of the B-1's airframe would be made up of various titanium alloys.

Based largely on these new requirements, on 18 January 1971, Secretary Seamans approved a $180 million program reduction, which also cut the number of test aircraft from five to three. One of the static test airframes was cancelled while the second was put on indefinite hold; the Air Force hoped that limited stress testing of specific structural items would suffice instead. In addition, the engine procurement was cut from 40 to 27, and the entire B-1A development program was stretched out. This last item would ultimately increase the total cost of the program, but it would help minimize individual year funding requirements.

As rescheduled, the B-1A's first flight would slip one month to April 1974, and a production decision would not be made before April 1975. The one-year period after first flight (instead of the six months originally planned) allowed double the number of flight test hours (to 200) flown prior to the production decision. Finally, the initial operational capability (IOC) date was moved to December 1979, when the Strategic Air Command would receive its 65th B-1A. This was a long delay. In 1970, the Air Force had planned that SAC would receive the 68th production aircraft and reach IOC by December 1977.

During 1970, Autonetics and IBM participated in studies under Project Junior Crown to analyze the effectiveness of various avionics packages, taking into consideration size, performance, and cost. It was realized that the complexity and cost of the avionics subsystems meant that early aircraft would be delivered with reduced capability, and Junior Crown identified incremental phases associated with the progression from the initial avionics subsystems to the final operational ones. Budgetary limitations were also forcing the B-1 SPO to investigate alternate design configurations; five were based on the initial Junior Crown subsystems, while four others used avionics equipment from various F-111 and B-52 models.

In mid-1971, Secretary Seamans stated that because the production decision had been postponed, the selection of a final avionics subcontractor was no longer considered urgent. The initial prototype B-1As would be fitted largely with FB-111A components, although the airframe would be designed with space, power, and cooling capacity to allow the installation of more advanced avionics at a future date. Industry was notified that the selection of an avionics contractor was being deferred, primarily to minimize near-year development costs.

The Air Force subsequently changed its mind, and on 29 September 1971 new avionics RFPs were released to 27 companies. Surprisingly, these RFPs separated the avionics subsystems into offensive and defensive functions instead of using the previous integrated approach. Only five companies chose to submit proposals for the offensive avionics, and all were received before the end of November. The evaluation of proposals took until late spring, and on 13 April 1972 Boeing was awarded a $62.4 million contract for the development and integration of the offensive avionics package. Like the airframe and engine contracts, this was a cost-plus-incentive-fee type with a sharing (90/10 percent) arrangement, and a $1 million award fee provision.

The RFPs for the defensive avionics brought even fewer responses. Only the Airborne Instrument Laboratory (AIL), a division of the Cutler-Hammer Corporation (later purchased by Eaton), and Raytheon responded. The evaluation of the two proposals was completed in February 1972, but no contract was awarded since the Air Force was not satisfied by either response and decided to release a revised RFP. Because of the system's complexity, the Air Force believed that development of the advanced defensive system needed for the B-1A would involve a great deal of technical risk, and the new RFP divided the project into two phases. The first would be a 10-month risk-reduction demonstration by two competing contractors working under fixed-price contracts for a maximum combined value of $5 million. The second phase would down-select to a single contractor to perform engineering development under a cost-plus-fixed-fee contract. The revised RFP listed the Air Force's operational objectives, with each given a descending priority, and set a price ceiling of $1.4 million per system in FY72 dollars. Each bidder was expected to structure its

A full-scale wooden mock-up of the B-1A was built at North American's Los Angeles facility. Note the open weapon bay doors and the crew access ladder. The left wing could pivot (manually) to various sweep angles. The cockpit was also fully finished. The raised walkway on the right side of the aircraft allowed visitors to look over the upper surfaces. *(Boeing North American via the Tony Landis Collection)*

Back to the future? Although the mock-up was very accurate in most details, the rear tail radome was not as it would appear on the first three B-1As. The blunt rear radome is a B-1B design feature, although it was also fitted to the fourth B-1A. *(Mick Roth)*

response in such a manner that the Air Force could "pick and chose" what capabilities would be included in the final system, based largely on cost and development schedule.

The revised RFPs were released to the same 23 companies on 17 May 1972, and the same two contractors (AIL and Raytheon) responded. Each was awarded a $2.49 million 10-month Phase I risk-reduction demonstration contract on 11 August 1972. Phase II was due to begin in mid-1973 and to run through December 1976.

In January 1971, North American Rockwell began constructing a 45,000-pound full-scale mock-up of the B-1A in its Los Angeles facility. The Air Force reviewed this mock-up in late October 1971, two months after the arrival of a full-scale mock-up of the General Electric F101 engine. The primary objective of the review was to determine if Air Force requirements and specifications were being met. Approximately 200 Air Force representatives also examined the location of equipment in the mock-up, with maintenance access and operational efficiency being primary concerns. The mock-up review board wrote 297 requests for alteration. Over 90 of those concerned maintenance aspects of the aircraft, 60 dealt chiefly with potential safety issues, and 10 involved the aircraft's logistical support. The rest fell in the operational category or were related to deficiencies in documentation. In addition, there were 21 requests for alterations to the engine, the most noteworthy involving a change in plumbing to make the engine mounts more accessible. A total of 257 of these discrepancies were resolved before the mock-up review ended.

In the meantime, various tests were undertaken to determine the radar cross-section (RCS) of the B-1A, including building a full-scale breadboard target and a 3300-pound, 36-foot-long RCS model to be tested at the Air Force Radar Target Scatter Facility at Holloman AFB, New Mexico. The B-1A was the first bomber where the RCS was a design consideration, and various parts of the airframe were subtly shaped in an attempt to lower the RCS.

The development of any major weapon system routinely encounters problems, and the Air Force did not expect the B-1A to deviate from this pattern. Yet, by the end of 1971,

The B-1A mock-up included a fully finished cockpit. Note the large moving map display in the center of the instrument panel, a feature that would not make it into any of the B-1A prototypes. The first B-1A used a very conventional instrument panel without the CRTs shown here, but the other three prototypes were generally similar to this layout. *(Mick Roth)*

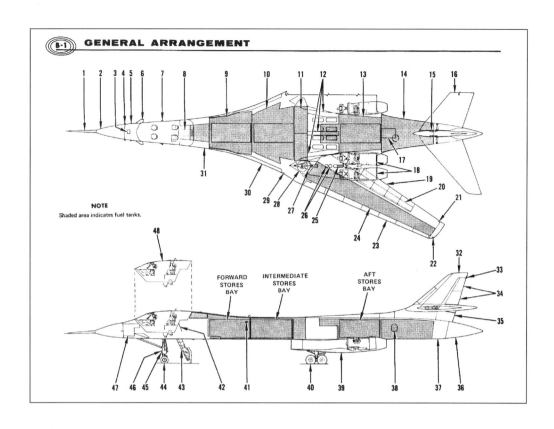

B-1 GENERAL ARRANGEMENT

NOTE
Shaded area indicates fuel tanks.

FORWARD STORES BAY

INTERMEDIATE STORES BAY

AFT STORES BAY

1. PITOT-STATIC BOOM (WITH AOA AND SIDESLIP VANES)
2. FORWARD RADOME
3. AERIAL REFUEL RECEPTACLE
4. PITOT-STATIC PROBE *
5. TOTAL TEMPERATURE PROBE *
6. STRUCTURAL MODE CONTROL SYSTEM VANE *
7. ANGLE-OF-ATTACK VANE *
8. CREW ENTRY WAY
9. FORWARD FUSELAGE FUEL TANK (TANK NO. 1)
10. FORWARD INTERMEDIATE FUSELAGE FUEL TANK (TANK NO. 2)
11. MAIN FUEL TANKS
12. MAIN WHEEL WELL EQUIPMENT (INTERMEDIATE AVIONICS) COMPARTMENT
13. AFT INTERMEDIATE FUSELAGE FUEL TANK (TANK NO. 3)
14. AFT FUSELAGE FUEL TANK (TANK NO. 4)
15. HORIZONTAL STABILIZER ACTUATOR *
16. HORIZONTAL STABILIZER
17. FLIGHT CONTROLS MIXER BAY
18. ENGINES *
19. FLAPS (6) *
20. SPOILERS/SPEED BRAKES (4) *
21. FUEL JETTISON OUTLET *
22. POSITION LIGHT *
23. SLATS (7) *
24. WING FUEL TANK *
25. APU *
26. HYDRAULIC RESERVOIRS *
27. INLET RAMP MECHANISM *
28. WING PIVOT
29. SUPPLEMENTAL POSITION AND ANTICOLLISION LIGHT *
30. WING GLOVE AVIONICS COMPARTMENT *
31. CENTRAL AVIONICS COMPARTMENT
32. VERTICAL STABILIZER
33. TAIL/ANTICOLLISION LIGHT
34. UPPER AND INTERMEDIATE RUDDERS

35. LOWER RUDDER
36. AFT RADOME
37. AFT AVIONICS COMPARTMENT
38. LN₂ DEWAR
39. ENGINE NACELLE *
40. MAIN LANDING GEAR *
41. AERIAL REFUEL/WING INSPECTION LIGHT *
42. ENTRY DOOR
43. ENTRY LADDER
44. NOSE LANDING GEAR
45. LANDING/TAXI LIGHT
46. LANDING LIGHTS (2)

47. FORWARD AVIONICS COMPARTMENT
48. EJECTABLE CREW MODULE
49. FORWARD CREW STATIONS
50. CREW SEAT (4) †
51. ESCAPE HATCH (SEVERABLE)
52. AFT CREW STATIONS
53. CONTROLS FOR ENTRY LADDER, APU, AND MAIN GEAR DOORS
54. SURVIVAL EQUIPMENT
55. SIDE WINDOW (SEVERABLE) *

* Both Sides (L and R)
† Right aft seat temporarily removed

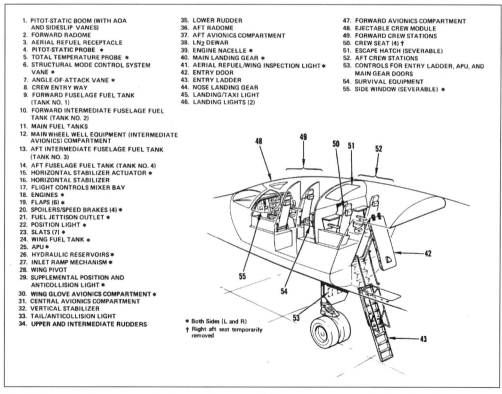

The B-1A general arrangement diagram from the flight manual shows the location of most major components aboard the first aircraft. Note how the fuselage fuel tanks surround the weapons bays, except on the bottom. *(U.S. Air Force)*

except for a minor weight increase (not an unusual occurrence) and difficulties with the crew escape system, problems were relatively few. For example, the aircraft's windshield, which included a thin polycarbon inner layer, had poor optical qualities and tended to shatter upon impact. However, two new windshields that used different stretched acrylics in the inner layers were ready for testing, and one of them would most likely be satisfactory.

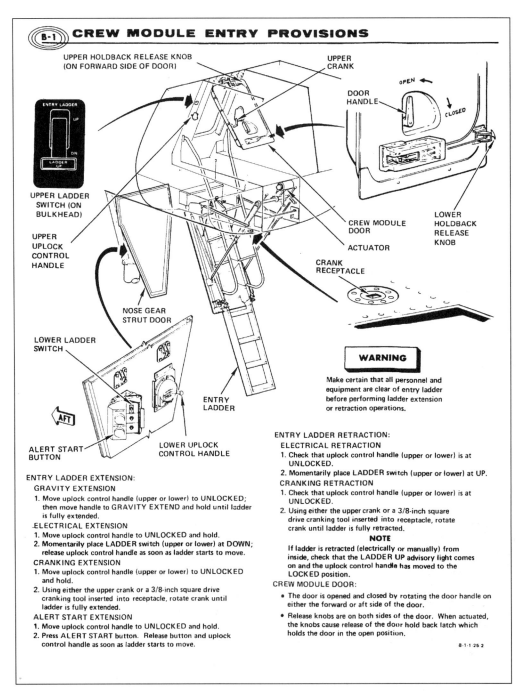

This flight manual illustration shows the crew module entry provisions. In the lower left is a diagram showing the "alert start button" on the nose-wheel strut—this would be pressed by the first crewmember arriving at the aircraft and would automatically start powering up the auxiliary power units, even prior to the crew arriving on the flight deck. The same panel has the switch that electrically opens the crew access hatch and extends the ladder. *(U.S. Air Force)*

Rocket sleds provided the best way to test the B-1A escape capsule at low levels. High-level testing was accomplished by having a B-52 carry the escape capsule to altitude and releasing it, much like the X-15 research airplane. *(Boeing North American via Steve Pace)*

As eventually installed on the first three B-1As, the crew escape system generally resembled the F-111's crew module, which had been hailed as a major advancement in aircraft design. Developed by the McDonnell Aircraft Corporation and initially tested in 1966, the F-111 crew module was fully automated. When forced to abandon the aircraft, the crew only had to press, squeeze, or pull one lever. This caused an explosive cord to shear the module from the fuselage. A rocket motor then ejected the module upward, and it parachuted to the ground or sea. The capsule was fully watertight and could serve as a shelter for the F-111's two crewmen, complete with radios, locating beacons, and survival gear.

Because of the increased size and weight required for the B-1A's four-man crew, the new module's research and development costs were expected to total $125 million. Nearly half of that amount had already been spent by the end of FY71, and test results had been disappointing. Consequently, during early 1972, the B-1 SPO planned once again to study various options for crew escape, knowing full well that no clear answer was likely to be forthcoming. The design and production of the initial B-1A prototypes was too far along to alter their escape systems, but the Air Force intended to evaluate the results of the study before deciding upon a production configuration.

The General Electric F101 engine had grown from the earlier GE9 demonstrator program that had been funded by the Air Force Systems Command, and the prototype YF101s also were experiencing some of the problems common to all development programs in their early stages. Specific difficulties centered on turbine blade failures, high-speed compressor stalls, and excessive oil consumption. All of the identified problems already had corrective action plans in place, and in mid-1972 Air Force engineers commented that the F101 had the potential to be the most durable high-performance engine the Air Force had ever procured.

The General Electric YF101-GE-100 engine for the B-1A had a remarkably trouble-free development program, although production versions for the B-1B would experience some early operational problems. Each engine was assembled in such a manner that it could only be installed in one location on the B-1A. *(General Electric Aircraft Engines)*

Assembly of the first B-1A (75-0158) began on 15 March 1972 at Air Force Plant 42 in Palmdale, California. Rockwell was using the industrial complex (Site 3) that had originally been built for the B-70 program, and all of the B-1A prototypes would be assembled here. An April 1972 review of the B-1A program at Los Angeles yielded encouraging results, leading the Air Force to conclude that the B-1A's first flight would occur on schedule in April 1974.

On 16 February 1973, the North American Rockwell Corporation merged with the Rockwell Manufacturing Company, creating the Rockwell International Corporation.

The optimism of the spring of 1972 did not necessarily prevail a year later. In July 1973, Secretary of the Air Force John L. McLucas, who had replaced Robert Seamans in May, notified Senator John C. Stennis, Chairman of the Senate Armed Services Committee, that fabrication of the first B-1A had fallen behind schedule. This was mainly because the effort involved in manufacturing and assembling the aircraft had been underestimated. The start of the second aircraft also had been delayed. The Air Force had become aware of such problems several months earlier and had turned down the contractor's request for overtime work, since this would raise costs. It now appeared that the initial flight of the first B-1A would slip by several months, the assembly and flight testing of the second and third aircraft would be slightly delayed, and the production decision would be postponed from July 1975 to May 1976. The new schedule would increase the total development cost by $80 million to $2490 million, but this was considered less expensive than attempting to adhere to the original schedule.

As a direct response to this news, the Research and Development Subcommittee of the Senate Armed Services Committee held a special hearing concerning the B-1A program on 27 July. Senator Thomas J. McIntyre, chairman of the subcommittee, expressed his concern about the state of the program. Even long-time supporter Senator Barry Goldwater commented on the Air Force's inability to adhere to schedule and cost estimates for the program and requested assurance that the Air Force would meet the new schedule. Secretary McLucas pointed out that the Air Force did not anticipate any major production problems and, except for increases caused by inflation, production cost estimates were not expected to rise. Major General Douglas T. Nelson, Director of the B-1 SPO since 13 August 1970, underlined the Air Force's own dissatisfaction, stating that Rockwell should have been better prepared to prevent or solve the problems that had come up. Ultimately, some of the blame was traced to the decrease in oversight brought about during the Project Focus streamlining.

Restructuring the B-1A development program required amending Rockwell and GE's contracts since both included specific schedule provisions. By supplemental agreements dated 15 July 1973, the first flight of the B-1A was moved from April to June 1974, and the initial flights of the second and third aircraft were scheduled for January 1976 and September 1975, respectively. This apparently odd sequence made sense since the second B-1A was to be used in a series of structural tests prior to its first flight. The contract amend-

An empty engine cart behind the left nacelle indicates that workers have just finished installing an engine in the first prototype. The long, pointed tail cone unique to first three B-1As is clearly evident here. *(Boeing North American via Steve Pace)*

ments specified that the structural tests were to be completed by February 1976, and the procurement of a dedicated full-scale structural test airframe was finally abandoned.

The General Electric contract was also modified in the summer of 1973, but involved more drastic changes. To save money, the number of experimental XF101 engines was reduced from 3 to 2, the quantity of prototype YF101s was cut again from 27 to 23, and an option for six additional YF101 qualification test engines was eliminated. As in the airframe's case, engine deliveries were stretched out over a longer period of time and overall costs increased, although, each fiscal year, costs either stayed the same or were reduced slightly. The delay allowed each engine to accumulate more test hours, reducing the number of engines needed to reach the 1105-hour qualification goal.

As of mid-1973, development costs totaled $1133 million including the amount spent since 1963 on AMPSS/AMSA studies and other related projects. Air Force budget analysts estimated that total development costs would reach $2628 million, while production costs for the planned 240 B-1As would total $8494 million. Hence, the Air Force anticipated the entire B-1A program would cost over $11 billion. This worked out to approximately $46 million per aircraft, inclusive of all development and production costs.

As 1973 came to a close, the future of the B-1A remained somewhat uncertain. In August, the Secretary of the Air Force asked Dr. Raymond L. Bisplinghoff, Deputy Director of the National Science Foundation, to conduct an independent review of the B-1A program. The Secretary's primary concern was the adequacy of the government and contractor management team to develop and produce the aircraft. This request led to the formation of a review committee, staffed with individuals from industry, the Air Force Scientific Advisory Board, other government agencies, and retired military and civilian federal employees. The

25 members of the Bisplinghoff Committee worked quickly, and on 4 October 1973 Dr. Bis-plinghoff and three committee members gave Secretary McLucas their findings.

The committee did not foresee any major technical problems that would prevent successful development or production of the aircraft, although the B-1A's complexity could not be overlooked. In this regard, except for wind-tunnel testing and engine development, the committee believed that the development program's new schedule was still very "success oriented," and the program was insufficiently funded, making it difficult to make the transition from the development to the production phase. There was also no reserve funding to cope with unforeseen problems. Moreover, the committee did not believe that three test aircraft were sufficient since the program's schedule risks would be greatly increased if any of the aircraft were destroyed during testing. The committee also noted that the revised development program would result in at least $300 million in total program cost growth.

Dr. Bisplinghoff described the B-1A as basically airworthy but heavy and costly, and the committee questioned the accuracy of Air Force estimates for the aircraft's empty weight, range, and takeoff distance. The Air Force responded that there were at least 100 airfields in the United States capable of supporting continuous B-1 operations, and an addition 220 airfields suitable for emergency dispersal. The aircraft, the Air Force noted, was always described as being capable of operating from runways sized for the Boeing 727 transport.

It is interesting to note that several technical features of the B-1 were specifically called out in Dr. Bisplinghoff's report. Among these were the overwing fairings, engine nacelles, and the electrical multiplex (EMUX) data bus. The first two would be substantially changed on the eventual B-1B, while the EMUX would evolve into a truly workable Mil-Std-1553B data bus.

If any further funding reductions were likely, Bisplinghoff believed that serious consideration should be given to cancelling the program. As time would show, a lack of funds and technical difficulties would continue to plague the B-1A program.

Joint Strategic Bomber Study

Despite the fact that construction of the B-1A prototypes was finally underway, the Air Force continued to study alternatives. Often this was at the request of Congress before it would release the next funding increment. At other times it was because some officials within the DoD and Air Force were not convinced that the B-1A could overcome its problems and lack of political support. The DoD Joint Strategic Bomber Study examined three alternatives: a stretched FB-111 (unofficially called the FB-111G, but not to be confused with the current F-111G), a re-engined B-52 derivative, and a standoff cruise missile launcher based on a wide-body transport. These alternatives were compared to the B-1A during three critical phases of a strategic bombing mission: launch, flight to the target area, and penetration to the target itself.

The three contractors that had originally responded to the B-1 RFP were asked to participate on a funded basis, with each contractor studying one alternative. A government review board then compared the three designs against various scenarios. Air Force Secretary McLucas presented the conclusions to the Senate Armed Services Committee on 17 April 1975.

General Dynamics proposed an FB-111G that used a stretched fuselage to contain almost twice as much fuel as the basic FB-111A. The stretch also allowed a larger weapons bay and additional space for avionics. The FB-111G did well in launch survivability but was seriously deficient during the flight to the target area. The problem was that the airframe was still too small, despite the fuselage stretch—its physical size was still only one-half that of the B-1A and it weighed only one-third as much. The FB-111G simply could not carry sufficient fuel or weapons to give adequate target coverage, or enough ECM equipment to defeat projected enemy defenses.

General Dynamics recognized this problem and proposed a further-stretched FB-111H version. Powered by a pair of F101 engines (the same as the B-1A) and carrying yet more fuel, this version was still found lacking. It could only carry half of the B-1A's weapons load, and when fully loaded it could not cross the Atlantic Ocean without refueling. Even assuming an aerial refueling on the edge of Soviet airspace, the FB-111H could not reach targets around Moscow with a full weapons load and still return to a friendly recovery base. And it still lacked sufficient ECM equipment to survive the Soviet defenses that were expected to be in place during the 1980s.

The stretched FB-111 was also shown to be less cost effective than the B-1A. The DoD analyses estimated that it would take 10 times as many FB-111G/Hs as B-1As to achieve comparable target effectiveness, plus more tankers, additional bases, and of course, 10 times the number of crews and maintenance personnel. Such an FB-111 force would be cost prohibitive.

Boeing had long proposed to re-engine the B-52G/H models with a version of the CFM-56 turbofan to increase their unrefueled range, as well as provide modest increases in speed and payload. Alternate engines, such as the Pratt & Whitney 2000 and Rolls Royce 535, had also been examined. The upgraded B-52I ("I" is seldom officially used as a designation suffix, so as not to confuse it with "1") also featured improved avionics (an ongoing process with the B-52) and minor structural strengthening (also an ongoing process).

The DoD analysis found that the B-52I would perform well during the flight to the target phase of the mission, but would be deficient in the other two phases. During the launch phase, the primary requirement was to be able to survive the short warning time of submarine-launched ballistic missiles (SLBMs). Quick reaction times, high flyaway speeds, and aircraft hardness to nuclear blast effects were the major factors. The ability to operate from a large number of dispersed austere airfields during crises was also considered important. The B-52I required a great deal of ground support equipment and offered comparatively low flyaway speeds. During the penetration phase, bomber survivability depends most on altitude, speed, and the ability to avoid or defeat interceptors with look-down, shoot-down capability. A low RCS was considered the primary way to defeat the interceptors. The B-52I would suffer from its relative slowness and large RCS, which would be difficult to conceal even with improved ECM equipment.

To counter these deficiencies, Boeing proposed a design that would include the new engines, a new supercritical wing, an extended bomb bay, improved avionics, and low-level ride control. Because so many major modifications would be required, a significant portion of the Air Force bomber force would be tied up in rework for years, seriously reducing the number of aircraft available for operations. In FY75 dollars, the estimate for the modifications was approximately $20 million per aircraft, almost half the price of a new B-1A—and the resulting aircraft would still be a 25-year-old B-52.

The third alternative was the most novel. A wide-body aircraft, such as the Lockheed C-5 or Boeing 747, could be modified to carry 50 to 100 air-launched cruise missiles (ALCMs) and launch them from well outside the borders of the target country. The DoD found these would be less effective than the B-1A in both the launch and penetration phases. During takeoff, the wide-body aircraft would be more vulnerable to SLBM attacks than any of the other designs, because transports would fly more slowly out to a safe distance and would be more difficult to harden against nuclear blast effects. (Boeing later disproved this theory with the E-4 and VC-25 versions of the 747.) Cruise missiles could also be expected to incur heavy losses while attacking targets protected by even relatively unsophisticated SAMs. The DoD study found that ". . . a force of primarily B-1s will place about twice as many weapons on target as will an equal cost all standoff cruise missile force. Moreover a purely standoff force would greatly simplify the enemy's defense architecture, allow-

One of the concepts that received serious consideration during the genesis of the B-1B was a wide-body transport filled with air-launched cruise missiles. This model of a Boeing 747 shows how cruise missiles would be carried on the main deck, then lowered via a trapeze at the rear and launched. The vulnerability of such aircraft to interceptors and other defenses eventually killed the idea. *(U.S. Air Force)*

ing a concentration on low altitude SAMs around targets, and perhaps, long range interceptors on the periphery. Such a concentration would severely damage an all-ALCM force."

The analyses showed the ALCM was not an alternative to the B-1A, but could effectively complement the manned bomber because it could help dilute the enemy's defenses. The existing FB-111As were also seen as a complement to the heavy bombers, because they were very good in their limited role of striking peripheral targets, but the stretched FB-111G/H would not be suitable as the primary strategic bomber. The study group felt the B-52 also was an extremely capable aircraft and would remain effective throughout the 1970s, however, ". . . the B-52 is getting old and the bomber study and the GAO review reaffirmed that for the threats postulated for the 1980s, and beyond, B-1 forces become more cost effective than even the B-52."

The Joint Strategic Bomber Study's two major observations were "(1) the low flying, fast, nuclear-hardened B-1, with its high-quality ECM, out performed all other vehicles examined by a wide margin, and (2) of the various equal cost forces examined, those consisting principally of B-1s performed substantially better. Based on these observations, we can reaffirm our conviction that the B-1 is the most cost effective way to modernize the strategic bomber force."

There were, of course, several flaws in the DoD analysis, which was largely predisposed to support the B-1A. Primarily, it assumed, incorrectly as it turned out, that the RCS reduction offered by the B-1A was sufficient to render it nearly invisible to Soviet radar. Secondly, it assumed, also incorrectly, that the defensive avionics (ECM) being developed for the B-1A would be capable of defeating all known Soviet defenses. In the end, the fully integrated ECM system, later installed on the B-1B, was never truly effective and is currently planned to be replaced by more conventional countermeasures equipment. But the DoD study, for a while at least, provided the necessary justification for Congress to continue authorizing funds for the B-1A program.

In early 1975, the AIL Division of Cutler-Hammer was finally selected to build the B-1 radio frequency surveillance/electronic countermeasures system (RFS/ECMS) and was awarded a $31,608,697 development contract. The AIL team also included Northrop, Litton Industries, and Sedco Systems. This system was intended to counter antiaircraft artillery, surface-to-air missile, and air-to-air missile fire control radars with deception jamming and to provide noise jamming to degrade the performance of early warning and ground intercept radars. The winning system was a major advance in concept since it relied heavily on digital components that could be easily reprogrammed to meet the ever-changing threat environment. For instance, changes in modulation techniques could be accomplished in software rather than changing the actual exciters and antennas. The first development system would be installed on the third B-1A prototype and AIL projected the system would cost $1.4 million per copy based on a 240 unit production run. From the "shopping list" of options, the Air Force configured a basic system that it could afford, but the contract included a number of additional options that could be exercised later to enhance capabilities. Several of these options had already been exercised by mid-1978.

On 26 October 1974, the first B-1A was rolled out at Palmdale. All four B-1As were initially painted in gloss "anti-flash" white, which was supposed to reduce the heat and radiation damage associated with nuclear blasts. At this point Rockwell still had high hopes for an extensive B-1A production program. *(Boeing North American via Steve Pace)*

The first flight of the third B-1A took place on 1 April 1976. The main landing gear was tucked into the space between the engine nacelles, resulting in a fairly narrow track for such a large aircraft. Note the configuration of the nose landing gear—unique to the three escape module equipped aircraft. The large black and white marking on the engine nacelle is a "photo reference marking" that provided a visual reference for engineers looking at photos of the aircraft. It was most likely applied for weapons drop tests. *(Boeing North American via Steve Pace)*

B-1A Flight Testing

The first B-1A prototype (74-0158) was completed just over two years after construction began, and it was rolled out at Palmdale on 26 October 1974 in front of a crowd of nearly 10,000 people. An extensive ground test program was followed by low- and high-speed taxi tests on the long runway at Palmdale.

The aircraft made its maiden flight on 23 December 1974 with pilot Charles C. Bock, Jr., copilot Colonel Emil "Ted" Sturmthal, and flight test engineer Richard Abrams. During the short hop to Edwards AFB, the landing gear was left down and the wings in their full-forward position. The second flight, which took place on 23 January 1975, was the first in which the landing gear was retracted and the wing sweep mechanism was activated.

The first two years of the Phase I flight test program was devoted to generating extensive test data to support a production decision that was scheduled for late 1976. This was a result of the DoD "fly-before-you-buy" program then in effect, which also resulted in the fly-off programs for the A-9/A-10 (A-X) and F-16/F-17 (LWF).

Flight testing was conducted by the B-1 Combined Test Force (CTF), made up of personnel from both the Air Force Systems Command and SAC. Test flights from Edwards took place approximately three times per month, allowing time for the engineers to assimilate each flight's test data before embarking on the next flight. The first six months were used to demonstrate the basic flight-handling characteristics of the aircraft, and confidence was soon sufficient to conduct terrain-following flights as low as 200 feet above the ground at

The first B-1A taxis back to its staging area after a test flight at Edwards. It was not unusual for the aircraft to taxi with their flaps and slats extended. Note the doors over the engine nacelles that cover the wing when it is in its fully aft position. *(Dennis R. Jenkins via the Mick Roth Collection)*

nearly the speed of sound. Twenty-five flights were flown during the first year, totaling slightly over 199 hours and covering approximately 57,000 miles. A speed of Mach 1.6 (1070 mph) had been achieved at 34,000 feet, and the aircraft had flown as high as 50,000 feet. The longest single flight, achieved with the aid of several in-flight refuelings, was 8 hours, 9 minutes.

Sensors and cotton "tufts" adorn the rear fuselage and vertical stabilizer of the first B-1A during turbulence testing. The aircraft is parked on the old XB-70 test stand at Edwards AFB. *(Dennis R. Jenkins via the Mick Roth Collection)*

Each of the three prototypes was assigned specific flight test responsibilities. The first aircraft (74-0158) was used to evaluate basic flight-handling qualities during its 79 flights, logging 405 hours, 18 minutes, of flight time. This aircraft also became the first B-1A to reach Mach 1.5, during October 1975, and also the first to reach Mach 2, during April 1976. Key test items included performance and flying qualities at high speed and low altitudes; heavyweight takeoff performance; in-flight refueling characteristics; and an initial assessment of takeoff, climb, subsonic cruise, and landing characteristics.

The second B-1A (74-0159) was not immediately taken to the air. Instead, the partially completed airframe was towed across Plant 42 to the Lockheed facility and subjected to a nondestructive structural loads test. Unlike many such studies, which test a dedicated airframe to destruction, the B-1A tests were simply intended to gather sufficient data to validate theoretical and model-derived results. After the loads tests were completed, the aircraft was towed back to the Rockwell facility to be completed. The second aircraft thus became the third B-1A to fly, making its maiden flight on 14 June 1976, not quite two months after its official rollout on 11 May. During the B-1A flight test program, the aircraft completed 60 flights totaling 282 hours, 30 minutes, before being placed in flyable storage. This aircraft attained the highest speed of any B-1A when it reached Mach 2.22 on 5 October 1978.

Following rollout on 16 January 1976, the third B-1A (74-0160) became the second to fly when it made its first flight on 26 March 1976. This prototype was used as an offensive avionics test platform, and was the first B-1A to successfully launch an AGM-69A Short-Range Attack Missile (SRAM). The SRAM was launched on 28 July 1977 over the White Sands Missile Range, New Mexico, from an altitude of 6000 feet and a speed of 500 knots. This aircraft flew the highest percentage of hours in the test program, with 829 hours, 24 minutes, accumulated during 138 sorties. The aircraft was placed in flyable storage on 15 April 1981.

One of the B-1A's major hurdles, an IOT&E that simulated SAC combat missions, was passed in early September 1976. Phase I flight testing was completed on 30 September 1976 with all major flight test objectives having been completed. In early November, the Defense Systems Acquisition Review Council (DSARC III) approved the full-scale production of the B-1A as a combat aircraft. The Air Force announced on 2 December that production contracts had been awarded for the construction of the first three operational aircraft and the purchase of long-lead items for the second lot of eight aircraft. The Air Force still intended to acquire 240 of the new bombers, in addition to the prototypes. Additionally, funds were authorized for the purchase and fabrication of production tooling.

However, like most major defense projects in the late 1970s, the B-1A was suffering from spiraling cost estimates. In 1970, the estimated unit price of production B-1As had been $40 million (FY70 dollars). By 1973 this had increased to $46 million (normalized FY70 dollars), and by the end of 1975 the figure had reached almost $70 million per aircraft. This was a 75 percent increase in price in just five years, and represented by far the most expensive combat aircraft ever contemplated for procurement.

The B-1A had been born mainly through the election of a new U.S. President (Nixon). It would die from a similar cause when Jimmy Carter took office. President Carter cancelled the program almost in its entirety on 30 June 1977. At a press conference Carter said, "My decision is that we should not continue with deployment of the B-1, and I am directing that we discontinue plans for production of this weapons system." This was primarily the result of Carter's concern over the ever-increasing cost estimates, and his steadfast belief that various types of missiles (ICBM, SLBM, and ALCM) could perform the mission more effectively without putting crewmembers at risk. Much like McNamara, Carter instead provided funds for a modest avionics and ECM upgrade for the remaining B-52G/H fleet.

Lagging well behind the first three aircraft, the fourth B-1A (76-0174) finally entered

All of the B-1As made their first flights from Plant 42 in Palmdale. Here the fourth aircraft departs on its maiden flight on 17 February 1979. The fourth aircraft is easily identified by the large black dielectric panels on the wing-root leading edge, and the lack of a long test boom from the nose. *(Boeing North American via Steve Pace)*

assembly on 25 August 1975 and made its first flight on 14 February 1979. The fourth B-1A was really a preproduction B-1A (in an earlier era the first three aircraft would have been designated XB-1A, while the fourth would have been a YB-1A), and did not fly until after the B-1A production program had been cancelled. It was the first B-1A to have full offensive and defensive avionics systems, and had been intended as a bridge between the three prototype aircraft and the planned 240 production aircraft. This aircraft was also manufactured using techniques and tooling more representative of the anticipated production program, and included improvements that had been planned for the production aircraft, including new software for the digital avionics, a modified fuel transfer system, new weapons bay doors, and a revised wing/fuselage interface.

The Air Force had finally conducted sufficient studies of crew ejection and decided to abandon the complicated escape module that had been used on the first three aircraft. On the fourth B-1A, the crew ejection module was replaced by four ACES II ejection seats that would have been standard on the B-1A production aircraft. The elimination of the escape capsule saved approximately $320,000 and 2000 pounds per aircraft.

By the summer of 1978, the installation of the first ALQ-161 system was under way on the fourth B-1A. Radiation pattern tests on the ALQ-161's three phased-array antennas, installed on a full-scale mock-up mounted on a pedestal, had been completed successfully at a facility in Weed Patch, California. A significant portion of the fourth aircraft's test flights were used for evaluating the ALQ-161.

Interestingly, at the same time the fourth aircraft was being manufactured, major subsections of a fifth aircraft were built in anticipation of the production contract. Some minor subsections for the sixth aircraft were also completed. These subassemblies were not assembled into an aircraft during the B-1A program, but would be used much later.

Although the B-1A program was effectively cancelled, flight testing continued using the third and fourth prototypes (74-0160 and 76-0174). Both aircraft were modified with an advanced Kuras Alterman Crosseye ECM system and a Doppler beam-sharpening modification to the forward-looking attack radar. The F101 engine program also continued at a reduced level, partially because the engines were needed to keep the two bombers flying, but also because the F101 had proven to be a remarkably good power-plant, and the Air Force anticipated some future need for it. In addition, wind-tunnel testing at AEDC continued, particularly to determine the separation characteristics of the stretched AGM-86B ALCM. Never had so much work been performed on a "cancelled" program. By 30 April 1981, when the fourth aircraft flew the last flight of the B-1A test program, the aircraft had made 70 flights and accumulated 378 hours. Since the maiden flight of the first B-1A on 23 December 1974, the four B-1As had logged 1895.2 hours in 247 flights. The YF101 engines had accumulated a total of just under 7600 flight hours.

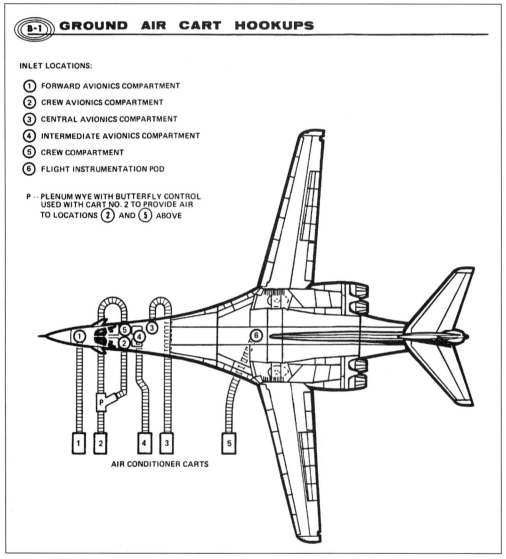

GROUND AIR CART HOOKUPS

INLET LOCATIONS:

① FORWARD AVIONICS COMPARTMENT
② CREW AVIONICS COMPARTMENT
③ CENTRAL AVIONICS COMPARTMENT
④ INTERMEDIATE AVIONICS COMPARTMENT
⑤ CREW COMPARTMENT
⑥ FLIGHT INSTRUMENTATION POD

P -- PLENUM WYE WITH BUTTERFLY CONTROL
USED WITH CART NO. 2 TO PROVIDE AIR
TO LOCATIONS ② AND ⑤ ABOVE

AIR CONDITIONER CARTS

Five air carts provided cooling air for the B-1As when they were on the ground without its engines running. In this illustration the fifth cart is dedicated to flight test instrumentation, but in operational aircraft would have cooled defensive avionics systems from the same location. *(U.S. Air Force)*

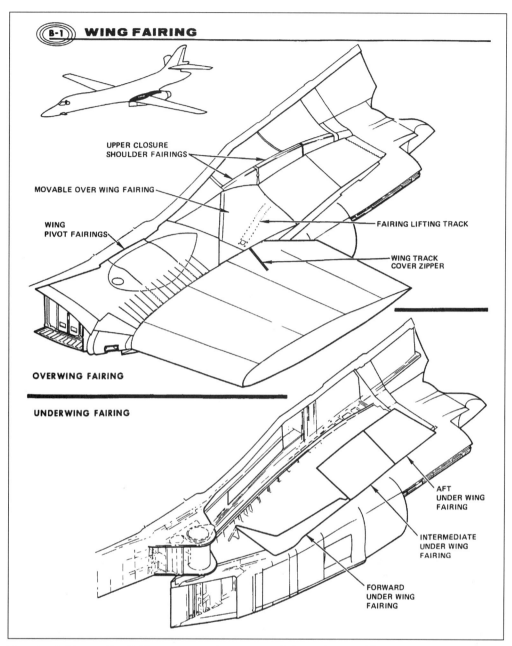

B-1 WING FAIRING

UPPER CLOSURE
SHOULDER FAIRINGS

MOVABLE OVER WING FAIRING

WING
PIVOT FAIRINGS

FAIRING LIFTING TRACK

WING TRACK
COVER ZIPPER

OVERWING FAIRING

UNDERWING FAIRING

AFT
UNDER WING
FAIRING

INTERMEDIATE
UNDER WING
FAIRING

FORWARD
UNDER WING
FAIRING

The wing fairing on the B-1A was a complex system of doors that would raise as the wing moved, then lower to seal the wing in its new position. The complexity was largely dictated by the high dynamic pressures encountered during high-speed flight at low altitudes. This would be changed to a much simpler system on the production B-1Bs. *(U.S. Air Force)*

B-1A Description

The four B-1As were prototype long-range supersonic bombers capable of Mach 2+ at high altitudes and Mach 1 at very low altitude. The B-1A was a major advance in technology from any strategic bomber that preceded it and incorporated many of the features that had made the F-111 a successful interdiction aircraft, including variable-geometry wings, a high thrust-to-weight ratio, advanced afterburning turbofan engines, automatic low-level terrain following, and an encapsulated crew escape module. New systems, including two auxiliary power units (APUs), an onboard oxygen generating system (OBOGS), and a central integrated test system (CITS) allowed the aircraft to be operated from dispersed austere bases. Careful shaping of the airframe was used to reduce the RCS, although no radar-absorbent coatings or materials were used specifically for this purpose. As eventually measured, the B-1A had an RCS of approximately 10 square meters (m^2), compared to the B-52's 100 m^2 and the FB-111A's 7 m^2. The internal weapons payload was theoretically greater than the total payload of the B-52G/H, and two external stores locations were also provided that could accommodate cruise missiles or other, as yet undeveloped, weapons.

The aircraft featured a blended wing-body fuselage with variable-geometry wings, a single vertical stabilizer with a three-section rudder, and horizontal stabilizers that operated independently to provide both pitch and roll control. The wings could vary their sweep from 15° to 67.5° and were equipped with leading-edge slats, spoilers that also functioned as speedbrakes, and trailing-edge flaps. The inboard wing did not have a defined airfoil profile, and its leading edge was very blunt in order to accommodate antennas for the defensive avionics system. Nonetheless, the inboard wing provided a significant portion of the total lift and was especially important at high angles-of-attack. Very small canards were mounted on each side of the forward fuselage as part of the structural mode control system, which was designed to reduce structural bending oscillations of the fuselage in pitch and yaw. A similar system had been flight tested on the XB-70A a decade earlier.

Each B-1A was powered by four YF101-GE-100 afterburning turbofan engines of 30,250 pounds-thrust mounted in two-engine nacelles below each wing pivot point. To allow supersonic speeds, an automated air induction control system varied the internal geometry of the inlets to maintain the required airflow to the engines under all flight conditions. Four auxiliary gearboxes, each shaft driven by a corresponding engine, were mounted in

The engine exhausts on the YF101-GE-100s were enclosed in tight-fitting "turkey-feathers." These were also included on the -102 engines used by the B-1B, but were later removed due to their high maintenance requirements. Their removal resulted in a slight drag penalty, but the overall cost savings was considered worth it. *(General Electric Aircraft Engines)*

In flight the B-1A was a graceful aircraft, appearing more like a large fighter than a bomber. The first two aircraft carried long nose booms with test instrumentation throughout their careers. *(Tony Landis Collection)*

separate compartments in the nacelles forward of the engines. These gearboxes were used to drive the hydraulic pumps and AC electric generators. An APU in each nacelle could also be used to drive the auxiliary gearboxes. The APUs provided engine starting, electrical power, and hydraulic power for ground checkout. This minimized the amount of ground equipment needed to support and launch the aircraft, especially at austere dispersal airfields.

A maximum of 150,000 pounds of fuel was carried in integral tanks in the fuselage, wing carry-through structure, and outer wing panels. A liquid nitrogen dewar provided gaseous nitrogen to inert the fuel tank ullage, minimizing fire and explosion hazards. Fuel transfer sequencing was automatic and also provided center-of-gravity control, especially during changes in wing geometry. The aircraft was equipped with single point refueling, and in-flight refueling was accomplished with a receptacle mounted on the nose ahead of the windscreen.

The fuselage was of conventional semimonocoque skin-frame-longeron construction made primarily of aluminum alloy. Titanium was used in the wing carry-through structure, the nacelle and vertical stabilizer supports, and other specific areas where high load-carrying capabilities were required. Titanium was also used for aft fuselage skins where engine exhaust generated high temperatures and acoustic levels. Other materials such as high-strength steel, fiberglass, polyimide quartz, and small amounts of boron composite were used where appropriate.

The cockpit was designed to provide the four crewmembers with a "shirtsleeve" environment. The forward crew station included a bird-resistant windshield and side and eyebrow windows, although no windows were provided for the rear crew stations. The cockpit was capable of maintaining a constant cabin pressure altitude of 8000 feet (the same as a modern airliner) throughout the aircraft operational flight envelope. The normal crew consisted of a

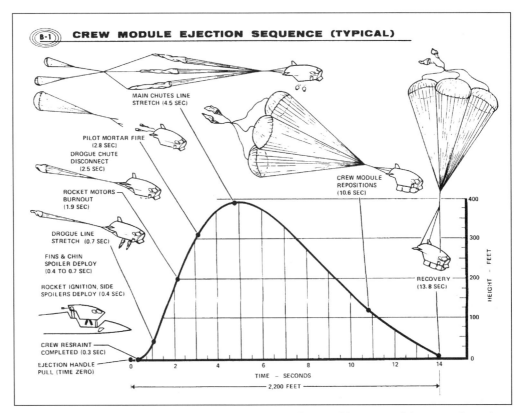

Like the F-111, the B-1A's escape module was supposed to provide successful escape throughout the aircraft's flight envelope. Unfortunately, the once it was called upon to do so, it did not completely work, resulting in the death of Doug Benefield. *(U.S. Air Force)*

pilot, copilot, defensive systems officer (DSO), and offensive systems officer (OSO), although on the first two B-1As, the DSO position was replaced by a flight test engineer (FTE). There were provisions for an instructor pilot (IP) sitting between and directly aft of the pilots, and an avionics instructor (AI) sitting between and directly aft of the FTE/DSO and the OSO.

The first three B-1As featured an encapsulated crew escape module, which normally formed an integral portion of the aircraft forward fuselage. The crew module was designed to provide safe escape from the aircraft at all speeds and altitudes within the operational flight envelope. The ejection process was initiated by pulling the ejection handles in the crew module. Automatic ejection could be initiated by either the pilot or copilot acting individually, or by the DSO and OSO acting together. If the automatic sequence failed after the ejection was commanded, the crew could initiate certain events (deploy parachutes, emergency oxygen, etc.) manually.

The crew module was severed by a linear-shaped explosive charge located behind the fairing strip that ran around the mold line and was propelled away from the aircraft by two rocket motors which produced 60,000 pounds-thrust for approximately 1.8 seconds. The motors could be gimbaled for directional control. After the module separated and was clear of the aircraft, the stabilizing fins deployed and the drogue parachute deployed, followed by deployment of three main parachutes. Large impact bladders inflated under the module to soften the landing. The module was designed to float and was equipped with uprighting and flotation bladders.

The fourth B-1A had four ACES II ejection seats instead of the escape module. These seats were essentially identical to the seats installed in the F-15 and F-16, except for the addition of armrests, comfort cushions, and limb restraints. A crewmember parachute and emergency oxygen system were included as part of each seat. The two instructor positions were not equipped with ejection seats; the instructors were expected to escape through the primary crew access hatch in the bottom of the fuselage—an unlikely scenario at low level.

The majority of the avionics were carried in the forward, central, and aft avionics compartments and in wing glove compartments. Internal ordnance was carried in three identical 15-foot-long weapons bays, two forward of the wing carry-through structure and one aft of the main landing gear wells. A total of 50,000 pounds of weapons could be carried between the three weapons bays on rotary launchers. Each weapons bay was technically capable of carrying 25,000 pounds of stores, but the maximum gross takeoff weight of the aircraft prohibited fully loading all three bays simultaneously. Structural provisions were provided in the fourth aircraft for two external pylons besides the forward weapons bay, but the pylons were never installed.

The B-1A was equipped with a conventional tricycle landing gear. The twin-wheel nose gear was mounted in the forward fuselage beneath the crew station and retracted forward. The nose-landing gear forward drag brace on the last B-1A differed from earlier aircraft due to some structural changes relating to the deletion of the crew escape module. The brace was shortened and had two short attaching arms that resulted in a "Y" shaped brace, rather than the one long straight arm on the first three aircraft. The twin-tandem main gear was mounted in the fuselage aft of the wing carry-through structure and retracted aft and laterally inboard for stowage in the fuselage between the intermediate and aft weapons bays.

Considered a major advance in technology at the time, an EMUX serial data bus was provided as a means of transmitting data throughout the aircraft on redundant transmission lines. This was an early attempt at a standardized bus implementation, and was generally similar to the eventual Mil-Std-1553B architecture used on the B-1B and most other modern military aircraft.

One of the key features that allowed the B-1A to operate from austere sites was the CITS, which functioned as an onboard test system for most of the aircraft systems. It performed test and control functions required to verify aircraft system performance both in-flight and on the ground, and it isolated and identified the fault down to a single line replaceable unit (LRU). Almost 20,000 individual parameters were monitored, and several thousand different diagnostic messages could be generated and recorded on a small printer in the cockpit.

The offensive avionics systems (OAS) allowed the aircraft to be flown on a preplanned mission in a fully automatic mode. The OSO could also change the mission based on new priorities or battle damage assessments. The AN/ASQ-156 offensive avionics system installed in the third and fourth aircraft consisted of a General Electric AN/APQ-144 (mod) forward-looking radar, Teledyne Ryan AN/APN-200 Doppler radar, a Honeywell AN/APN-194 dual channel radar altimeter, two Litton LN-15S inertial navigation systems, and a Hughes forward-looking infrared (FLIR) electro-optical viewing system (EVS). The avionics control unit complex (ACUC) used data from all the sensors in conjunction with prestored information to determine navigation, weapon delivery, and stores management functions. The APQ-144 forward-looking radar was similar to that in the F-111F but modified to allow it to scan 60° on either side of the centerline. As in the F-111, the forward-looking radar was separate from the terrain-following radar (TFR) system. The EVS, although completely repackaged, was essentially identical to the one installed in the B-52G/H. The EVS turret was on the bottom of the fuselage behind the nose landing gear.

The Texas Instruments AN/APQ-146 TFR system was the same as that used in the F-111F. This proven system gave the B-1A an impressive low-level penetration capability. As in the F-111, the TFR system allowed near-supersonic flight at altitudes as low as 50 feet, although the larger B-1A was essentially restricted to 200-foot minimum altitudes. An automatic flight control system (AFCS) provided pitch and roll control, various pilot assist modes, and included automatic throttle control.

The third B-1A as it appeared on 30 July 1985. The Crosseye ECM system on top of the fuselage was very prominent, but was considered inappropriate for a bomber-class aircraft and was not included in the B-1B production plan. *(Craig Kaston via the Mick Roth Collection)*

The defensive avionics system (DAS) was only installed in the last B-1A. The DAS comprised the Boeing AN/ASQ-184 management system and the ALQ-161 RFS/ECMS. The ALQ-161 was the first airborne electronic warfare system to have been designed as a fully integrated system from the start, in contrast to the B-52 system, which was a loose collection of subsystems that had been added over the years. The ALQ-161 included a variety of airborne jamming equipment, as well as the receivers for detecting the characteristics and approximate location of enemy radars. This information was used to automatically determine the relative priority of each emitter, so that available airborne jamming power could be applied effectively. The effectiveness of the jammers was greatly enhanced by the use of phased-array antennas that could direct the radiated energy at the appropriate enemy radar, instead of radiating it inefficiently from omnidirectional antennas. Further, the ALQ-161 was designed to continuously monitor the enemy threat situation and automatically adapt to the shutdown of one radar or the appearance of a new threat.

In 1978, AIL's Edwin M. Drogin presented a paper at the National Aerospace and Electronics Conference in Dayton that said the ALQ-161 is "designed primarily for use against pulse-type radars over a very wide bandwidth, roughly from 200 mc [MHz] to over 10 gc." The ALQ-161 was designed to evaluate the frequency of the incoming threat radar signal and automatically adjust the jamming signal with a 1 MHz accuracy. The system could also be used to jam continuous-wave emitters, such as Doppler radar or enemy radio communications. The ALQ-161 contained three sets of phased-array antennas used on a time-shared basis for both receiving and transmitting. In order to provide full 360° azimuth coverage, one antenna array was located in the tail and the other two in the wing-root leading edges. Using these antennas, narrow beams could be generated and electronically aimed at each threat radar within a few microseconds, then quickly shifted to direct jamming energy at another threat.

Drogin indicated that time was "the most critical parameter, because we must use a few transmitters to jam many threats . . . There may be 50 to 100 enemy radars looking at the

Although the nose radome was eventually painted to match the rest of the aircraft, the fourth B-1A's distinctive wing-root leading edge dielectric panels remained gloss black throughout its career. These covered the forward antenna arrays for the ALQ-161 defensive avionics system. *(Mick Roth Collection)*

With its wings swept fully aft, the third B-1A shows its high-speed configuration. The wing-sweep mechanism did not experience any significant problems during the development program, a tribute to the robustness of the design. The engine exhaust nozzles are in their fully "closed" position. *(Boeing North American)*

Suffering from an identity crisis, the fourth B-1A is shown at the Air Force Museum in November 1990. Many details represent the final B-1B design—the nose radome, the placement of the pitot tubes on the nose, and the vortex generators around the aft fuselage. But the pointed rear tail cone is pure B-1A, as is the gloss white paint scheme. This aircraft spent its entire flight test career with a B-1B-style blunt rear tail cone, but the Museum let Rome Labs use it to assist in antenna measurement tests. *(David W. Menard via the Terry Panopalis Collection)*

The September 1976 Edwards' air show offered the opportunity for the public to see the B-1A, seen here being towed into position before the show began. Although the aircraft did not fly during the show, it was still one of the star attractions. *(Mick Roth)*

aircraft." Rather than try to jam each radar continuously, the ALQ-161 was designed to determine when each radar would be looking at the aircraft and transmit only during that window. The ALQ-161's Litton LC-4516D minicomputer calculated how much radiated power was needed to screen the aircraft and obscure its natural radar echo (i.e., skin return). Then the system could automatically adjust the power radiated against each threat to the exact level required for screening. "By modulating the radiated energy we can achieve 'range-denial' as well as 'angle-denial' protection," Drogin said. The processor also determined the relative priority of each threat, the window during which each should be jammed, the beam pointing angle to the radar, the optimum power level, and the required modulation techniques.

Within any one of the three azimuth sectors, each of the four different frequency band jammers (bands 4, 5, 6, and 7) had three transmitters controlled by a high-speed microcomputer. The processor allocated each group of three transmitters to the highest-priority threats, on a pulse-by-pulse basis, based on data collected on each radar being monitored. These data included the time at which the radar was next expected to illuminate the aircraft and the duration of the desired jamming window. When there were relatively few enemy radars to be jammed, every known threat was allocated to a transmitter. When there were more known threats than transmitters or power available to the ALQ-161, the lower-priority threats are ignored, or reduced in time or power, in order to concentrate on the higher-priority ones.

After the cancellation of the B-1A production program, the Kuras Alterman Crosseye defensive jamming system and its accompanying dorsal spine waveguide was installed on the third and fourth aircraft. The waveguide was very prominent on top of the fuselage, stretching from just behind the cockpit area to the base of the vertical stabilizer. Details of this system are still classified, and very few details have been released on the installation or its function. However, the term "crosseye" is fairly generic ECM terminology to describe an "angle deception" system. Using this concept, two widely spaced locations on the aircraft have interconnected transponders installed. The receiver normal to the direction of the victim radar receives the victim radar pulse and triggers the transponder on the opposite side of the unit, which then transmits a copy of the victim radar pulse with a 180° phase shift. The result is a reversal of the sign of the angular error measured at the victim radar, causing the radar positioning mechanism to drive in the wrong direction (perfectly clear, right?).

From the Ashes: The B-1B

During early 1979, Rockwell began an examination of various derivatives of the B-1 with reduced cost and expanded mission roles. The result was a "core" concept that could be used to build a family of four different strategic aircraft. The core aircraft would have about 85 percent in common with the basic B-1A airframe, and many subsystems would be substantially similar. During the manufacturing process, each aircraft would be configured with various components that would adapt the airframe to a specific strategic mission. Rockwell stated that this family—consisting of a strategic weapons launcher, near-term penetrator, conventional bomber, and tanker—would be a very cost-effective strategic force because of the commonality among the variants. The cost effectiveness would come from an increased production run, common engines and basic avionics, crew cross training, and a simplified logistics system. Rockwell pointed out that this design would take advantage of the state of the art technology and nuclear hardness of the basic B-1A design, and it could use the estimated $5900 million already invested in the overall B-1 program.

The projected cost for the new aircraft, based on 100 aircraft at a production rate of four per month, was $43.3 million for the strategic weapons launcher, $48 million for the penetrator, $45 million for the conventional bomber, and $42.2 million for the tanker. This compared favorably to $68.5 million for the B-1A, although much of the apparent savings was illusory. The B-1A cost had included amortizing the research and development costs at roughly $24.6 million per aircraft based on a 240-aircraft production run. The "core" aircraft cost did not include this figure since it had already been written off as part of the B-1A cancellation.

Externally, the core aircraft was similar in appearance to the B-1A, but used a fixed-wing with 25° of leading-edge sweep. The fixed-wing was significantly simpler, cost less, and offered a significant weight reduction. Elimination of the fairing required for the variable-geometry wings also resulted in a significant reduction in base drag at subsonic speeds, improving the fuel efficiency of the design. By limiting the aircraft to subsonic speeds, the use of titanium could be reduced from 21 percent of the total airframe weight in the B-1A to approximately 8 percent in the core aircraft. Maximum altitude would be decreased to

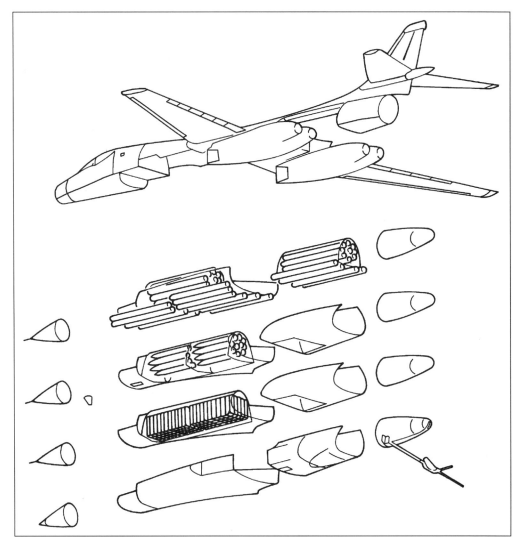

The core aircraft concept was put forward by Rockwell as a way to produce more B-1 derivatives than would otherwise be ordered. The basic airframe was tailored on the production line to serve one of four possible missions—strategic weapons launcher, near-term penetrator, conventional bomber, or tanker. *(Boeing North American)*

42,000 feet and the low-level penetration speed reduced to Mach 0.80 at 500 feet. The fixed-wing and lower speeds meant that independent operation of the horizontal stabilizers was no longer required, allowing a more conventional flight control system that used the horizontal stabilizer for pitch, a nonsegmented rudder for yaw, and ailerons and spoilers for roll.

The strategic weapons launcher was designed to carry as many as 30 ALCMs. The components added to the core airframe were two weapons bays, one forward and one aft of the wing and main landing gear, each equipped to carry eight missiles on a rotary launcher. Hardpoints for 14 external missiles were located on the weapons bay doors, requiring that the external missiles be launched before the weapons bays could be opened. A forward avionics compartment and radome would house an attack radar, while an aft avionics compartment contained ECM equipment. This aircraft was also capable of conventional warfare missions.

The near-term penetrator was optimized for low-level interdiction into the Soviet Union. It would be fitted with 16 SRAMs carried on two 180-inch rotary launchers in weapons bays located forward of the wing, and a fuel tank would be installed in place of the aft weapons bay. The B-1A structural mode control system and its forward-mounted canards would be retained to allow low-level operation. The same avionics and ECM equipment installed on the strategic weapons launcher were included with the addition of a terrain-following radar and FLIR/EVS. The penetrator could be assigned a split mission role with the addition of hardpoints on the weapons bay doors for 14 externally mounted cruise missiles.

The conventional bomber would be fitted with a weapons bay forward of the wing to accommodate such weapons as Mk 82 bombs, mines, and Harpoon missiles on normal vertical bomb racks. The other components added to the conventional bomber version were an aft-mounted fuel tank module and a relatively simple bombing and navigation system and ECM equipment.

An aerial tanker version of the core aircraft could be developed incorporating the B-1A's nuclear hardness and fast launch capability. The main components added to the core aircraft were a weather/rendezvous radar, three fuel tanks (where the B-1A had weapons bays), a boom operator's station, and a tail cone boom section.

Cruise Missile Carrier Development

In 1979, the Boeing AGM-86B and General Dynamics AGM-109 were in competition for the ALCM production contract. Each of the new missiles had twice the 745-mile range of the first-generation AGM-86A. With the new missiles demonstrating significant advances in accuracy and reliability, the Air Force began looking for the best platform from which to deploy them. A wide variety of possible aircraft were considered, with the B-52G/H being the obvious near-term choice. For the longer term, variants of the B-1A were compared with modified wide-body transport aircraft, as well as new design dedicated ALCM carriers. These were largely the same options that had previously been investigated during the Joint Strategic Bomber Study, although the individual designs differed somewhat.

In November 1979, as a result of the DoD cruise missile studies, the Air Force asked Rockwell to submit a proposal to fly a prototype strategic ALCM launcher. The prototype would be modified from the third B-1A (74-0160) and include two weapons bays capable of carrying eight ALCMs each. This design was similar to the strategic weapons launcher version of the B-1 core aircraft except it would retain the variable-geometry wings. Fourteen additional missiles could be carried externally in a configuration that differed from the B-1 core aircraft—six missiles would be mounted on single missile pylons on the bottom of the fuselage, and a pair of two-missile pylons on the underside of each inner wing. This configuration gave the aircraft the capability to carry a total of 30 cruise missiles.

Long-Range Combat Aircraft (LRCA)

While work on the strategic ALCM launcher study was in progress, Rockwell continued to investigate various other B-1 derivatives. Simultaneously, the DoD initiated a study by the Air Force Scientific Advisory Board (SAB) to determine the future direction of manned bomber development. The SAB concluded that the next bomber should be a versatile aircraft capable of undertaking a variety of missions, and that it should not be developed only to carry cruise missiles or to deliver free-falling nuclear weapons. Additionally, the SAB noted that a B-1 derivative probably offered the best overall design for a near-term (1987 IOC) aircraft that could conduct the missions outlined in the Board's recommendation.

To validate the SAB's conclusions, proposals were solicited from various contractors to fulfill the requirements for a Long-Range Combat Aircraft (LRCA). Rockwell's proposal was a modified version of the B-1A while General Dynamics proposed the FB-111B/C, very similar to the FB-111H developed for the Joint Strategic Bomber Study in 1975. The third option was an all-new concept, the Advanced Technology Bomber (ATB), although it did not represent any specific design (Lockheed and Northrop were competing for the ATB contract at the time).

The DoD also reviewed the issue of whether a single aircraft could meet all of the objectives. If not, could the objectives be satisfied by producing a multirole bomber first, with the ATB phased in at a later date? The review focused on bomber payload and range, penetration capability, multirole application, flexibility, cost, IOC date, and the maturity of the necessary technology. The general conclusion was that the ATB would require a considerable development program, and that some interim bomber was necessary to replace the B-52 until the ATB would be ready.

Rockwell did not feel compelled to adhere to any of the previously established requirements, and lowered the maximum speed of the LRCA from the B-1A's Mach 2.25 to only Mach 1.25, greatly simplifying the engine inlet systems and over-wing fairings. At the same time, a major strengthening of the basic airframe allowed the gross takeoff weight to increase from 395,000 to 477,000 pounds. This permitted the aircraft to carry an additional 50,000 pounds of weapons and 24,000 pounds of fuel (the other 8000 pounds represented the additional weight of the beefier airframe). This meant that the LRCA could carry a maximum load in each weapons bay, something the B-1A had not been able to do. The two forward weapons bays were redesigned to increase their flexibility by allowing the bulkhead separating them to be moved. The aircraft could carry 14 ALCMs externally and eight ALCMs in the forward weapons bay. The aft weapons bay would still be available to carry eight gravity nuclear bombs, eight SRAMs, or an auxiliary fuel tank. Significant attention was paid to configuring the new fixed inlets to minimize the radar cross-section of the design, and some amount of radar-absorbing material (RAM) was included in the final design.

Creating the FB-111B/C would entail stretching the fuselage of 66 FB-111As and 89 F-111Ds from 73 feet to 88 feet. An additional 31,822 pounds of fuel would be added, bringing the total fuel capacity to 64,574 pounds, and the main landing gear would be strengthened and moved outboard to accommodate the increased gross weight. The aircraft would be equipped with new defensive avionics as a retrofit after delivery to meet the IOC date. An auxiliary power unit would be added in the tail cone to meet the austere dispersal-basing requirement, and a pair of F101 engines would replace the TF30 turbofans. The weapons load would be increased from six weapons (two in the weapons bay, and one each on four under-wing pylons) to six external weapons and either four SRAMs, five B61 nuclear bombs, four B57 nuclear bombs, or three B43 nuclear bombs in the weapons bay. The FB-111B/C could not carry ALCMs internally, and carrying ALCMs externally would increase drag, severely decreasing the aircraft's range. Also, ALCMs carried on wing stations were a nuclear safety concern because they would be dangerously close to the ground during takeoff and landing. The stretched FB-111 would also depend heavily on tanker support, even with its increased fuel capacity.

The B-1A and its LRCA derivative used some design features, such as its blended wing-body, to reduce its radar signature. Both the B-1 LRCA and the stretched FB-111B/C would also use RAM to reduce their RCS. In both cases this produced an estimated signature of less than 2 m^2, compared to the original B-1A's 10 m^2.

The Advanced Technology Bomber would not need to further reduce its radar signature. The whole concept was based around building a "stealth" bomber that was essentially immune from detection by conventional radar and infrared sensors. Ideally, the total signature would be less than 0.1 m^2. Lockheed had successfully demonstrated one version of this concept with the Have Blue demonstrator and the F-117A Nighthawk stealth fighter. Although aerodynamically crude, the concept worked, and Lockheed believed it could be scaled up to meet LRCA requirements. But advances in computer technology allowed Northrop to propose a different style of stealth bomber that used a much more aerodynamically refined flying-wing design. This design also appeared to meet all the LRCA requirements.

Both the B-1 LRCA and FB-111B/C appeared to be able to meet the 1987 IOC date, while the ATB would represent, at best, a high-risk development program with an IOC in the early 1990s or later. The modified B-1 and stretched FB-111 presented different issues that affected Air Force confidence in reaching the 1987 IOC. General Dynamics had a production base in place for the F-16, which meant skilled workers and tools were available, and the Fort Worth facility was large enough to accommodate the additional work. However, extensive modifications would be required to convert the FB-111A and F-111D since the entire mid and aft fuselage sections would be new, as would be the engines. An extensive flight test program would be necessary to validate the design and determine the performance of the stretched aircraft. On the other hand, the B-1A prototypes were still flying, and while the modifications required were substantial, they were relatively straightforward. But Rockwell did not have any ongoing production programs other than the small-scale manufacture of Space Shuttle Orbiters, and would have to recruit and train people as well as procure tooling, and perhaps, a new facility. Neither situation was ideal.

On 30 April 1981, while the DoD and U.S. Congress deliberated the budget elements that would dictate the possible procurement of the LRCA, the last flight of the original B-1A program took place at Edwards. The fourth prototype was now placed in flyable storage alongside the other three, left there to wait for future developments.

The Bomber Penetration Evaluation (BPE) began in 1979 and ran through early 1981. This was a largely theoretical study of how some hypothetical aircraft might perform against projected Soviet air defenses. This final study led the Air Force to recommend the selection of the B-1B as the next strategic bomber on 1 June 1981, and on 2 October 1981 President Ronald Reagan announced that the Air Force would acquire 100 B-1B aircraft as part of the Strategic Modernization Program. The ATB program was also authorized to proceed, with plans to eventually procure 132 Northrop B-2A Spirit stealth bombers.

Development of the ALQ-161 ECM system had been cancelled in 1977 along with the B-1A production program. However, unlike many of the contractors, AIL had been authorized to continue its participation in the follow-on flight testing. Realizing the need for an advanced ECM system for whatever new bomber would ultimately replace the B-52, in October 1981 the Air Force reinstated the ALQ-161 program in a totally concurrent devel-

The second B-1A was used during the B-1B test program. For the first few months it retained its original gloss white paint scheme but with new "B-1B Test Program" markings on the vertical stabilizer. It was later repainted in the "strategic" version of the European One camouflage that would be used on the B-1Bs. (U.S. Air Force/DVIC DF-SC-85-03085)

opment and production program. There had been 95 flights of the prototype ALQ-161 aboard the B-1A, resulting in over 400 flight hours of experience. The initial 1981 contracts covered investigations on what new technology could be inserted into the existing ALQ-161 design without major development.

On 20 January 1982, Rockwell and the Air Force signed two contracts. The first of these was a $1317 million full-scale development (FSD) agreement that required Rockwell to finalize the B-1B design and modify two of the B-1A aircraft (74-0159 and 76-0174) as B-1B prototypes. The second was an $886 million production contract covering the construction of the first production B-1B and procurement of long-lead items for early full-scale production lots. The overall acquisition costs were set at $20.5 billion for 100 aircraft, including spares, support, and training. Nobody seemed to notice that this worked out to $205 million per aircraft. Concurrently, the Air Force awarded a contract to General Electric for production of the initial batches of F100-GE-102 engines, with a total of 469 engines to be procured (400 installed and 69 as spares). The first of the engines was delivered on 30 September 1983. These contracts were expected to generate work for some 3000 companies and provide employment for 58,000 people, including 22,000 at Rockwell.

The configuration of the B-1B was quite similar to the fourth B-1A prototype. In fact, 85 percent of the airframe was common to the B-1A, while over 90 percent of the offensive avionics was common to the equipment installed on the B-52H. The defensive avionics were derivative of the system used on the B-1A. Externally the most obvious differences were the B-1B's swept leading edge on the engine inlets and nacelles, the redesign of the over-wing fairing area, and the blunter nose and tail radomes. The first two changes were a result of simplifying the basic design since the original supersonic low-level requirements had been deleted. The B-1A over-wing fairing had been made up of a series of doors on the upper fuselage over the engine nacelle area, which raised during wing sweep and then closed down to fair the wing in its new position. The B-1B over-wing fairing was closer in design and function to that of the F-111, and used a large two-piece door edged with an inflatable bladder to fair the wing into the fuselage. Additional external weapons stations were also added, allowing the B-1B to carry more cruise missiles.

To further reduce the frontal RCS, the B-1B engine inlets were equipped with radar-deflecting vanes inside their ducts. These vanes were designed to prevent radar energy from being reflected off of the front of the engine and back to the transmitting radar. By all accounts the devices have been remarkably successful. Initially the B-1B was reported to have an RCS of less than 1.0 m^2, although this was subsequently revised in January 1993 to be approximately 1.45 m^2. This compares very favorably to the B-52 (100 m^2) and even the Russian Tu 160 Blackjack (15 m^2). However, it pales in comparison to the dedicated stealth aircraft. The B-2A reportedly has an RCS of only 0.1 m^2, while the F-117A has a truly remarkable 0.025 m^2.

Now that the Air Force knew the B-1B was going to happen, AIL was awarded a $1700 million contract to complete development of the ALQ-161A and deliver 100 systems to equip the new bombers. Each copy would cost over $10 million.

The first two complete ALQ-161As were installed on the fourth B-1A and the first B-1B during mid-1984 for continued flight testing. In addition, two partial systems were delivered for laboratory testing. The first was installed in a full-scale metal mock-up at the Rockwell facility at Weed Patch, California, to measure antenna radiation patterns. The other system was to be delivered to the Integrated Facility for Avionics System Test (IFAST) at Edwards AFB. The original schedule called for the delivery of seven ALQ-161A systems ordered under Lot 2 in late 1984, with the production rate increasing to two systems a month by August 1985 and reaching the peak rate of four per month in May 1986. Development problems would soon change this schedule. Due to the demanding concurrent scheduling necessary to achieve the desired 1987 IOC, significant problems were being reported by early 1986, and the first 22 operational B-1Bs would be delivered without the system.

It should be noted that many sources list the B-1B as carrying the Westinghouse AN/ALQ-153 tail-warning radar (as in the B-52G/H). This is not the case. Originally the ALQ-153 was in competition with a similar AIL AN/ALQ-154 system. Both systems had been flight tested in 1978 as part of the B-52G upgrade program. However, subsequent investigation by AIL showed that the tail-warning function could be integrated into the ALQ-161 with a considerable savings in cost and weight. Following a three-month evaluation, AIL was awarded a $9.1 million contract in September 1983 to incorporate this function into the ALQ-161A. A brass-board unit was installed on a Lockheed C-141 for flight evaluation at Eglin AFB. Originally, the TWF was scheduled to be included on the B-1B beginning with the seventh aircraft and to be retrofitted on earlier aircraft. Other problems ultimately resulted in the ALQ-161A not being installed on the B-1B until the 22nd aircraft.

AIL established an elaborate system test facility at its Deer Park, New York, plant that included cable runs identical to those used in the B-1B. To allow the hardware and software to be tested under realistic conditions, the Defensive System Integration Facility made it possible for the ALQ-161A to fly a simulated B-1B mission that even took into account changing surface topographies. Included was a threat generator that could simulate more than 70 enemy radars, including multibeam emitters and complex scanning radars, with a variety of modulations such as frequency slide, pulse-Doppler, and continuous-wave. At the time, AIL claimed that the simulation was so accurate the facility could potentially be used to train B-1B defensive system operators. AIL also built mobile test vans capable of simulating enemy threat emitters and delivered them to Edwards AFB, along with about 250 company personnel, to check out the ALQ-161A installed in the test aircraft.

B-1B Flight Testing

Modification of the second B-1A (74-0159) to include various B-1B subsystems took just over a year. The modifications did not include any of the aerodynamic changes to the air intakes, over-wing fairings, or the nose or tail radomes. On 23 March 1983 the modified B-1A made its first flight, marking the beginning of the B-1B test program. At this point the aircraft was still painted white, but had special "B-1B Flight Test" markings on the vertical stabilizer. It was subsequently repainted in the strategic camouflage that production B-1Bs would use. The initial series of flights was intended to verify the B-1B flight control law changes, and also to provide flight envelope expansion data relative to the increased gross weight of the B-1B. The planned 275 hours of flight tests were divided into stability and control (60 hours), vibration and acoustics (50 hours), dynamic response (45 hours), propulsion (15 hours), and weapons (105 hours). Additionally, this aircraft was planned to be used for cruise missile separation tests.

Unfortunately, the second B-1A crashed at Edwards on 29 August 1984. The aircraft was investigating minimum control speeds, and the center-of-gravity (cg) was allowed to creep too far aft (the pilot was controlling cg manually at the time). There was insufficient altitude available to recover the aircraft, which crashed into the desert. Rockwell test pilot Doug Benefield was killed when the crew escape module recovery parachute malfunctioned, causing the module to hit the ground in a nose-down attitude, preventing the bladders on the bottom of the module from damping the impact with the ground. The malfunction also caused serious injury to pilot Major Richard Reynolds and flight test engineer Captain Otto Waniczek. This accident led to a number of changes in the B-1B's fuel management and flight control system, most of which were incorporated beginning with B-1B No. 19 as part of the SIS1 modification.

On 30 July 1984, the fourth B-1A (76-0174) flew for the first time since being equipped with the full B-1B offensive and defensive avionics systems. This aircraft was selected as the primary B-1B tested since it was generally similar to the B-1B design and already contained a fairly complete set of avionics. The large dorsal spine associated with the Crosseye system was removed prior to it joining the B-1B test program, and the aircraft was still wearing its desert camouflage scheme. Initially, 420 hours of flight test time were scheduled: offensive avionics (135 hours), defensive avionics (245 hours), aircraft development (25 hours), and adverse weather performance (15 hours). The externally visible differences that identified 76-0174 as a B-1A were the over-wing fairing design, the lack of windows at the OSO and DSO stations, the supersonic engine intakes, and the lack of the antenna array under and on the sides of the rear fuselage. But some things were not quite B-1A either; for instance, the blunt rear radome that covered some of the ALQ-161A antennas was new.

The first production B-1B (82-0001—coincidentally, the first B-52A was 52-0001, and the first XB-70A was 62-0001) was rolled out on 4 September 1984, five months ahead of schedule. The early delivery was due in part to the use of existing subassemblies originally manufactured for the planned, but never completed, fifth B-1A. Although this permitted the B-1B program to proceed at a rapid pace, it also meant that there would be some substantial differences between the first B-1B and subsequent aircraft.

The first B-1B made its maiden flight on 18 October 1984, well ahead of the original March 1985 schedule date. The crew on this flight consisted of pilot M. L. Evenson, copilot Lieutenant Colonel L. B. Schroeder, DSO Captain D. E. Hamilton, and OSO Major S. A. Henry. The first flight had no major problems, with the aircraft leaving Palmdale and flying for 3 hours, 20 minutes, before landing at Edwards AFB.

The flight report said, "The first flight of aircraft B-1B No. 1 was successfully accomplished on 10/18/84. Following two delays, takeoff occurred at 1438 PDT. All planned avionics systems were operating at takeoff. The primary objectives of the flight were to evaluate flying qualities of the aircraft and assess in-flight operation of avionics systems. The aircraft was flown to the Edwards area and all testing was conducted in this region. The entire avionics system operated as expected throughout the flight with the exception of the radar. The radar was turned on approximately 10 minutes following takeoff and locked up 40 minutes later. . . ."

The aircraft was assigned to the B-1 CTF at Edwards and continued to undergo test flights to evaluate the aerodynamic characteristics of the B-1B. A considerable amount of specialized flight test equipment, including a pitot boom on the tip of the radome and "flutter wands" on the wing tips, the horizontal stabilizer tips, and the upper rudder, was installed on the aircraft. The flutter wands could be oscillated in flight to induce flutter as needed to obtain test objectives. An aft-facing camera pod was mounted on the crew access door and camera pods were added to the engine nacelles to record weapon releases. The original black air refueling markings on the nose did not show up well during night operations and were replaced during May 1985 with a spiderweb of white lines. These were later simplified to the present markings. While at Edwards, the aircraft was named *Leader Of The Fleet*, with the name painted on the outside of both nose gear doors.

Aerodynamic and weapon release testing continued through 28 April 1988, by which time the first B-1B had logged 617 hours in 138 test missions. The aircraft was placed in flyable storage at Edwards, awaiting a decision as to what to do with the somewhat unique airframe. There were several structural and systems differences between the first B-1B and the remainder of the B-1B fleet, due mostly to the use of B-1A No. 5 subassemblies and the installation of flight test equipment. The substantial costs involved in modifying the basic structure could not be justified, and on 2 August 1988 the aircraft was flown to Ellsworth AFB, where it was removed from flying status and became a weapons-loading trainer.

In February 1995, the B-1 SPO sponsored a meeting with other Air Force and Navy programs to develop a plan for investigating issues associated with the proposed change from JP-4 to JP-8 fuel. The B-1 SPO developed a JP-8 characterization test program that included a series of ballistic tests against replica aircraft to provide data on both ullage and dry bay

The first B-1B (82-0001) was named "Leader of the Fleet." For most of its career it simply carried its name on the nose wheel doors, but later it received nose art on the left side only. Note the cooling air hoses. *(Craig Kaston via the Mick Roth Collection)*

JP-8 fire characteristics. This data would be subsequently confirmed in a series of tests using sections of the first B-1B. In 1995, the aircraft was disassembled in accordance with the Strategic Arms Reduction Treaty (START), and portions were transported to Wright-Patterson AFB for use in the JP-8 fire propagation tests. The remainder of the airframe was subsequently scrapped.

B-1B Production

During 1982, the Air Force awarded contracts for five production batches (lots) of B-1Bs. Lot I consisted of only the first aircraft (82-0001). The first true production batch was Lot II, consisting of seven aircraft (83-0065/0071) funded in the FY83 budget. An additional 10 aircraft (Lot III, 84-0049/840058) followed in FY84, 34 aircraft (Lot IV, 85-0059/0092) in FY85, and the remaining 48 (Lot V, 86-0093/0140) of the requested 100 aircraft in FY86. By the spring of 1986, eight B-1Bs had been delivered. Deliveries increased to a peak rate of four aircraft per month in October 1986, and continued at that rate throughout 1987 and the first four months of 1988. The last production aircraft (86-0140) was delivered to the 384th Bomb Wing (Heavy) at McConnell AFB, Kansas, on 2 May 1988.

The facility at Plant 42's Site 3 where the B-1As had been built (and the XB-70As before them) was not considered large enough to house all of the B-1B production work, so a new facility was built across the runway for B-1B production. Nevertheless, the two main buildings (301 and 307) at Site 3 were used to manufacture the forward and forward intermediate fuselage sections. Painting was also accomplished at Site 3. The new facility (unofficially called Site 9) was built by Rockwell on land leased from the Los Angeles Department of Airports (which, in the 1970s, had planned to built a replacement for LAX adjacent to Plant 42). The final assembly building at Site 9 has 264,000 square feet (660 × 400 feet) of unobstructed floor space and is 73 feet high. It could accommodate nine B-1Bs in section assembly, five in fuselage mate, two in aircraft mate, and two in final assembly.

The B-1B underwent structural testing in the Lockheed facility at Plant 42 in Palmdale. Like the B-1A and Space Shuttle this was nondestructive testing, and the airframe was later completed as an operational aircraft. *(Tony Landis Collection)*

Assembled aircraft were then moved to an adjacent 254,000-square-foot checkout building capable of performing tests on four B-1Bs simultaneously.

The B-1B manufacturing program was perhaps one of the smoothest in Air Force history. It ran on or ahead of time and was generally below cost estimates in constant-year dollars (the actual total exceeded the estimate by 14 percent, mainly due to inflationary adjustments). On 6 April 1987, the Air Force presented the Manufacturing Productivity Award to Rockwell's North American Aircraft Division in recognition of the B-1B production program. This annual award focuses on increased efficiency, initial quality, effective management, and the implementation of actions to reduce weapon system costs. Rockwell made a capital investment of $600 million to support B-1B manufacturing, mainly in state-of-the-art production machinery. These advanced production machines plus enhancements in computer-aided manufacturing contributed to Rockwell's increased productivity. Another major contributing factor was a dedicated work force and management team. The first production batch (Lot II) took an average of 22,000 labor hours per aircraft to produce, a figure reduced to 11,000 hours per aircraft in the last production batch. This represented an estimated $1000 million cost savings.

At the peak of production, approximately 167,000 production tools were used by Rockwell and its suppliers. When the last production B-1B was delivered, all critical tooling essential for after-production needs, including battle damage repair, structural modifications, and spares, was placed in storage. The most expensive tooling was kept, and only tooling that could be replaced quickly and inexpensively was discarded. All long-lead-time tooling was also retained. Some of the nondimensional special tooling was sent to Air Force operational and maintenance bases for continued use but the balance was scrapped. Nondimensional tooling includes work platforms, ramps, and large cargo containers for shipping major subassemblies. Approximately 57 percent (96,000 items) of the production tooling was retained in government storage or with the manufacturer. It is interesting to note that this retained tooling represented 80 percent of the total value (cost) of all B-1B tooling.

The B-1B was officially named "Lancer" on 15 March 1990 after a long campaign that had started with the B-1A. The B-1 SPO decided that the name Lancer evoked the spirit of the B-1's mission, and as then–Air Force Secretary Donald Rice said, "Much like the Lancers of yesteryear, the B-1Bs of today provide the same speed, maneuverability, and shock needed to penetrate well beyond an adversary's defenses and deliver a decisive blow to his war fighting means." Other suggested names had included Peacemaker II, Excalibur, Phoenix, and Centurion. A more popular, but very unofficial, nickname is simply "Bone." This name came about when a reporter writing an article on the Rockwell B-ONE accidentally left out the hyphen. When people associated with the B-1B program talk about it, they use "Bone"—the term Lancer is most often used in press releases.

Test Programs

The Air Force Operational Test and Evaluation Center (AFOTEC) provides assessments of the operational effectiveness and suitability of weapon systems to the Air Force Chief of Staff, Secretary of the Air Force, and the Secretary of Defense to assist in the acquisition decision process. AFOTEC testing traditionally consists of initial operational test and evaluation (IOT&E) and follow-on operational test and evaluation (FOT&E). This testing is designed to evaluate how well weapon systems will perform when operated and maintained by normal Air Force personnel in a realistic training and combat environment. AFOTEC testing usually occurs after the development command and manufacturer completes the developmental test and evaluation (DT&E).

But the B-1 SPO decided to break from tradition. In order to reduce B-1B program costs and compress the development schedule, IOT&E was accomplished at Edwards AFB in conjunction with the DT&E. Five B-1Bs, No. 1 (82-0001), No. 9 (84-0049), No. 17 (84-0057), No. 28 (85-0068), and No. 40 (85-0080), were used. The combined test series was completed in April 1988.

The subsequent FOT&E consisted of 144 missions from Dyess AFB, Texas, using B-1B No. 32 (85-0072—*Polarized*). These missions included three live AGM-69A launches, five inert B83 drops, five inert B61 drops, four conventional weapons missions that dropped a total of 276 inert 500-pound Mk 82 AIR bombs, two polar navigation missions ("70 Degree North Mission"), one long-range over-water deployment to the western Pacific and the southern hemisphere (Exercise Distant Mariner), and 90 ECM test missions against airborne and ground-based threats throughout the United States.

The FOT&E evaluated the operational effectiveness of the B-1B's navigation reliability and accuracy, low-level penetration capability, survivability, weapons delivery, mission reliability, and diagnostic capability. Although coming too late to affect the acquisition strategy for the B-1B program, the FOT&E effort was generally considered successful and resulted in several changes to software and procedures.

Operational test and evaluation (OT&E) actually continues for the life of a weapons system. As each new capability or significant modification is made, a formal OT&E is conducted to verify its effectiveness. In many cases this is a requirement levied by Congress prior to releasing production funding for the new capability. In all cases it is a requirement from the Office of the Under Secretary of Defense for Acquisition and Technology (USD/A&T). The OT&E of the B-1B continues in full force as of this writing, evaluating the various modifications that continue to be made to the aircraft.

During July and August 1986, the 10th B-1B (84-0050) underwent environmental testing in the McKinley Climatic Laboratory at Eglin AFB, Florida. Additional climatic testing was accomplished at McKinley during July and August 1987 using B-1B No. 88 (86-0128). The aircraft were parked inside the climatic hangar and operated at temperatures ranging from 125°F to –65°F. Various types of precipitation, including rain and fog, were also created in

The 10th B-1B covered in ice at the McKinley Climatic Laboratory at Eglin AFB during July 1986. Additional testing was conducted using the No. 88 aircraft the following year. *(U.S. Air Force via the Tony Landis Collection)*

the laboratory. To permit engine operation during these tests, the engine exhaust was ducted to the outside of the building. Only minor problems were uncovered during the first series of tests, and these had been corrected by the second series.

The 28 September 1987 crash of the 12th aircraft (84-0052) resulted in the death of three crewmembers, including two riding in the instructor seats. Due to the low-level nature of the flight, it is unlikely that anybody could have bailed out using established procedures, but questions nevertheless arose about the bottom bailout capability of the B-1B. To determine if safe bailout from the crew entry hatch was possible, tests were conducted using aircraft No. 81 (86-0121) during January 1989. The crew ladder and bottom hatch were removed and the nose-landing gear was locked down to configure the aircraft as it would be if the bottom bailout handle in the crew entryway had been pulled. The nose-landing gear and its door are designed to act as a spoiler, allowing crewmembers to drop below the level of engine nacelles before hitting the slipstream. An instrumented dummy was released through the open crew hatch at various speeds and altitudes within the bottom bailout envelope (speeds below 300 knots). The testing demonstrated that a crewmember could successfully escape from the B-1B if time permitted.

The Air Force Anechoic Facility (AFAF) at Edwards is large enough to accommodate any aircraft smaller than the C-5 and is designed to simulate free-space electromagnetic characteristics. The AFAF consists of a $250 \times 264 \times 70$-foot shielded anechoic chamber enclosed in a metal building that also houses offices and shops. The walls, ceilings, and floor of the anechoic chamber are covered with over 204,000 square feet of radio frequency (RF) absorbing material cut into 816,000 pyramid-shaped foam cones that vary in height from 12 to 36 inches. In the center of the AFAF is an 80-foot diameter turntable that can be rotated 190° in either direction. Aircraft are towed onto the turntable through a door in the east wall, put on

The first aircraft to use the Air Force Anechoic Facility at Edwards AFB was B-1B No. 40 (85-0080). In this photo the aircraft has its wings swept back and landing gear up—the aircraft is supported on jacks hidden beneath layers of radio frequency (RF) absorbing material. Even the hoses carrying cooling air into the aircraft have been covered with RF absorbent material. *(U.S. Air Force via the Tony Landis Collection)*

jacks, and the landing gear is then retracted. Jacks and other equipment on the turntable are covered with RAM to reduce the number of reflective surfaces. The signals hitting the aircraft come from three separate threat antennas located on the north, south, and west walls. The AFAF took just under two years to build at a cost of $58 million, all of it B-1B program money. Silhouettes of the B-1B are cast in the concrete at various places throughout the building to remind future users who originally paid for the facility. Appropriately, during mid-1990, a B-1B (85-0080) became the first aircraft to be tested in the facility.

Electromagnetic Pulse

Electromagnetic pulse (EMP) is one of the effects of any large explosion, but is most often associated with high-altitude nuclear detonations. When an aircraft encounters EMP, very large electrical currents are created on the outside skin, which can flow through cables and antennas, potentially damaging electronic components. The B-1B design counters EMP by shielding the electronic subsystems and the interconnecting cabling, and designing the electronics to either accept any remaining currents or pass them to a ground.

To verify the effectiveness of the design, a B-1B was tested on the "Trestle" at Kirtland AFB, New Mexico. This 118-foot-high, 40,000-square-foot platform is large enough to hold a C-5 and can support an aircraft weighing up to 550,000 pounds. It is constructed completely of wood and other nonmetallic materials—glue, wood pegs, and fiberglass bolts were used instead of metal nails, nuts, and bolts. The facility simulates the electromagnetic pulse using two 5-million volt pulsers that discharge their energy into wires surrounding the aircraft on the trestle. Special sensors measure aircraft response to EMP and transmit data via fiber optic cable (which is immune to EMP) to computers inside a shielded enclosure for recording and later analysis.

Two different B-1Bs were tested at the electromagnetic pulse "trestle" at Kirtland AFB, New Mexico. The No. 66 aircraft (86-0106) and the last B-1B (86-0140) was tested from November 1987 to September 1989. *(Boeing North American)*

The B-1B underwent three phases of EMP testing from November 1987 to September 1989. Phase 1 was accomplished during November and December 1987 and verified access to the test locations within the aircraft using aircraft No. 66 (86-0106). The second phase lasted from July until December 1988 and provided the majority of the data used to evaluate the design and implementation of the EMP protective measures. This phase also established a baseline against which future test data can be compared to detect changes in the system. The last B-1B (86-0140) was used for Phase 2. The third phase repeated selected tests and measurements on the last aircraft, and compared the results to the Phase 2 baseline to evaluate the repeatability of the test procedures. This phase took place from July through September 1989.

The data collected by the EMP testing are also used by the Oklahoma City Air Logistics Center (OC-ALC) for maintenance of the B-1B fleet. Using simplified test procedures developed from these data, aircraft undergoing routine maintenance are screened for changes from the established baseline to determine if additional maintenance is required to maintain the EMP integrity of the aircraft.

B-1B Antenna Measurements

When the B-1A production program was cancelled in 1977, the Air Force's Rome Laboratory requested one of the B-1A prototypes for a series of antenna measurement tests at its Stockbridge Facilities. Even though the B-1A would not enter the active inventory, the Laboratory believed the aircraft would prove to be a valuable research tool. For a variety of reasons, the B-1 SPO declined the request. When the B-1B program was initiated in 1981, Rome Labs renewed its request, but the B-1 SPO did not want to eliminate a possible flight test aircraft from the inventory, and again declined the request.

In 1987, the Rome Laboratory was finally authorized by the B-1 SPO to acquire one of the B-1As as a testbed. In fact, the entire antenna measurement program had become an urgent matter to support finding solutions to problems being encountered during the development of the defensive avionics system. After reviewing the condition of the three remaining B-1As, Rome Labs stated their preference for the fourth aircraft since it most closely resembled the production B-1B. However, this aircraft had already been turned over to the Air Force Museum at Wright-Patterson AFB, leaving the first two prototypes to choose from. After a careful review of these two airframes, Rome Labs decided the first aircraft was in overall better condition and selected it.

On 1 June 1987 the first B-1A (74-0158) was formally assigned to the Rome Laboratory. The next major issue was how to transport the aircraft from Edwards to the Rome Laboratory facilities near Griffiss AFB, New York. Although the aircraft had been in "flyable" storage, it had been heavily scavenged for parts to support the initial B-1B flight test program. It was determined that it was not cost effective to return the aircraft to flight status for one more flight, since after that flight it would again be stripped down for conversion to an antenna measurement testbed.

A number of alternatives were investigated. The fact that the aircraft was not flightworthy did not rule out transport by air, and the use of NASA's modified Boeing 747 Shuttle Carrier Aircraft (SCA) was examined. The shuttle fleet was grounded due to the Challenger accident, and the SCA was, in theory, available for use. It was technically feasible that the B-1A could be transported atop the SCA basically intact. However, this would involve modifications to the SCA and flight qualifying the combined vehicle, which would take longer than the B-1 SPO was willing to wait. Also, since there was, at the time, only a single SCA, NASA was hesitant to allow another program to use it in such a manner.

The next option was to break the B-1A apart into sections that would fit into a C-5 transport. The B-1A was a large aircraft, and although it was again technically feasible, this option was not considered cost effective. Movement by rail was also investigated, but the costs involved were greater than anticipated due to the use of specialized rail cars and special routing requirements. In addition, the aircraft could not be delivered by rail near enough the Rome Laboratory without resorting to the extensive use of trucks. Transport by helicopter was reviewed, but again the aircraft would need to be completely disassembled, this time into even smaller pieces. The distances involved, along with the economic and logistics considerations, ruled out this possibility. Movement by barge was considered. Again, the aircraft would have to be completely dissembled and trucked to the nearest port where it would be loaded aboard a barge and transported through the Panama Canal, then up the river and canal systems of the eastern United States. This option was also determined not to be cost effective.

The one thing all of the options (except the SCA) had in common was that the B-1A would need to be disassembled to the point where it could be transported at least some distance by truck. For the most part, the amount of disassembly necessary for the trucking portion of the trip was the same, only the distances involved varied. Since trucking was necessary anyway, it was determined that it was most cost effective to simply use this mode of transportation all the way across the country.

But nobody had ever disassembled a B-1 before, and there were no manuals on how to accomplish this task. At the same time, the aircraft would be stripped of most internal systems (wiring, fuel lines, hydraulics, etc.) to lighten it as much as possible. This saved transportation costs, but was also necessary so as not to exceed the limitations of Rome Lab's mounting pylons. The ground rule was to preserve the external electromagnetic characteristics of the airframe as much as possible. Any parts removed from the aircraft that were deemed to be in serviceable condition were returned to the B-1B logistics system for use on operational aircraft.

Originally, only the rear fuselage was mounted (upside-down) for testing. Later in the test series the vertical stabilizer was reattached to the rear fuselage and the entire assembly was mounted right-side-up for more antenna measurements. These measurements were undertaken in support of the new tail warning function being included in the horizontal stabilizer fairing. *(U.S. Air Force/Rome Labs)*

Eventually Rome Labs intended to utilize the entire B-1 airframe at its Stockbridge Facilities. However, the B-1 SPO's first priority was to conduct measurements relating to the ALQ-161A's tail-warning function, so the tail section was needed first. The tail section was broken down into the aft fuselage section, tail radome, vertical stabilizer, and the horizontal stabilizers. This worked out to be two oversized truck loads, which were quickly packed and shipped overland to the Newport Facilities.

In parallel, arrangements were made with the Air Force Museum to swap tail radomes. The museum's No. 4 B-1A had been built with a B-1B-style tail radome (blunter and of different material than the original B-1A unit), and the museum decided that a swap of tail radomes would not detract from its aircraft's historical value, although it adds some confusion for historians.

The tail section arrived at Griffiss AFB in late November 1987 and was modified internally to allow power and RF hardware to be installed. The tail section was installed at the Newport Facilities in January 1988. The first tests to be conducted concerned the effects of the horizontal stabilizers, rudder position, and radar-absorbing materials on various TWF antenna configurations.

Meanwhile, back at Edwards, the remainder of the airframe was being disassembled beginning with the engine nacelles (the engines were returned to the manufacturer for modification to the -102 configuration and subsequently returned to the inventory). The removal of the nacelles also provided easier access to the wing pivot points in the wing carry-through structure. This was the most controversial aspect of the disassembly process since Rockwell was certain that the wing pivot pin could not be removed in the field. During the manufacturing process, the pin sleeve had been heated and the pin frozen in liquid

The first B-1A was dismantled at Edwards AFB and transported to Rome Laboratories for antenna measurements. Disassembling the aircraft was an adventure for those involved since nobody had ever disassembled a B-1 before, and no technical manuals existed on how to do it. *(U.S. Air Force/Rome Labs)*

Other tests at Rome Labs have used only the extreme forward fuselage. The Laboratory has tested most every modern Air Force aircraft type, including F-111, F-4, F-15, and the A-10. *(U.S. Air Force/Rome Labs)*

nitrogen. The frozen pin was inserted in the heated sleeve and an extremely tight fit resulted after both items returned to ambient temperature. Rockwell and others did not believe this process could be reversed in the field.

Nevertheless, it was decided to attempt freezing the pin with liquid nitrogen while a crane took the tension off the pin by lifting up on the wing. A hydraulic jack was placed under the pin to push up on it, and a crane was hooked to the top of the pin to pull on it simultaneously. When everything was in position, the liquid nitrogen was poured into the pin (which is hollow, just for this reason). After allowing an hour for the pin to cool down, it was easily extracted, and the same procedure was repeated on the other wing. Upon completion of this major task, the remainder of the disassembly was relatively easy. In addition to allowing the B-1A to be transported to Rome Labs, this exercise also provided valuable experience for the Air Force in how to recover and repair a B-1B in the field.

The next section removed was the aft intermediate fuselage, which was further broken down into center and side pieces to reduce its width to a size suitable for trucking. The forward fuselage section containing the cockpit was removed next. In addition, the nose radome was removed. The main landing gear was removed from the wing carry-through structure next. After this, the structure itself was removed from the forward intermediate fuselage section and was further broken down by slitting it down the middle. As each section was removed, it was secured and/or crated, then loaded onto trucks for the journey from Edwards to Griffiss. The last trucks arrived at Griffiss in December 1988.

It should be noted that disassembling the B-1 at its production break/assembly points was not a straightforward task. No technical orders were available, so the disassembly was accomplished basically by trial and error based on the prior experiences of all the parties. Fortunately, the combined expertise of all involved proved to be more than adequate for the task. Not only nuts, bolts, rivets, sealer, and paint had to be removed, but all electrical harnesses, fuel and hydraulic lines, and pyrotechnics had to be disconnected and removed or disabled in order to break the fuselage sections apart.

Once at Griffiss, the forward intermediate fuselage and engine nacelles were superficially modified to match the B-1B configuration. Quick-look tests were conducted on the forward intermediate fuselage and cockpit section at the Newport Facilities. Continued testing has involved both the forward fuselage and aft fuselage being mounted upside-down and right-side-up, but as of the end of 1998 there has not been a reason to completely reassemble the aircraft. The entire B-1 could be reassembled at the Stockbridge Facilities to support B-1B testing if it is ever required. Both upside-down and right-side-up mounts were constructed capable of supporting the weight of the entire airframe.

Y2K Testing

On 27 October 1998, the B-1 SPO completed a year 2000 (Y2K) demonstration at the Birk Flight Test Facility at Edwards. The Y2K compliance team comprised contractor and government personnel from the B-1 SPO, Boeing, the 419th Flight Test Squadron (FLTS), and the 46th Test Group (TG) from Holloman AFB. The team's primary objective was to answer questions about the computer systems' ability to successfully make the transition to the year 2000. A secondary objective was to verify the validity of the Y2K compliance certifications already completed on various B-1B subsystems. The B-1B was the first major weapons system to accomplish an end-to-end test demonstrating Y2K compliance.

The most extensive testing was accomplished on the ground, where significant Y2K and global positioning system (GPS) rollover dates were tested. Some of the test scenarios included 31 December 1999 to 1 January 2000, 28 February to 29 February 2000, and GPS almanac/week rollovers. The 46th TG provided equipment capable of simulating the GPS satellite constellation, and the ground test was conducted using procedures developed by

Boeing in conjunction with 419th FLTS and culminated with the simulated launch of a GBU-32 JDAM. This test ensured that proper mission data were passed from the aircraft to the weapon following a rollover from 31 December 1999 to 1 January 2000.

Following the successful ground test segment, the flight segment focused on overall B-1B system operation. The B-1B flew its demonstration mission on 23 October 1998, but the mission clock was rolled forward to 11 October 2000. The demonstration included a weapons release, terrain following, navigation legs, and operation of all B-1B systems. The 419th FLTS crew noted no anomalies in system performance.

Support Aircraft

The B-1B program used two transport aircraft for avionics flight testing. Westinghouse tested the APQ-164 offensive radar set in a modified BAC-111 (N164W) with an extended radome mounted on the nose that contained the low observable antenna and with consoles in the passenger cabin for operation and display of the radar. The third YC-141A (61-2777) was used by Aeronautical Systems Division (ASD) as a flying testbed for development of the ALQ-161A defensive avionics system. This aircraft used various external antennas over the course of development.

During the flight test program, the B-1 CTF used General Dynamics F-111s stationed at Edwards as safety chase aircraft since the F-111's performance closely matched that of the B-1B. However, the F-111 did not have the endurance of the B-1B, and two or three F-111 sorties were required for each B-1B test flight. A single F-111A (66-0053), three F-111Ds (68-0085, 68-0087, and 68-0089), and one F-111E (71-0115) were used in support of the B-1B program.

The B-1 CTF also used various McDonnell Douglas F-4 Phantom IIs assigned to Edwards as photo chase aircraft, especially for flight tests with planned weapon releases. Five F-4Cs (63-7407/7409, 67-0727, and 64-0869) and five F-4Es (66-0284, 66-0286, 66-0289, 66-0291,

Various Convair (General Dynamics) F-106 Delta Darts were used as chase aircraft during the B-1B production program. These were the last "manned" F-106s in operational service with the Air Force (others had been converted as target drones). Special tail markings celebrated their service. *(Mick Roth Collection)*

When the B-1B production program ended, the F-106s were ferried to Davis-Monthan AFB in Arizona for storage. After a while they were earmarked for conversion into target drones. Four single-seat F-106As and three two-seat F-106Bs were used by the B-1B program. *(U.S. Air Force/DVIC DF-ST-91-02481)*

Wings fully swept, a B-1B banks away from the camera during a training flight. The strategic camouflage wrapped completely around the aircraft, although the bottom colors were different than the topside ones. *(U.S. Air Force)*

A white Christmas for the 7th BW at Dyess AFB, Texas. Unlike the B-2A, the B-1Bs stay outside except during heavy maintenance, meaning they get wet—or in this case, cold. *(7th BW Public Affairs)*

One of the aircraft retained at Edwards AFB for continued testing shows the large deflection on the horizontal stabilizers during braking. The wing spoiler panels are also deflected upward. *(Erik Simonsen)*

One of the B-1Bs (84-0049) retained at Edwards shows the full-span leading-edge slats and the almost full-span flaps in their fully deployed position. Noteworthy is the ALE-50 dispenser on the bottom of the rear fuselage. *(Terry Panopalis)*

A careful examination will show a conventional weapons module being loaded into the aft weapons bay of this B-1B (86-0137) at McConnell AFB on 21 August 1992. *(Don Logan via the Mick Roth Collection)*

The blue and white checkerboard pattern has always been used by the B-1B training squadron, although the squadron itself has changed several times. This is 86-0105, assigned to the 28th BS of the 7th BW at Dyess AFB, on 12 May 1997. *(Don Logan via the Mick Roth Collection)*

Most B-1Bs carry nose art on the left side of the forward fuselage, while some also carry it on the right side. The nose art is at the discretion of the aircraft commander, and changes occasionally as new commanders are assigned to the aircraft. The permanent B-1B bases (such as Ellsworth AFB, here) have the cooling air supply (part of the central aircraft support system—CASS) built into the ramp, eliminating the need for the large ground carts seen at Edwards AFB and other operating locations. *(Don Logan via the Mick Roth Collection)*

The lower forward fuselage is flattened slightly around the weapons bays to simplify the door interface, which had to remain a constant section to allow the bays to be reconfigured to accommodate larger weapons. The nacelles are contoured to tightly envelop the engines and minimize drag. *(Boeing North American via Steve Pace)*

The B-1B is capable of supersonic flight at high altitudes, although changes to the air intakes and engines to minimize costs resulted in a significant loss of top speed potential. Most B-1B mission scenarios have it attacking at low or medium altitudes where supersonic speeds are of less value. *(U.S. Air Force)*

The fuel management system pumps fuel between the forward and aft fuselage tanks to maintain an optimum center-of-gravity (cg) as the wings move or weapons are deployed. Fuel can also be dumped through the wingtip vents as needed to ensure cg limits are not violated. *(U.S. Air Force)*

The two ECM antennas on the fuselage sides behind the cockpit show up well in this view from a tanker. The early black refueling markings, however, do not show up well, which is the primary reason they were changed to white. *(Tony Landis Collection)*

The B-1B is capable of refueling from KC-135s and KC-10s. This perspective gives a good comparison of size to the KC-10, which is the military version of the McDonnell Douglas (now Boeing) DC-10 commercial transport. *(Tony Landis Collection)*

and 66-0377) were used at various times. Like the F-111s, the F-4s were not dedicated to the B-1B test program and so did not wear any special markings.

Initially, the F-111s from Edwards were also used as safety chase aircraft to accompany B-1Bs on their acceptance test flights, but the rapid B-1B production rate necessitated the need for a replacement. The General Dynamics F-106 Delta Dart was being retired from the Air Force inventory at the time and several were available. F-106s were used to support acceptance test flights from 10 October 1986 until 30 June 1990. Unlike the Edwards aircraft that supported multiple test programs, the F-106s were dedicated to the B-1B program and carried special tail markings. The basic layout of the markings did not change, but the colors used on the single-seat F-106As differed from those used on the two-seat F-106Bs. The F-106A markings were blue and white, while the F-106B tails were initially black with white markings, but were later changed to red with black and white markings. Four F-106As (58-0795, 59-0008, 59-0060, and 59-0061) and three F-106Bs (57-2509, 57-2513, and 57-2535) were used.

Operational Service

Throughout the Cold War the Strategic Air Command, headquartered at Offutt AFB, Nebraska, maintained bombers and tankers on nuclear alert and was the keeper of the Single Integrated Operations Plan (SIOP), which established targets for the initial phase of an nuclear war. In the spirit of Curtiss LeMay, SAC was still led by the "bomber generals" who had pioneered the strategic bomber.

The B-1Bs were initially assigned to four SAC Bombardment Wings: the 96th BW at Dyess AFB, Abilene, Texas (initially assigned 29 aircraft); the 28th BW at Ellsworth AFB, Rapid City, South Dakota (35 aircraft); the 319th BW at Grand Forks AFB, Grand Forks, North Dakota

The first B-1A prototype taxies past the tower at Edwards AFB on its way to the active runway. Note the Strategic Air Command (SAC) stripe and badge on the nose. The gloss white paint stood up well under the desert sun, something that could not be said for the "strategic" camouflage used on the B-1B. *(Dennis R. Jenkins via the Mick Roth Collection)*

The second prototype provides a good view of the pointed rear radome and horizontal stabilizer fairing used on the B-1A. The blunter shapes on the B-1B provide one of the most obvious external clues. Note the deployed spoilers on the upper wing surfaces. Another B-1A is in the background. *(Dennis R. Jenkins via the Mick Roth Collection)*

Sunrise at Edwards AFB shows the first B-1A being checked out. The high daytime temperatures at Edwards result in many test flights taking place at day-break when it is still cool. The escape modules' stabilizing fins had to be raised in order to access some electronic components. *(Erik Simonsen Collection)*

Afterburners blazing, the first B-1A departs Palmdale for its maiden flight on 23 December 1974. The flight ended at Edwards AFB 1 hour, 18 minutes later. The complex over-wing fairings show up well here. All four B-1As had black wheels, while all B-1Bs have used white wheels. *(U.S. Air Force via Steve Pace)*

The third B-1A shows two unusual fairings, one of each side of the forward fuselage just behind the radome. Each obviously houses a forward-looking antenna, but nothing explaining their purpose has been uncovered. Although the Crosseye ECM system had been installed on this aircraft, it is unlikely the antennas are associated with it. *(U.S. Air Force/DVIC DF-ST-82-01173)*

The fourth B-1A shows the large waveguide associated with the Crosseye ECM system installed on top of the fuselage. The rear fuselage radome uses the blunt shape later installed on all B-1Bs, but the horizontal fuselage fairing retains the pointed shape common to all B-1As. The addition of the ALQ-161A tail warning function on the B-1B would dictate a change to a blunt shape. Note that the forward radome is camouflaged, not black. *(U.S. Air Force/DVIC DF-ST-82-08092)*

The wing carry-through structure is removed from the first B-1A in preparation for it being transported to Rome Laboratory for antenna measurement tests. Note the large wing pivot points, and the "hi-tech" stand used to support the aft fuselage. *(U.S. Air Force/Rome Labs)*

Surplus F-106 interceptors were used as chase aircraft during the B-1B production program. Note the early "B-1B Chase" markings on the aircraft in the background, and the newer markings on the two closer aircraft. Four single-seat F-106As and three two-seat F-106Bs were used. *(Mick Roth Collection)*

Members of the 96th and 28th Organizational Maintenance Squadrons close an engine cowling from a B-1B. Barely visible at the top right is the fact that the "turkey feathers" have been removed from the exhaust nozzle. *(U.S. Air Force/DVIC DF-ST-88-03483)*

A B-1B (83-0067) shows the phased-array antenna inside the forward radome. This antenna is angled slightly down in order to deflect enemy radar signals downward, away from the original transmitter. *(Don Logan via the Mick Roth Collection)*

Despite their high cost, the B-1Bs spend their time outside, unlike their B-2A counterparts. The amount of radar-absorbing material on the B-1B is relatively small (at least compared to the B-2A), and has proven to withstand weather relatively well. *(Don Logan via the Mick Roth Collection)*

The cockpit of the B-1B is conventional, although the designers chose to use control sticks instead of the yokes found in most large aircraft. The large moving map display shown in the early B-1A mock-up was not included in either the B-1A or B-1B production plans. *(Mick Roth Collection)*

A maneuvering B-1B dumps fuel to maintain its center-of-gravity. Pilots like the B-1B for its "fighterlike" performance, at least at low gross weights. The European One camouflage carried over to the bottom of the aircraft, although the colors differ. The three weapons bays show up as white outlines. *(U.S. Air Force via Steve Pace)*

The two large hatches in the ramp at the lower left contain connections to the central aircraft support system (CASS) that provides avionics and crew compartment cooling, shop air for power tools, electrical power for aircraft systems, and coolanol for the defensive avionics system while the aircraft is on the ground. This was one of the primary facility modifications made at each of the permanent B-1B bases prior to the aircraft arriving. The CASS pads at Dyess AFB are unique since they are housed above-ground—at the other B-1B bases everything is totally underground. *(U.S. Air Force photo by MSgt Buster Kellum)*

A single BDU-46/E practice bomb (simulating a B83 nuclear store) is dropped from a B-1B over the Edwards AFB range. The drogue chute has already pulled the main chute out, although it is not fully reefed yet. The chute slows the bomb's descent sufficiently to allow the bomber to escape. *(U.S. Air Force via the Tony Landis Collection)*

The General Electric F101-GE-102 engine for the B-1B was a direct descendent of the YF101-GE-100 used by the B-1As. The major changes to the engine involved relocating various components so that any engine could be placed in any engine location, eliminating the need to build up unique engines for each location. *(General Electric Aircraft Engines)*

(17 aircraft); and the 384th BW at McConnell AFB, Wichita, Kansas (17 aircraft). The B-1 CTF at Edwards maintained B-1B aircraft Nos. 9 and 28 for flight test work.

On 21 December 1983, President Reagan announced that Dyess AFB would receive the Air Force's first operational B-1Bs. A ceremony, attended by 50,000 people, was held at Dyess as SAC's 96th BW formally accepted its first B-1B on 29 June 1985. The ceremony was held 30 years to the day after the delivery of the first operational B-52 to Castle AFB, California. However, the first operational B-1B (83-0065—*Star of Abilene*) had been temporarily grounded at Offutt AFB on 27 June 1985 after an engine ingested debris. The bomber had been on its way from Palmdale to Dyess to be the centerpiece of the acceptance ceremonies. As a substitute, the first B-1B (82-0001) was flown from Edwards to Dyess during the early morning of 29 June. Following the arrival at Dyess of the *Star of Abilene* on 7 July, 82-0001 returned to Edwards.

The first unit at Dyess to receive B-1Bs was the 4018th Combat Crew Training Squadron (CCTS), which had the mission of training all future B-1B crewmembers. This unit had been activated on 15 March 1985 and was deactivated on 1 July 1986 when the training responsibility was transferred to the 338th Strategic Bombardment Training Squadron (SBTS), which was later redesignated the 338th CCTS.

The 96th BW's first operational squadron was the 337th Bombardment Squadron, Heavy, and the squadron achieved its IOC on 1 October 1986, even though its crews had yet to launch a SRAM or ALCM. That same day the B-1B stood its first nuclear alert at Dyess as part of the SIOP. A little less than two years had passed since the first flight of the B-1B, and only 60 percent of the scheduled flight test activities had been completed at Edwards. The automatic terrain-following system had not yet been certified, resulting in restrictions prohibiting flight below 1000 feet. The complex defensive avionics system did not work, fuel tanks leaked, and engines were subject to constant inspections in an attempt to prevent in-flight failures. But problems with new weapons systems are common and expected. The Air Force was content to finally have a replacement for the workhorse B-52.

Although SAC was happy with its new bomber, even if the early examples lacked some of the eventual capabilities, the popular press was less than supportive. Between November 1986 and March 1987 headlines read: "The B-1 Bomber: A Flying Lemon" (*U.S. News and World Report*), "Debut of the Wrong Bomber" (*The New York Times*), and "The World's First Self-Jamming Bomber" (*Armed Forces Journal*). Every publication from *Aviation Week* to *Popular Science* was reporting on the B-1B's problems, and seldom focusing on its capabilities. To some extent this was to be expected of what had proven to be the most expensive combat aircraft ever built—an amortized cost of $283 million per aircraft. Congressional investigations continued to fuel public criticism of the bomber. Nevertheless, with a great deal of professional pride, SAC crews just shrugged off the publicity and got on with proving the bomber could do its job.

By the end of October 1986, the 96th BW had received only 17 B-1Bs, but deliveries were increasing, and on 27 February 1987 the Wing received its last aircraft. The launch of the first AGM-69A SRAM by an operational B-1B crew occurred on 3 June 1987, and three weeks later an operational B-1B took part in its first Red Flag exercise. The 96th BW passed its first operational readiness inspection (ORI) on 29 October 1987, a little over a year after its IOC. This was the first time in SAC history that a wing transitioning to a new aircraft had passed its first ORI, although the tempo of the ORI differed somewhat from the days of Curtiss LeMay.

The second unit to receive B-1Bs was the 28th BW at Ellsworth AFB, with the arrival of *Wings of Freedom* (85-0073) on 21 January 1987. The Wing operates two squadrons of B-1Bs, the 37th BS and the 77th BS. Interestingly, the 77th BS was deactivated on 31 March 1995, only to be reactivated again on 1 April 1997, this time with a single B-1B assigned. The unit is scheduled to have 12 B-1Bs before 1 April 2000, drawing aircraft mainly from the 7th BW at Dyess.

On 14 April 1987, a B-1B (85-0072—*Polarized*) flew the "70 Degree North Mission" to test the navigation system's operations in northern latitudes and around the north pole. The aircraft covered 9411 miles in 21 hours, 40 minutes, flying from Dyess north across the United States, along the Canadian Pacific coast, across Alaska, over the Beaufort Sea within 160 miles of the Soviet Union, and around the Arctic circle above 70° north latitude. The aircraft turned back at Coronation Gulf, south of Victoria Island in far north central Canada. The crew consisted of three pilots, Lieutenant Colonel Larry Jordan, Lieutenant Colonel Larry D. Autry, and Major Kevin Clifford; two OSOs, Major Bob Sutton and Captain James Meier; and DSO Lieutenant Colonel Paul Hendricks III. Five air refuelings were accomplished, but on a combat mission to the same area, only two refuelings would have been required. The average speed for the mission was 440 knots. The DSO reported very little activity from Soviet early warning radars as the B-1B flew within 160 miles of the Soviet border. This surprised the crew as they had thought that the Soviet Air Force would have taken advantage of this flight to get a close-up look at the United States' latest strategic bomber.

The 319th BW at Grand Forks AFB began transitioning to the B-1B with the arrival of the first (86-0107) of 17 aircraft on 26 October 1987. On 1 October 1993, the wing was redesignated the 319th Air Refueling Wing and transferred to the Air Mobility Command (AMC), which also assumed responsibility for the base itself. But in an odd move, on 1 October 1993 the ACC activated the 319th Bomb Group, separate from the 319th ARW, to continue operating the remaining B-1Bs at Grand Forks. On 16 July 1994, the B-1Bs were transferred to the 34th BS at Ellsworth, and the 319th BG was deactivated.

The last of the original B-1B operational units was the 384th BW at McConnell AFB. The 28th BS received the Wing's first B-1B (86-0124) on 29 February 1988. Proving even the Air Force has a sense of humor at times, the 28th BS used "OZ" tailcodes (Kansas being the "Land of Oz"). On 1 October 1994, the 384th Bomb Group (which had replaced the 384th BW on 1 January 1994) was deactivated, and the 28th BS was transferred to the 7th Wing at Dyess. Most of the squadron's B-1Bs, however, went to the 184th BW of the Kansas ANG, located just a little further down the flight line at McConnell.

Polarized (85-0072) has been used for a variety of missions, including the "70 degree North Mission," "Distant Mariner 88," and AFOTEC weapons drop testing. This is the nose art in use on 30 December 1993. *(Don Logan via the Mick Roth Collection)*

As a complement to the polar mission, "Distant Mariner 88" was flown 10–22 May 1988 to test the navigation system while crossing the Equator and the International Dateline (although exactly why this should bother modern electronics is unknown). Again *Polarized* (85-0072) was selected, and the aircraft left Dyess on 10 May and flew direct to Hickam AFB, Hawaii. Several sorties were flown from Hickam before *Polarized* flew to Anderson AFB, Guam, on 14 May. The B-1B remained at Guam through 18 May, flying sorties over the western and southern Pacific including one sortie to Australia. Additional sorties were flown after the aircraft returned to Hickam until 22 May, when *Polarized* departed for Dyess.

As part of the general thawing of the Cold War, the Air Force underwent a comprehensive reorganization. SAC was disestablished on 1 June 1992, and its bomber force was transferred to the newly formed Air Combat Command (ACC), headquartered at Langley AFB, Virginia. On the same day, SAC transferred its tankers to the Air Mobility Command. The ACC was officially a merger of two equals, the tactical assets of Tactical Air Command (TAC) and the bombers of SAC. In reality, however, the bombers had effectively come under the control of the "fighter generals" from the old TAC. As if to emphasize this, bombers were assigned tailcodes for the first time.

The 96th BW at Dyess was deactivated on 1 October 1993, and its facilities, people, and aircraft were transferred "in place" to the 7th Wing, and the 338th BS was absorbed into the 9th BS. As of 1 October 1995, the 7th BW was the only B-1B unit with a SIOP commitment, and two years later the unit stood its last nuclear alert, marking the B-1B's total commitment as a conventional bomber.

Also on 1 October 1993, the 7th Wing's 337th BS absorbed the training functions previously assigned to the 338th CCTS, although this was rather short-lived, with the 337th BS being deactivated on 1 October 1994 and the training function transferred to the 28th BS. The 28th BS had been assigned to the 384th BW at McConnell AFB and was transferred to Dyess on 1 October 1994. This is the current B-1B training squadron and uses the blue and white checkerboard tail stripe long associated with the B-1B training unit.

The "Air Intervention Wing" at Mountain Home AFB, Idaho, is also equipped with the B-1B. The 366th Wing is one of three composite wings in the Air Force, but is configured differently than the other two. A mixture of B-1B, F-15E, F-15C, F-16C, and KC-135 aircraft allows the wing to conduct combat operations with little or no support from any other units. The 366th Wing was activated on 1 June 1992, and on 4 April 1994 the 34th BS was activated at Ellsworth AFB as part of the 366th Wing. The B-1Bs were physically based at Ellsworth since that base had the facilities, tools, and spare parts to support the aircraft and the Air Force did not want to spend the money to duplicate the infrastructure at Mountain Home. Despite being based at Ellsworth, the squadron's aircraft wore "MO" tailcodes.

Four B-1Bs from the 9th BS deployed to RAF Fairford on 1 June 1994 to participate in the NATO exercise "Central Enterprise," which ran 13–17 June. The B-1B deployment was called "Coronet Pluto '94" and involved more than 250 people from Dyess. During the exercise, the B-1B crews became familiar with air traffic control procedures in European airspace, and dummy 500-pound bombs were dropped over the Vlievors range in The Netherlands. Two of the aircraft (84-0057—*Hellion* and 86-0103—*Reluctant Dragon*) also took part in the ceremonies surrounding the 50th anniversary of the D-Day invasion on 6 June.

To reduce the cost of operating the strategic bomber fleet, the Air Force decided to transfer some B-1Bs to the Air National Guard (ANG). This marked the first time a heavy bomber had been assigned to the ANG. Although U.S. doctrine prohibits members of the ANG or Reserve forces from being assigned to a nuclear mission, the decision to dedicate the B-1B to conventional warfare made it sensible and cost effective to transfer the B-1B to the ANG. During peacetime, the ANG augments the ACC by participating in various exercises and operations. In wartime, Air Force strategic bombers committed to the SIOP would be assigned to U.S. Strategic Command (Stratcom) at Offutt, while those engaged in conventional missions would come under unified commanders in chief with regional responsibilities.

The 28th BS at McConnell AFB was transferred to the 7th Wing at Dyess on 1 October 1994 when the 384th BW became the 384th Air Refueling Wing. But McConnell still has B-1Bs, courtesy of the 184th BW of the Kansas ANG. On 1 July 1994, the 184th Fighter Group was redesignated a Bomber Group and became the first ANG unit to be equipped with a heavy bomber. The unit was subsequently redesignated 184th Bomb Wing, with its sole squadron becoming the 127th BS.

The last unit to receive B-1Bs was the 116th BW of the Georgia ANG at Robins AFB, Georgia. The 116th Fighter Wing had previously flown F-15As from Dobbins AFB in Marietta, Georgia, before being moved to Robins AFB and equipped with B-1Bs. The Wing's 128th BS became the second ANG squadron to operate the B-1B.

On 22 August 1996, Mountain Home finally began to receive the B-1Bs that are assigned to the 366th Wing, and all nine aircraft had arrived by March 1997. Various modifications had been made to the facilities at Mountain Home to accommodate the bombers.

On 21 April 1997, B-1Bs participated in a joint exercise with the U.S. Navy and dropped Mk 62 mines for the first time. This role had previously been performed by the B-52. Although most Navy aircraft have the capability to carry the Mk 62 mine, the B-1B allows larger areas to be mined on a single mission.

In May 1997, an aircraft from the 7th BW (86-0132—*Oh! Hard Luck*) became the first B-1B to reach 4000 flight hours. The aircraft was displayed at the Golden Air Tattoo at Nel-

On 4 October 1989, *Excalibur* (85-0070) was forced to make an emergency landing at Edwards AFB after the nose landing gear would not deploy. Pilots Captain Jeffery K. Beene and Captain Vernon B. Benton managed to keep the nose up until 105 knots, after which it gently settled to the lakebed, causing the bomber to veer off course slightly. The crew was awarded the MacKay Trophy for their efforts in getting the bomber back onto the ground intact. *(Tony Landis Collection)*

Excalibur was remarkably undamaged, with the only structural damage being suffered by the lower portion of the forward bulkhead used to mount the radar antenna. The aircraft was repaired at Edwards AFB and returned to Dyess AFB on 23 January 1990, flown by the same crew that had made the emergency landing. *(Tony Landis Collection)*

lis AFB, Nevada, shortly thereafter. A team from the OC-ALC also carefully examined the aircraft to determine how the airframe was holding up. No particular problems were discovered.

The B-1B supported two Air Expeditionary Force (AEF) deployments to Bahrain during 1997. The 366th Wing sent two aircraft to join the 366th AEF in September 1997, where they participated in live bombing missions in the Persian Gulf. Then, beginning on 17 November 1997, two B-1Bs from the 28th BW joined the 347th AEF as tensions with Iraq rose again after UN inspectors were denied access to certain locations. In February 1998, a third B-1B was sent to Bahrain as tensions rose further. No military action was taken at the time, however.

Of the original 100 aircraft, one has been scrapped and six have been lost in accidents. As of mid-June 1998, the remaining 93 are assigned to six operating locations. The 7th BW at Dyess AFB has 39 aircraft (15 in the 9th BS and 24 in the 28th BS); the 28th BW at Ellsworth AFB has 21 aircraft (17 in the 37th BS and four in the 77th BS); the 366th Wing at Mountain Home AFB has nine aircraft (all in the 34th BS); the 116th BW at Robins AFB has 10 aircraft (all in the 128th BS); the 184th BW at McConnell AFB has 12 aircraft (all in the 127th BS); and the 412th TW at Edwards AFB maintains two aircraft for follow-on testing.

First Combat

The first combat use of the B-1B occurred on the evening of 18 December 1998 (Oman time) against targets in Iraq during Operation Desert Fox. This was the second day of a

On the second night of Operation Desert Fox, two B-1Bs were part of a joint-service strike package that attacked Republican Guard barracks. The next night, two B-1Bs attacked other Republican Guard targets. President Clinton called off the raids prior to the last two aircraft flying their assigned sorties. *(U.S. Air Force)*

This was the bomb damage assessment photo released by the Air Force after the B-1B's first combat sortie against the Al Kut Barracks in Iraq. The nine arrows show the most significant damage. The attack was made with Mk 82 500-pound bombs from medium altitude (~20,000 feet). *(Department of Defense)*

A load of Mk 82 bombs awaits loading on a B-1B from the 28th BW at RAF Fairford. The bomber will attack military targets in the former Yugoslavia as part of NATO Operation Allied Force. *(U.S. Air Force)*

four-day air campaign against Saddam Hussein. An integrated air package consisting of EA-6Bs, F-14Bs, F/A-18Cs, and two B-1Bs was launched against Republican Guard barracks in west-northwest Iraq. The B-1Bs were *Wolf Pack* (86-0096) from the 37th BS of the 28th BW with aircraft commander (AC) Lieutenant Colonel Steve Wilborsky, pilot Captain Chris Wright, and WSOs Captain Fred Bivetto and Captain Peter Bailey; and *Watchdog* (86-0135) from the 9th BS of the 7th BW with AC Captain Jeff Hoyt, pilot Lieutenant Bob Mankus, and WSOs Captain Jason Xiques and Captain Gordon Greaney.

The B-1Bs took off from Oman and dropped Mk 82 iron bombs from medium altitudes of approximately 20,000 feet. The strike package encountered heavy antiaircraft artillery (AAA) fire during portions of the six-hour missions, but did not sustain any damage. The Air Force did not immediately release any information on the results of the raids, other than to say they were "very successful." Later reports indicated that several barracks were destroyed.

A second mission was flown by B-1Bs on the third day of the strikes. This mission was flown by *Watchdog* (86-0135) from the 28th BS with AC Lieutenant Colonel Gary Harencak, pilot Major Brian Dodson, and WSOs Captain Rod Todaro and Captain John Newby and *Lady Hawk* (86-0102) from the 37th BS with AC Captain Jeff Taliaferro, Captain Randy Kaufman, and WSOs Captain Joe Reidy and Captain John Martin. Kaufmann indicated the two aircraft attacked different targets in the same general area as the first strikes. Poststrike assessments showed that the bombers destroyed several more buildings on this raid. All bombs were dropped on a single pass to minimize exposure to Iraqi air defenses. The B-1 pilots noted that coordinating with the Navy aircraft was successful, and that this demonstrated that the B-1B could operate effectively as part of a strike package.

The following day two additional B-1Bs (86-0109 from the 7th BW and 85-0084 from the 28th BW) were dispatched from the United States to Oman to bolster the forces, although President William J. Clinton announced later that evening that the bombing raids were being concluded. Air Force officials felt comfortable using the bombers even though the

ALQ-161A was still not totally functional, and the bombers deployed to the region had not been modified to carry the ALE-50 towed decoy. Following the end of Desert Fox, all six B-1Bs in theatre had returned to the United States by the end of 1998.

Allied Force

The B-1B saw its next combat during the air war over the former Yugoslavia beginning in March 1999 in Operation Allied Force. Along with the B-2, the B-1B dropped CBU-87 and CBU-89 cluster bombs and Mk 82 dumb bombs on military and dual-use targets throughout Serbia and Kosovo. At least six B-1Bs were flying combat missions from the NATO base at RAF Fairford in the United Kingdom. The use of precision-guided weapons was limited to the B-2 simply because there were not many of them in the inventory yet, and stockpiles were quickly depleted. Conventional Mk 82s (and possibly some Mk 84s) were dropped on most later missions.

The Science: Construction, Systems, and Weapons

The B-1B is a high-performance long-range bomber designed for speeds in excess of Mach 1 at altitude and very high subsonic speeds at altitudes as low as 200 feet. It has an intercontinental range without refueling.

Fuselage

The fuselage is an area-ruled semimonocoque structure made primarily of 2025 and 7075 aluminum alloys. The basic structure includes a steel/boron-filled/titanium sandwich dorsal spine, aluminum longerons, and a large number of closely spaced frames. The fuselage is manufactured in five sections: forward, forward intermediate, wing carry-through structure, aft intermediate, and aft. Polyimide quartz is used for the nose and tail radomes, and composite materials are used for the wing root leading-edge antenna fairings.

The wing carry-through structure is internally sealed to serve as an integral fuel tank and is constructed primarily of diffusion bonded 6AL-4V titanium alloy. Diffusion bonding is a technique in which individual pieces of titanium are heated in a vacuum furnace to the point when the atoms just become mobile, and then the pieces are squeezed together, effectively becoming a single piece of metal. Each wing pivot mechanism uses a hollow 36-inch-long, 17-inch-diameter pin made from a single 6AL-4V forging, supported by spherical steel bearings. Machined titanium plates cover the pin. To attach the outer wing panels, the wing carry-through sleeves are heated by electric blankets while the pin is soaked in liquid nitrogen. After the pin is inserted, the parts are returned to ambient temperature, resulting in a tight fit.

The forward equipment bay, central equipment bay, two wheel-well equipment bays, and an aft equipment bay provide space for most avionics components. There are also two smaller bays just aft of the central bay, and a smaller side-fairing bay is located in each fuselage wing root. In addition, a bay has been incorporated into the horizontal stabilizer fairing to house the tail-warning ECM equipment.

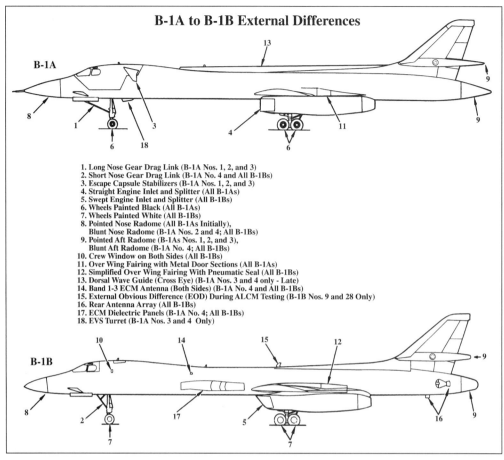

B-1A to B-1B External Differences

B-1A

B-1B

1. Long Nose Gear Drag Link (B-1A Nos. 1, 2, and 3)
2. Short Nose Gear Drag Link (B-1A No. 4 and All B-1Bs)
3. Escape Capsule Stabilizers (B-1A Nos. 1, 2, and 3)
4. Straight Engine Inlet and Splitter (All B-1As)
5. Swept Engine Inlet and Splitter (All B-1Bs)
6. Wheels Painted Black (All B-1As)
7. Wheels Painted White (All B-1Bs)
8. Pointed Nose Radome (All B-1As Initially),
   Blunt Nose Radome (B-1A Nos. 2 and 4; All B-1Bs)
9. Pointed Aft Radome (B-1As Nos. 1, 2, and 3),
   Blunt Aft Radome (B-1A No. 4; All B-1Bs)
10. Crew Window on Both Sides (All B-1Bs)
11. Over Wing Fairing with Metal Door Sections (All B-1As)
12. Simplified Over Wing Fairing With Pneumatic Seal (All B-1Bs)
13. Dorsal Wave Guide (Cross Eye) (B-1A Nos. 3 and 4 only - Late)
14. Band 1-3 ECM Antenna (Both Sides) (B-1A No. 4 and All B-1Bs)
15. External Obvious Difference (EOD) During ALCM Testing (B-1B Nos. 9 and 28 Only)
16. Rear Antenna Array (All B-1Bs)
17. ECM Dielectric Panels (B-1A No. 4; All B-1Bs)
18. EVS Turret (B-1A Nos. 3 and 4 Only)

Superficially the B-1B looks very similar to the B-1A, but in reality there are many detail changes between the two aircraft. This diagram shows the visible changes, but under the skin there are a host of others. *(Courtesy of Don Logan)*

There are two weapons bays forward of the wing carry-through structure and a single 15-foot-long weapons bay aft of the main landing gear wheel wells. The two forward weapons bays in the last 91 aircraft (84-0049 through 86-0140) were manufactured with a movable bulkhead and two-section forward weapons bay doors. This bulkhead may be positioned to provide two 15-foot bays, one 22-foot intermediate bay plus an 8-foot forward bay, or a single 31-foot bay. The long intermediate bay allows installation of the 256-inch cruise missile launcher. To date, only aircraft No. 9 (84-0049) and No. 28 (85-0028) have been modified to the 22-foot intermediate bay configuration, and both were reconfigured to the standard three-bay configuration following completion of cruise missile testing. Aircraft No. 2 through No. 8 (83-0065 through 83-0071) were modified after production to incorporate the movable bulkhead. The first B-1B was never modified before it was broken up. In addition to the weapons capability, all bays have provisions to carry internal fuel tanks.

Except for the first aircraft, there are structural provisions for 6 two-missile pylons and two single-missile pylons on the bottom of the fuselage. The last 91 aircraft were equipped with wiring and interface provisions for the 6 two-missile pylons from the factory. Because of START treaty limitations, no provisions were included for activating the two single-missile pylons. Aircraft Nos. 2 through 8 were subsequently modified to the same standard. The first B-1B was never modified. The forward-most six stations are also capable of carrying jettisonable external fuel tanks, although none have ever been observed fitted to an aircraft.

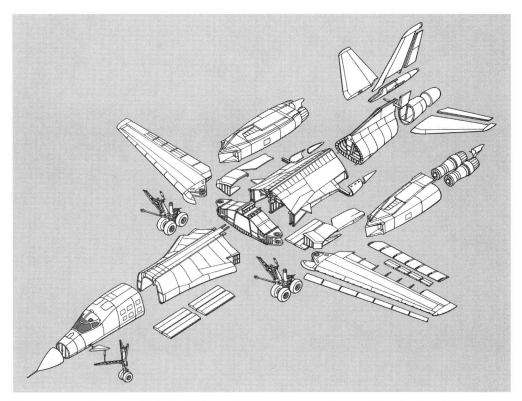

Like most modern aircraft, the B-1B is made up of various subassemblies that are built-up separately then joined together on the final assembly line. *(Boeing North American)*

Crew Compartment

The crew compartment provides for a basic crew of four: pilot, copilot, offensive systems officer (OSO), and defensive systems officer (DSO), plus two instructors. The two instructor seats are seldom used since they do not have any ejection capabilities. By the end of 1998, the Air Force had begun cross training the OSO and DSO crewmembers and redesignated them weapons systems operators (WSO). The two crew stations are still dedicated to their respective functions, but the crewmembers are largely interchangeable. A toilet and a galley are installed for crew comfort on long missions. The crew compartment is pressurized to an equivalent of 8000 feet altitude to provide a shirt-sleeve environment. Crew entry is through an electrically operated hatch located on the bottom of the fuselage just aft of the nose landing gear.

The forward windscreens are sharply raked and are designed to resist heavy birdstrikes at high speeds. Each rear crew station has a small side window, something missing from the original B-1A design, but incorporated into the B-1B after the crewmembers complained of feeling claustrophobic. Special darkening panels were provided for use during nuclear strikes, replacing the traditional blackout curtains. The panels provided small 5.5-inch portholes for crew visibility and allow only 0.003 percent of the normal light to pass through. The pilots are provided with control sticks instead of the more conventional yokes usually found in large aircraft.

Individual ACES II ejection seats are provided for the four primary crewmembers. The ACES II was developed by McDonnell Douglas, although the B-1B seats are manufactured by Weber Aircraft. The seats are essentially identical to the ACES II seats installed in the F-15 and F-16 except for the addition of armrests, a comfort cushion, and limb restraints. A crewmember parachute and an emergency oxygen system are included as part of each

By modern standards the B-1B cockpit is almost archaic, but it serves its purpose well. The aircraft still features many electromechanical instruments instead of more modern electronic displays, and does not have heads-up displays (HUDs) for the pilots. It does, however, provide some situational data electronically on a CRT directly in front of each pilot. *(U.S. Air Force/DVIC DF-ST-88-03482)*

seat. Seat ejection occurs through four hatches located on the top of the fuselage after actuation of either or both of the side-mounted ejection control handles. The system has an automatic mode that allows either the pilot or copilot to initiate ejection for all four crewmembers. Successful ejections are possible through most of the B-1B's flight envelope, including during high-speed, low-altitude flight.

A bottom bailout system is provided for any instructor personnel who may be aboard the aircraft during training missions. When activated, the bottom bailout system jettisons the crew entry hatch and ladder and extends the nose-landing gear to allow the instructors to manually bail out from the bottom entry hatch. The two flight instructors are provided with individual parachutes that are equipped with an emergency oxygen bottle similar to the ones mounted on the ejection seat. The bottom bailout envelope is fairly large and covers a reasonable range of speed (up to 300 knots) and altitude. However, successful escape during extreme low-altitude flight is very unlikely.

Wings

As with the B-1A, the fuselage blends into the fixed inner wing section. The inner wing does not have a defined airfoil section, and its leading edge is quite blunt to accommodate antennas for the defensive avionics system and to provide additional volume for a variety of electronic boxes located behind it. Nonetheless, the inner wing section provides a significant amount of lift, especially at high angles-of-attack.

The outer wing can vary its sweep from 15° to 67.5°, and is equipped with leading-edge slats, spoilers (which also function as speedbrakes), and trailing-edge flaps. The thickness/chord ratio of the outer wing section varies between 6 and 9 percent, depending on the wing angle. The wing is a conventional aluminum alloy structure with two main spars,

The third B-1A was the first aircraft equipped with the offensive avionics system. This is the OSO station. The tracking handle and round CRT are from an F-111, while the rectangular scope (above round scope) is from a B-52. This configuration would change considerably for the B-1B. *(Mick Roth Collection)*

28 forged and machined ribs, and one-piece integrally stiffened skins and is sealed to form an integral fuel tank. The inboard trailing edge of the outer wing is cut away to facilitate stowage at maximum sweep. The wings sweep at approximately 1° per second as the fuel center-of-gravity management system (FCGMS) transfers fuel to maintain the aircraft center-of-gravity (cg) as the center of lift changes. There are detents in the control handles at 15° (full forward), 20°, and 67.5° (full aft), although the wings have the capability of being stopped at any position between full forward and full aft. The cockpit wing sweep control lever is shaped like a wing and moves in the natural sense—forward to bring the wings forward, and backward to sweep the wings aft. This is the opposite of the prototype F-111 system where the designers thought the wing sweep control should mimic the throttle (i.e., forward to go fast—wings back; rearward to go slow—wings forward). Production F-111s used the more natural system, similar to the B-1.

The Fowler-type wing flaps are divided into six sections that are mechanically connected and operate as one unit. Each wing is equipped with a leading edge slat that is divided into

The production B-1B OSO Panel. The stick is used to designate areas of interest for the radar. *(Jay Miller via the Mick Roth Collection)*

The production B-1B DSO Panel. The nearest panel controls the ALQ-161A RFS/ECMS. The displays and controls are actually part of the ASQ-184 management system. *(Jay Miller via the Mick Roth Collection)*

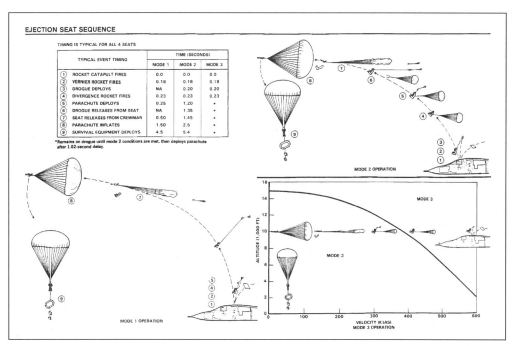

The following table is part of the figure:

TYPICAL EVENT TIMING	TIME (SECONDS)		
	MODE 1	MODE 2	MODE 3
① ROCKET CATAPULT FIRES	0.0	0.0	0.0
② VERNIER ROCKET FIRES	0.18	0.18	0.18
③ DROGUE DEPLOYS	NA	0.20	0.20
④ DIVERGENCE ROCKET FIRES	0.23	0.23	0.23
⑤ PARACHUTE DEPLOYS	0.25	1.20	*
⑥ DROGUE RELEASES FROM SEAT	NA	1.35	*
⑦ SEAT RELEASES FROM CREWMAN	0.50	1.45	*
⑧ PARACHUTE INFLATES	1.50	2.5	*
⑨ SURVIVAL EQUIPMENT DEPLOYS	4.5	5.4	*

*Remains on drogue until mode 2 conditions are met, then deploys parachute after 1.02-second delay.

The ACES II ejection seats in the B-1B can provide successful ejection throughout the aircraft's performance envelope, including during high-speed, low-altitude flight. This has been demonstrated on several occasions. Several different escape modes are available depending upon the flight regime. (U.S. Air Force)

seven sections that are mechanically connected and operate as one unit. Advanced composite materials are used for the wing flaps, slats, and inboard spoilers. Graphite-reinforced composites are used for the wingtips.

Flap operation is constrained by the wing sweep positions, and flap extension is impossible with the wings swept more than 20°. Conversely, any extension of the flaps restricts the wing sweep to less then 20° by means of a mechanical interlock. At full extension the inner flap section is well outboard of the engine nacelle. The slats can extend to a maximum of 20°, and the flaps can extend up to 40°.

On the B-1A, the opening into which each outer wing panel slid was sealed by a complicated series of doors that were individually raised during wing sweep and then lowered tight against the wing. The B-1B uses a simpler system with a hinged upper and lower door, both provided with an inflatable seal. The inboard leading edge of each wing terminates in a curved knuckle that covers the mechanical drive and prevents any gap appearing at maximum sweep. Wing sweep is provided by two irreversible screwjacks driven by dual hydraulic motors. The four motors have been tested to a push/pull rating of 1,000,000 pounds, although this is greatly in excess of the power necessary to move the wings. The two screwjacks are linked by a torque shaft to ensure both wings always move in unison. Each drive motor is powered by a different hydraulic system, and any two motors can fail without loss of wing sweep control.

The upper surface of each outer wing contains four spoiler panels. Each panel has the same span and approximately the same chord as the flap section behind it. The wing spoilers serve a dual purpose, acting as flight control surfaces in the air and as speedbrakes on the ground. Full travel (0 to 70°) of the spoiler panels, when acting as speedbrakes, requires approximately 2.7 seconds. All four pairs of spoiler panels act as speedbrakes on the ground; however, only the inboard pair on each wing can be used as speedbrakes in the air.

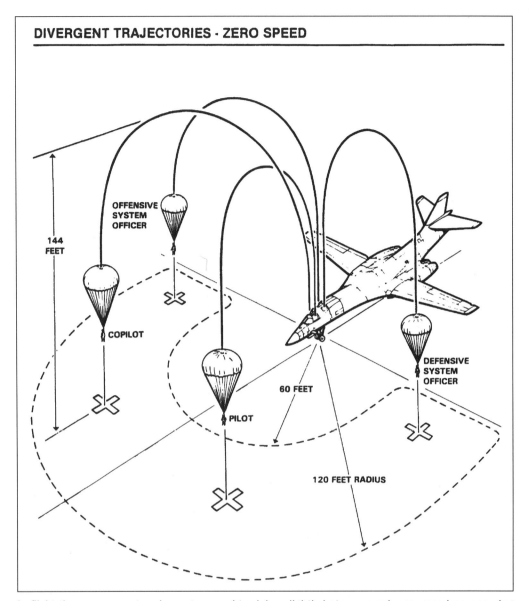

DIVERGENT TRAJECTORIES · ZERO SPEED

144 FEET

OFFENSIVE SYSTEM OFFICER

COPILOT

PILOT

60 FEET

DEFENSIVE SYSTEM OFFICER

120 FEET RADIUS

In flight the escape system is programmed to delay slightly between each crewmember, ensuring proper separation during ejection. On the ground, however, simply delaying does not necessarily help. Therefore, the escape system is programmed to vector each seat in a different direction, ensuring the crewmembers do not hit each other during ejection. *(U.S. Air Force)*

A speedbrake mixer allows the inboard spoilers to operate as both speedbrakes and roll control devices simultaneously. Operation of the outboard spoiler panels in the speed-brake mode requires weight on all three landing gear (nose gear momentarily only).

Structural Mode Control System

The structural mode control system (SMCS) detects and automatically dampens structural bending mode oscillations in the pitch and yaw axes of the aircraft. Bending oscillations are dampened through displacement of small composite control vanes mounted at 30° anhedral on each side of the forward fuselage. Fuselage bending in pitch is dampened by symmetrical displacement of the vanes, and bending in yaw is dampened by asymmetrical displacement of the vanes, along with displacement of the lower (third) rudder section.

Tail Surfaces

The vertical stabilizer is a conventional aluminum and titanium torsion box structure with hardened steel spindles for attaching the horizontal stabilizers. The horizontal stabilizers can be moved together from 10° leading edge up to 25° down for pitch control, and differentially ±20° for roll control. The vertical stabilizer has a three-section rudder capable of moving 25° to either side. The upper two sections are used to control yaw, and the lower section is controlled by the SMCS to damp out yaw motions in turbulence. All tail surfaces are hydraulically powered and mechanically signaled with electrical backup. There are no separate trim panels, the main surfaces simply being minutely adjusted instead.

Engines

The General Electric F101-GE-102 afterburning turbofan engine is an improved version of the YF101-GE-100 used in the B-1A. The main engine bleed air port is located in a neutral position on the engine, eliminating the need for a left and right engine buildup, thereby allowing any engine to be installed in any engine position on the aircraft. Compared to the exhaust nozzle used on the -100, the 12-petal nozzle originally fitted to the B-1B was simpler and 85 pounds lighter. Nevertheless, the complex "turkey feathers" proved difficult and expensive to maintain and have been removed from operational engines, resulting in a slight drag penalty.

The original F101 was a development of the GE9 demonstrator program that had been funded by the Air Force Systems Command. The GE9 also provided the basis for the F110 fighter engine. From its inception, the F101 was designed to incorporate technology that would lessen the impact of exhaust emissions and noise, and enhance fuel economy. The

Like the F-15's F100 engine, the B-1B's F101 has lost its "turkey feathers." The titanium covers provided slightly better drag characteristics, but proved to be maintenance intensive and expensive to repair. The Air Force elected to accept the slight increase in drag for the reduction in cost and complexity. Interestingly, in this photo the inboard left engine still has its feathers, while the other three do not. *(Craig Kaston via the Mick Roth Collection)*

The General Electric F101-GE-102 engine for the B-1B was a direct descendant of the -100 engine used in the B-1A. Problems with blades separating from the fan section early in its career caused several groundings of the B-1B fleet, but a redesigned blade section and containment shroud have largely eliminated the problem. Otherwise the engine has proven very reliable. *(General Electric Aircraft Engines)*

engine is virtually smokeless. The engine is 181 inches long and 55 inches in diameter and weighs 4450 pounds (dry). Each engine is a dual-rotor design with a bypass ratio of approximately 2 and a maximum mass flow of 352 pounds per second. The afterburning turbofan is rated at 17,000 pounds-thrust at sea level without afterburner and 30,780 pounds-thrust with afterburner.

A pair of engines are mounted side by side in a nacelle attached to the lower surface of the fixed inner wing section. The nacelle structures are manufactured from aluminum and titanium alloys with various panels made of glass-fiber composites. A significant portion of the air intakes is covered with radar-absorbing material (RAM), and an internal array of baffles deflects any remaining radar signals and prevents them from reaching the highly reflective fan blades on the engines.

Secondary Power System

A Garrett auxiliary power unit (APU) is located in the front of each engine nacelle. The APUs for the B-1B have been modified from those used on the B-1A to provide more operational flexibility and better performance during engine start. In the B-1A, the APU was mechanically connected by a drive shaft to both engines in the nacelle, and under some conditions did not have enough power to simultaneously start both engines. In the B-1B, only the right engine in each nacelle (engines No. 2 and 4) is mechanically connected to the APU. The left engine in each nacelle (engines No. 1 and 3) is started using bleed air from the APU. The APUs are also capable of providing hydraulic and electrical power when the engines are not operating.

Fuel System

The fuel system supplies JP-4 to the engines and APUs, controls the aircraft center-of-gravity (cg), and provides a heat sink for various systems and the hydraulic fluid. JP-5 may be used as an alternate fuel under some restrictions, and a move is under way to use low-emission JP-8 as the normal fuel in all Air Force aircraft. A maximum of 34,532 gallons (224,496 pounds) of fuel is contained in six integral fuselage tanks and a single integral tank in each wing. The fuselage tanks are the 4747-gallon (30,855-pound) No. 1 forward tank, 5785-gallon (37,606-pound) No. 2 forward intermediate tank, 3556-gallon (23,116-pound) No. 3 aft intermediate tank, 7759-gallon (50,435-pound) No. 4 aft tank, 3127-gallon (20,324-pound) wing carry-through structure tank, and a 4779-gallon (31,065-pound) integral tank in each outer wing panel.

In addition, 2950-gallon (19,176-pound), 15-foot auxiliary tanks can be installed in each of the three weapons bays, or a 1285-gallon (8352-pound), 7.5-foot tank can be installed in the "short" forward weapons bay. The aircraft has the capability, including plumbing and jettison circuits, for carriage of jettisonable 2975-gallon (19,339-pound) external fuel tanks at six external tank pylon locations on the bottom of the fuselage. Fuel dump outlets are located at the trailing edge near the tip of each wing. The liquid nitrogen pressurization and inerting system developed for use on the B-1A was not used on the B-1B.

Aircraft data, such as dry weight, flight control positions, stores and weapons information, and the like, are preprogrammed into the Simmonds Precision, Inc., fuel/center-of-gravity management system (FCGMS) to establish the initial cg. As fuel is used, wing sweep changed, or weapons released, the FCGMS will transfer fuel between tanks No. 1 and No. 4 to maintain an acceptable cg. If a weapon is selected for release that will cause an out-of-cg condition, the "Selected Store Out-Of-Limits" light at the pilot's and OSO's stations will come on. The aircraft cg may be managed manually or by one of three automatic modes.

Landing Gear System

The tricycle landing gear is essentially identical to that introduced on the No. 4 B-1A. The twin-wheel nose gear is mounted in the forward fuselage beneath the crew compartment and retracts forward under two gear doors. The nose gear has two 16-inch wheels with 22-ply 35 × 11.5-16 tires inflated to 210 psi, and can be steered hydraulically. The twin-tandem main gear are mounted in the fuselage aft of the wing structure and retract aft and laterally inboard for stowage in the fuselage between the intermediate and aft weapons bays. Each main gear strut carries four 30-ply 46 × 16-325 tires inflated to 220–275 psi. All landing gear has an emergency extension system using high-pressure nitrogen. Interestingly, the wheels on all four B-1As were painted black, while all 100 B-1Bs have used white wheels. Goodyear supplies the wheels and carbon brakes, while B.F. Goodrich supplies the tires.

The B-1 in-flight refueling receptacle is directly in front of the windscreens, and the pilots have a great view of the procedure. The original black markings around the receptacle were too difficult for the boom operator to see, especially at night, so this complex set of white markings was developed. Note the outline around the forward windscreen, helping to ensure the boomer does not place the boom through them into the cockpit. The markings were subsequently toned down, and the outline around the windscreen was removed. *(U.S. Air Force/7th BW Public Affairs)*

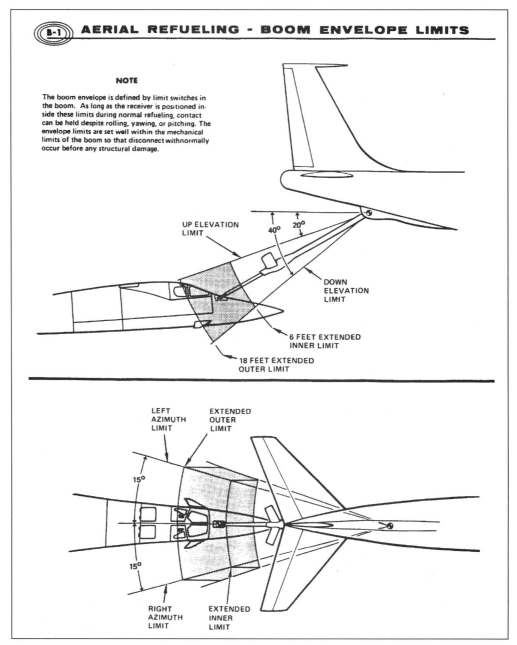

This diagram shows how much the boom on the tanker can move during refueling operations. This diagram is for a B-1A and KC-135, but the B-1B and KC-10 are generally similar. The general performance of the B-1B during refueling is highly satisfactory. *(U.S. Air Force)*

Hydraulic System

The hydraulic system consists of four completely independent, equal-status, 4000-psi hydraulic systems. Each system has two hydraulic pumps (one primary and one secondary) located on different engines. The systems are completely independent, and there is no interchanging of oil between the systems. Hydraulic pressure is used to power landing gear retraction and extension, wheel brakes, nose wheel steering, opening and closing of the weapons bay doors, weapon launcher rotation, wing sweep, flaps, slats, and the spoiler movement.

Central Integrated Test System

The aircraft has a central integrated test system (CITS), which provides 95 percent fault detection and 75 percent fault isolation. CITS provides ground readiness testing, ground fault isolation, in-flight failure detection, and in-flight fault isolation of aircraft systems and components. The system monitors over 22,000 parameters and is capable of providing over 10,000 different messages to assist in troubleshooting onboard systems. Any failures are printed in the cockpit, listing the malfunctioning line replaceable unit (LRU) along with various status information. These data are also recorded to magnetic tape for ground troubleshooting.

Automatic Flight Control System

The quadruplex automatic flight control system (AFCS) controls flight path, roll attitude, altitude, air speed, autothrottle, and terrain following. The system provides a variety of pitch and roll, automatic guidance and pilot-assist modes of flight control operation, as well as automatic throttle control. A split-axes feature allows independent operation in a single axis (pitch or roll) if one axis fails. The basic mode of operation is pitch and roll attitude hold. Alternate modes include altitude hold, air-speed hold, Mach hold, heading hold, automatic navigation, and automatic throttle.

Offensive Avionics System

The B-1B uses radar and navigation equipment technology developed for the latest generation of fighter aircraft such as the F-16, as well as avionics technology from the B-52H bomber's updated offensive avionics system. Boeing Military Airplane Company is respon-

As delivered, the B-1B only had two pitot tubes on each side of the fuselage. The upper one was added as part of the SIS2/SEF (stall inhibit system 2/stability enhancement function) modification to improve performance at increased gross weights. This is 86-0096 at Ellsworth AFB on 25 July 1990. *(Don Logan via the Mick Roth Collection)*

sible for the B-1B's AN/ASQ-184 offensive avionics system (OAS), which also provides controls and displays as well as management functions for the DAS. The OAS includes a Singer Kearfott SKN-2440 inertial navigation system (INS); GPS system; Teledyne Ryan AN/APN-218 Doppler velocity sensor; Honeywell AN/APN-224 radar altimeter; Westinghouse AN/APQ-164 multimode offensive radar system (ORS); four IBM AP-101C/F avionics control units (ACU); Sperry offensive display sets, similar to those in the B-52H, comprising three 6.5 × 6.5-inch multifunction displays [two at the OSO's station and one for the defensive systems operator (DSO)], an electronics display unit, and a video recorder (all are similar to the B-52H units); Sanders electronic CRT display units, modified from those developed for the B-1A, to allow the defensive systems operator to analyze threat situations and assign appropriate countermeasures; and Sundstrand data transfer units (similar to those in the B-52H) to gather and store mission and flight data.

The APQ-164 was developed by Westinghouse based on the AN/APG-66 used in the F-16. It uses a single 28.4 × 14.2-inch, fixed-position, electronically scanned 1526-element antenna that is rigidly mounted to the forward fuselage to perform both attack and terrain-

The main antenna for the Westinghouse AN/APQ-164 offensive radar system is a phased-array ("electronically agile") antenna that is mounted at an angle to reflect incoming radar energy from enemy defenses down and away from their receivers. This single antenna serves both the offensive avionics and the terrain-following system. *(Don Logan via the Mick Roth Collection)*

following functions. The antenna is mounted in such a way as to reflect unwanted energy (such as that received by an enemy surveillance radar) downward toward the ground, hopefully minimizing the possibility of detection. The APQ-164 is a multimode radar capable of high-resolution synthetic aperture radar (SAR) ground mapping, real-beam ground mapping, weather depiction, beacon, terrain avoidance, and terrain following. The system is dual-redundant in all subsystems except for the phased-array antenna.

Communications and Navigation Equipment

The B-1B is equipped with a Magnavox AN/ARC-164(V) VHF radio, Collins AN/ARC-210 VHF/UHF radio (initially an ARC-171), Collins AN/ARC-190 HF radio, King KY-58 secure voice system (for the ARC-164), King KY-100 secure voice system (for the ARC-210), AN/ASC-19 AFSATCOM, Litton AN/APX-101A IFF transponder, and an AN/APX-105 rendezvous beacon. The B-1B also has a Collins AN/ARN-118 TACAN and a Collins AN/ARN-108 ILS system installed as radio navigation aids.

Defensive Avionics System

The defensive avionics system (DAS) consists of portions of the Boeing AN/ASQ-184 management system, AIL AN/ALQ-161A radio frequency surveillance/electronic countermeasures system (RFS/ECMS) and tail warning function (TWF), and an expendable

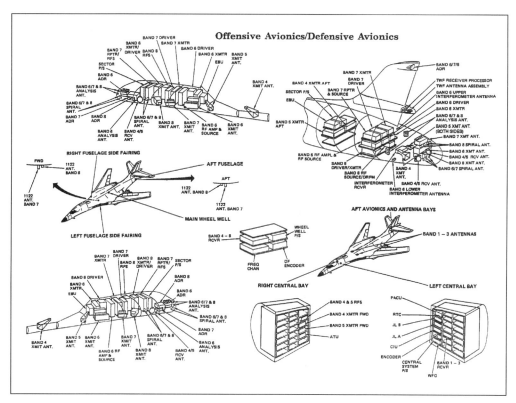

The offensive and defensive avionics systems use almost all available space in the B-1B to house the different "black boxes" necessary to perform their functions. This diagram shows the locations of most of the major components. Note the location of the ALQ-161A antenna arrays in the wing-root leading edge. If the ALQ-161A is replaced by the ALR-56M and IDECM systems as part of the DSUP, the number of components will be reduced significantly, a tribute to the great strides in technology over the past 20 years. *(U.S. Air Force)*

countermeasures (EXCM) system. As originally installed, the system consisted of 120 separate elements weighing over 5200 pounds and consumed about 120 kW of power in "all-out" jamming mode.

The ASQ-184 management system is shared between the offensive avionics and the DAS. It provides the controls and displays that allow the DSO to interface with the RFS/ECMS, TWF, and EXCM, and also provides an automatic interface between the OAS and DAS to prevent the two systems' transmissions from interfering with each other.

The original requirements included threats covering the spectrum from 200 MHz to 15 GHz. Using the traditional designation system, these extended from B-band to K-band, but in the B-1B these were referred to as Band 1 through Band 8, with the highest emphasis on Bands 4–8. The RFS was designed to receive these signals, record them, compare them with a known threat library, positively identify each one, assign each one a priority, and then command the ECMS portion of the system to jam the highest priority threats. The system is controlled by a IBM AP-101F digital computer communicating over a common Mil-Std-1553B serial data bus.

The major subcontractors for the ALQ-161A include Raytheon's Sedco Systems Division, which provides the phased-array antennas used for Bands 6, 7, and 8; Northrop Grumman, which provides the drivers and transmitters for Band 6 and 7 and a hybrid driver-transmitter for Band 8; and General Electric, who supplies the new Band 8 exciters. All of the subcontractors, except GE, also worked on the original ALQ-161 team.

An IBM 101D (and still later, an AP-101F) computer replaced the Litton LC-4516D as the ALQ-161A's central system manager because the same IBM computer is used elsewhere on the B-1B, including its offensive avionics system. Beyond achieving hardware commonality, this also permits the use of a common Jovial J-83 software environment. The system was subsequently upgraded with the same AP-101F that will replace the other aircraft computers under the CMUP program.

Three sets of electronically steerable Sedco phased-array antennas each provide 120° of azimuth coverage for a total of 360° for Bands 6, 7, and 8. One set of phased-array antennas is installed in the tail of the B-1B, and the other two are located in the wing-root leading edges. Antennas for lower frequencies are located around the rear fuselage and on the upper fuselage sides just behind the cockpit area and thus do not provide broadside coverage. For Bands 4 and 5, each of the forward and aft-looking antennas has two transmitters to share the jamming workload. Each of the 120° sector phased-array antennas for Bands 6 and 7 is fed by three transmitters, while each of Band 8's 120° sector phased-array antennas is powered by two transmitters. The time-sharing of these transmitter resources in each band for each threat in terms of its priority is the most critical parameter controlled by the central IBM computer.

If the optimum strategy for countering a specific radar is to deceive it as to the B-1B's azimuth position, for example, by transmitting through the enemy radar antenna's side-lobe, the AP-101 must determine the precise instant that the antenna sidelobe will be aimed at the aircraft, as well as its relative bearing so that the phased-array antenna beam can be pointed in that direction. Additionally, the transmitter must be tuned to the enemy radar's frequency, and the level of power must be set so that it corresponds to the skin-echo level as well as being "smeared" in time to enhance the deception.

The task is complicated by frequency-hopping enemy radars that shift frequency slightly for each pulse or that stagger the time interval between each pulse, especially where deceptive countermeasures are desirable rather than brute-force jamming. Initially, the ALQ-161A resorts to continuous-wave jamming until it acquires data to determine the new radar's characteristics including such things as scan and pulse rate. Once this has been done, the ALQ-161A shifts to a more efficient strategy and radiates only when the radar is illuminating the aircraft.

A variety of antennas are located on the rear fuselage of the B-1B. The small radome behind the horizontal stabilizer housed the tail-warning function of the ALQ-161A, while the large rear radome contained various antennas for the DAS. This photo shows the vortex generators in their original configuration. Subsequently, the three lowest generators were moved to a position directly behind the upper three, and an 11th generator was added. *(Mick Roth Collection)*

Operation of the ALQ-161A is primarily in an automatic mode, where the system receives, identifies, and jams threat radars instantaneously. However, the WSO can manually intervene when desired. Complete situational awareness is provided on two threat display formats to the WSO that include constant information of threat type, mode, location jamming status, frequency, and relative amplitude. Other additional system and/or threat information is available on call to the operator through a correlated joystick that allows the WSO to designate specific threats and request data from either display format. Additional manual functions such as jamming modifications, receiver attenuation changes, and threat characteristic changes are available to the WSO.

The system is highly reprogrammable, on the ground and in the air, which allows it to adapt to any scenario in minimum time. The receiver continually observes the entire environment to detect most conventional threats at a moderate sensitivity. For those emitters that require higher sensitivity for detection, the receiver uses its directed high sensitivity search routine that is programmed by the user for maximum effectiveness.

The TWF is a function of the ALQ-161A system that monitors the hemisphere directly behind the aircraft through antennas in the fairing behind the horizontal stabilizer. It uses a pulse-Doppler radar, which detects airborne threats approaching from the rear of the aircraft. When a threat is detected, the TWF discriminates between aircraft and missiles, the associated azimuth and range information is displayed to the DSO, and a missile warning tone is provided to the crew through the aircraft intercom. The TWF is capable of automatically dispensing flares or chaff.

The DAS is being largely replaced by more conventional ECM equipment as part of the DSUP upgrade program initiated in 1995 and scheduled to be complete in 2009. This program will replace the ALQ-161A RFS/ECMS and portions of the ASQ-184 defensive management system with an Loral/Litton AN/ALR-56M radar warning receiver (RWR) and the

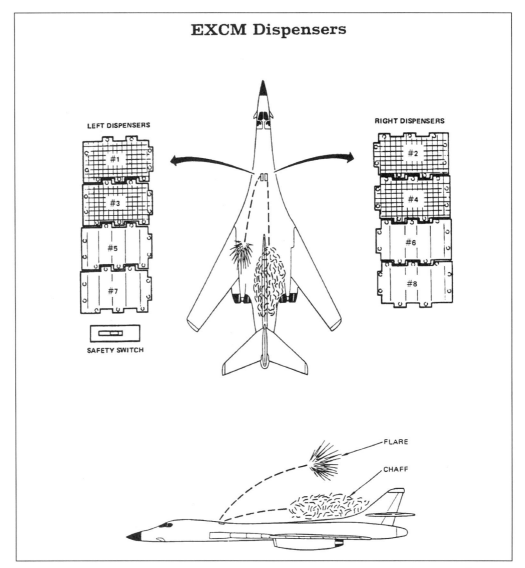

EXCM Dispensers

LEFT DISPENSERS

#1
#3
#5
#7

SAFETY SWITCH

RIGHT DISPENSERS

#2
#4
#6
#8

FLARE

CHAFF

There are two sets of four expendable countermeasures dispensers on top of the B-1B fuselage. Each dispenser can carry chaff or flares. Due to the extreme low level the B-1B operates at, the dispensers eject the countermeasures upwards. This also ensures that FOD does not get ingested into the engines when countermeasures are dispensed. *(U.S. Air Force)*

Navy's Integrated Defensive Electronic Countermeasures (IDECM) system. The existing TWF and EXCM dispensers will be retained and integrated with the new equipment. In addition, an interim ALE-50 towed decoy system is being added to the aft fuselage pending the installation of the IDECM's fiber-optic towed decoy (FOTD).

The ALE-50 decoy is a repeater jammer that is towed several hundred feet behind the B-1B. The decoy uses various techniques to provide a radar signature that is easier to detect from most angles than the B-1B itself, luring most missiles towards the decoy. The distance from the decoy to the B-1B is sufficient to avoid collateral damage to the bomber from a missile impacting the decoy.

The ALR-56M includes a fast-scanning superhet receiver, a superhet controller, an analysis processor, a low band receiver/power supply, and four quadrant receivers. The ALR-56M is designed to provide high performance in a dense signal environment and excellent detection of modern threat signals and is currently installed in F-16C Block 40 aircraft. The system is essentially a miniaturized version (hence the "M") of the F-15's ALR-56C.

The Sanders IDECM suite is intended to provide self-protection and increased surviv-ability for tactical aircraft against radio frequency (RF) and infrared (IR) surface-to-air and air-to-air threats. The IDECM was initially developed for the Navy's F/A-18E/F, and is cur-rently undergoing tests in that aircraft. The major hardware component of the IDECM is the radio frequency countermeasure (RFCM) system. In the B-1B the RFCM will integrate with the ALR-56M and the existing TWF and EXCM, as well as the ALE-50 decoy. Integration of these systems is intended to provide threat system warning, threat missile detection/warning, and the most effective countermeasure response to increase surviv-ability of the B-1B against all anticipated RF and IR threats. The RFCM will also include an onboard receiver/processor/techniques generator that stimulates the FOTD. The FOTD is intended to be compatible with the ALE-50 dispenser and will eventually replace the interim ALE-50 installation on the B-1B.

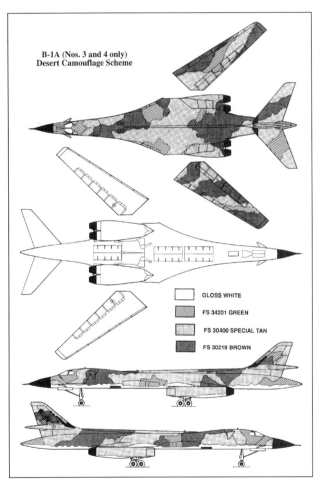

All four B-1As were delivered in overall gloss white, but this desert camouflage scheme was applied to the last two B-1As late in their careers. The three-tone camouflage was only applied to the top of the aircraft—the bottom remained gloss white. All four B-1As were eventually repainted into the standard B-1B strategic camouflage. *(Courtesy of Don Logan)*

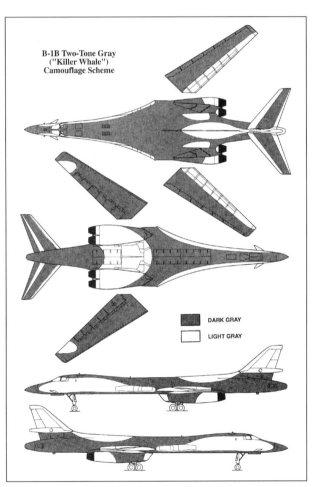

This was the camouflage scheme that was supposed to appear on the production B-1Bs. It was designed to accom-modate the conflicting requirements of nuclear "antiflash" protection and visual stealth. The light gray areas provided antiflash protection of critical areas. The scheme was never applied to any aircraft when the Air Force decided the anti-flash requirements were no longer important. *(Courtesy of Don Logan)*

Expendable Countermeasures System

The expendable countermeasures (EXCM) system consists of eight interchangeable IR flare or chaff dispensers located on top of the fuselage aft of the crew compartment. Dispensing of chaff or flares is controlled manually by the DSO or automatically by the ALQ-161A or TWF. The eight dispensing locations are organized in two banks of four, identified as the left bank (dispensers 1, 3, 5, and 7) and the right bank (dispensers 2, 4, 6, and 8). Each location may be loaded with a dispenser containing up to 12 flares or up to 120 chaff cartridges. The flares are capable of being ejected at a rate of up to 16 per second, two at a time, from opposite sides of the aircraft.

Color Schemes

All four B-1As were initially painted overall gloss ("anti-flash") white. The third and fourth aircraft had black nose radomes since both were equipped with the offensive avionics system, and the fourth aircraft had black dielectric panels on the wing-root leading edges to cover antennas for the ALQ-161. The second aircraft received distinctive "B-1B" markings on the vertical stabilizer when it began flying as part of the B-1B flight test program. The last two B-1As were repainted into a three-tone desert camouflage of tan, green, and brown with flat white undersides. All four B-1As were eventually painted in the B-1B strategic camouflage.

The originally proposed B-1B camouflage was a two-tone gray "killer whale" scheme that used a very pale gray to cover the flash-sensitive areas such as the crew compartment and avionics bays. This scheme, however, was never applied to any aircraft, and all production B-1Bs left the factory with a "strategic" variation of the "European One" scheme of very dark green (FS34086) and dark gray (FS36081) upper surface and two-tone gray (FS36081 dark gray and FS36118 gunship gray) lower surface. The nose radomes were very dark gray. Interestingly, on some aircraft the dark green faded to an almost reddish brown, especially under sunset or dawn lighting.

Beginning in late 1990 the B-1Bs began receiving an overall gunship gray (FS36118) scheme very similar to that used on the B-52G/H. As the aircraft were repainted, many retained a very dark gray radome, but these are slowly being replaced by units that more closely match the overall paint color.

When they entered service, the B-1Bs did not have conspicuous markings, carrying the SAC badge on the left forward fuselage, below the OSO's window, and the wing badge on the right side, below the DSO's window. Wing insignia were soon adopted and applied to the vertical stabilizers. The 96th BW used the Texas state flag with the skull of a Texas Longhorn superimposed. The 28th BW carried the outline of Mount Rushmore, between parallel blue bands (the upper one joined

B-1B Strategic ("European One") Camouflage Scheme

FS 34086 DARK GREEN
FS 36081 DARK GRAY
FS 36118 GUNSHIP GRAY

This strategic camouflage scheme (a variation of "European One") was used by all B-1Bs as they came from the factory. This scheme was later replaced by a single-tone dark gray, which is currently used by the entire fleet. *(Courtesy of Don Logan)*

below a thin orange stripe) and with the word "Ellsworth" in orange. The 319th BW used an orange and blue stripe with a "sunflake" design forward, consisting of the upper half of a sunburst and the lower half of a snowflake. The 384th BW used the "Keeper of the Plains" motif with a Native American holding wheat sheaves and lightning bolts, superimposed on a three-tone blue band. This unit also applied its World War II "triangle P" insignia on some aircraft for bombing competitions.

The transfer of the B-1B to the ACC saw the introduction of two-letter tailcodes, and squadron tail stripes replaced the old wing identities. The SAC badge was replaced by the appropriate squadron badge. Serial number presentation was also changed from the old SAC style, which ran the second digit of the year prefix together with the "last four" below the "USAF" legend. In ACC service the aircraft wear the two-digit year prefix below the letters "AF," with the last three digits of the serial being roughly twice the height. Aircraft received the ACC badge on their vertical stabilizers, between tail stripe and tailcode, freeing up the space below the OSO window (previously used by the SAC badge) for application of squadron insignia, or, more usually, to repeat the wing badge. Many B-1Bs soon acquired names, painted on the undercarriage doors. After a while, B-1Bs began to pick up nose art, usually only on the left side (but on both sides, mirror fashion, on aircraft from the 96th BW). Between 1988 and early 1991 the 384th BW did not use nose art, instead having aircraft names on both sides of the fuselage painted in red or blue according to flight allocation.

Rethinking the Mission: More Acronyms

A lthough the B-1B's manufacturing program was one of the smoothest in Air Force history, its introduction into service was not without its problems. Some of this was related to the ever-decreasing defense budget and an inability to provide proper tools and spare parts to the operational users. Other problems could be traced directly to inadequate testing or overambitious requirements, things not uncommon to many modern weapons systems. Despite a great deal of bad press, the B-1B's service introduction was actually not as trouble plagued as the general public thought, although some of the problems made national headlines (perhaps deservedly so).

Incidents and Accidents

The B-1B's central integrated test system (CITS) monitors about 22,000 parameters and issues more than 10,000 different maintenance codes to assist crews in troubleshooting the aircraft after a mission. When the B-1B first entered service, as many as 350 false reports were issued on each flight. Part of the trouble lay in faulty sensors, wiring, and other hardware shortcomings, but the major problem was the software. Subsequent releases of software reduced the false-report rate per flight to 120, then 95, and finally to less than five per flight beginning in 1990. In recent years, most flights have been completed with no CITS false indications.

On 10 March 1986, the first B-1B delivered to SAC (83-0065) was returning from a training flight when the wings refused to move from the 55° position. After several practice approaches, the aircraft landed safely at Dyess, touching down at a well-above-normal 238 knots. The problem was traced to an interconnect cable that had broken after being improperly routed and kinked. The cable was part of the device that determines the wing-sweep angle. When the system could not determine the wing position, the wings were locked in their current position. It was found that there were no drawings showing the correct routing for the cable, so a standard kink-free routing was quickly designed, and all aircraft were modified.

The overall gray paint scheme is weathering much better than the earlier "strategic" camouflage. Providing an unusual bit of official humor, the "OZ" tail codes represent Kansas. *(Terry Panopalis)*

Another wing-sweep anomaly was encountered in an early aircraft (84-0051) during the pretaxi check when the left wing continued to rotate forward past the 15° setting and penetrated the No. 2 fuel tank. The cause was a combination of incorrect rigging of the wing-sweep system, a broken left gearbox quill-shaft, worn splines on the right-angle gearbox joining the drive shafts, and a damaged control shaft linking the left and right hydraulic drives. This appeared to be an isolated incident, and the aircraft was repaired and returned to service.

Bird strikes are always a threat to high-speed aircraft, especially by ones that fly at extremely low altitudes. Engineers go to great lengths to determine areas susceptible to bird strikes and design them to minimize the strikes' potential impact. The first operational B-1B loss occurred on 28 September 1987, near La Junta, Colorado, when the 12th B-1B (85-0052) crashed following a suspected bird strike. A catastrophic fire broke out and the crew abandoned the aircraft. The six-man training crew from the 338th SBTS was made up of three instructors and three students. Neither instructor had time to egress through the bottom hatch and both were killed, as was the copilot, whose ejection seat malfunctioned. The subsequent investigation centered on the possibility that a large bird impacted the support between an engine nacelle and the wing, penetrating the structure and breaking fuel, hydraulic, and electrical lines. Although no conclusive evidence was uncovered, the Air Force temporarily suspended low-level training and launched an engineering evaluation of areas where bird strikes could cause critical damage. Five vulnerable locations were identified, including each wing-nacelle junction, the base of the vertical stabilizer ahead of the horizontal stabilizer power unit, and the inner-wing leading edge immediately inboard of each wing pivot. Hardened steel and/or Kevlar shields were designed for each area, and by February 1989 Rockwell had modified 29 aircraft and OC-ALC had modified the remaining 67.

On 8 November 1988, another B-1B (85-0063) was on a training mission near Dyess AFB when an uncontrolled fire broke out in the over-wing fairing area above the left engines. The crew of four ejected safely, and the aircraft crashed about three miles from the base. There was no indication of a bird strike, and the crash investigation subsequently deter-

The white outlines around the tail codes are unusual, and indicate a commander's or special Wing aircraft. In this case some liberty has been taken with the serial number (86-0138) to make "384th BW." *(Terry Panopalis)*

mined that the cause was most probably a fuel leak, possibly due to failure of a fuel manifold. This conclusion led to an investigation as to whether the same failure might have been responsible for the B-1B lost over La Junta a year earlier. The investigation was inconclusive, but prompt action was initiated to prevent any recurrence. Modifications included adding two fire-detection circuits, various baffles and drains to prevent fuel from accumulating, and two Halon extinguisher bottles to each over-wing fairing.

On 18 November 1988, a B-1B (85-0076—*Black Jack*) crashed while trying to land in adverse weather at Ellsworth AFB. All four crewmembers ejected safely. The cause of the crash was determined to be a combination of bad weather, a restricted (i.e., not fully functional) aircraft ILS system, and pilot error.

On 4 October 1989, a B-1B (85-0070) suffered an in-flight failure of the No. 2 hydraulic system, losing nosewheel steering and 20 percent of braking capacity, and requiring the alternate (No. 3) hydraulic system to be used for gear extension. After two hard touch-and-go landings on the main gear in attempts to shake the nose gear loose failed to rectify the situation, a nose-gear-up landing was made on the lakebed at Edwards. The aircraft suffered only minor damage to the radome and forward fuselage. It was later determined that an electrical cable supplying power to the nose-gear emergency (alternate) selector valve had become disconnected.

On 14 October 1990, a B-1B (86-0128) was on a training mission when there was a loud explosion as the engines were commanded to MIL power. Various caution and warning alarms followed, and the crew became aware of a fire outside the left side of the aircraft. After shutting down the No. 1 engine and actuating that engine's fire extinguishers, a night landing was made at Pueblo, Colorado. A postaccident investigation showed that the uncontained failure of the No. 1 engine fan had caused extensive local damage, including severing the forward engine mounts. The engine had completely broken away from the aircraft, fortunately without hitting anything, but the burning main fuel line damaged the tail section and aft radome. After some local repairs, the aircraft was ferried on three engines to OC-ALC for final repairs.

Just over two months later, on 19 December 1990, another B-1B (83-0071) was practicing landing approaches when the crew felt a sharp jolt after advancing the engines to MIL power. The No. 3 engine was shut down, and its fire extinguishers activated. Again, the cause was determined to be an uncontained fan failure.

The following day, all B-1Bs, except those aircraft on nuclear alert status, were grounded. After only 100,000 flight hours, there had been six F101 fan failures. General Electric began to completely redesign the first-stage fan blades with part-span dampers. As an interim measure, the 0.06-inch stainless-steel first-stage fan retaining ring was replaced by a ring made of 0.125-inch Inconel 718 in an effort to contain any future failures. Furthermore, all B-1Bs were required to undergo an inspection before each flight and an eddy-current check every 25 hours. The grounding was lifted on 6 February 1991. The fleet was subsequently equipped with the modified engines and no further fan failures have been experienced.

A B-1B (86-0106—*Lone Wolf*) crashed on 30 November 1992 during a low-level night flight near Van Horn, Texas. All four crewmembers were killed when the aircraft collided with a mountain in the Sierra Vieja range. Subsequent analysis of the flight data recorder indicated that everything had been functioning normally prior to the impact, leading investigators to declare the incident the result of "pilot error."

On 19 September 1997, a B-1B (85-0078—*Heavy Metal*) from the 37th BS at Ellsworth crashed 25 miles north of Alzada, Montana, while flying over the Powder River Military Operating Area. All four crewmembers were killed. The board of inquiry determined that the aircraft impacted the ground while carrying out a defensive maneuver that involved slowing down and turning sharply to avoid a threat.

Defensive Avionics System Problems

The B-1B had one truly deficient area that would not prove easy to fix. The defensive avionics system (DAS) was one of the most complex electronic systems ever fitted to a combat aircraft. The production ALQ-161A is an enhanced version of the advanced development model that underwent flight test on a B-1A. The enhancements include adding a Band 8 radar warning and jamming capability to extend frequency coverage further into K-band; extending the receive-warning function (but no jamming) below 200 MHz; adding the tail-warning function (TWF), a pulse-Doppler radar to detect aircraft and missiles approaching the rear quarter; and incorporating a digital radio-frequency memory to permit deception jamming of more advanced Soviet radars, such as those that employ pulse-Doppler techniques. The majority of these changes were made to address changes in the perceived threats. The ALQ-161A retains the basic system architecture of the original system designed in the early 1970s. Therefore, the basic architecture and hardware were already almost 15 years old when the B-1B was first introduced to squadron service. Although the requirement changes were probably reasonable, the Air Force insisted that the DAS be operational for the planned B-1B IOC in 1986, allowing very little time to test the integrated DAS, and even less to test the interaction between the DAS and the offensive avionics system.

On the B-1A, all of the pieces of the DAS were to be integrated by Boeing, but on the B-1B the Air Force assumed the role of integrator. It should be noted that the Boeing ASQ-184 is a "shared" system, performing functions for the offensive and defensive avionics, which explains why Boeing had initially been assigned the role of integrator on the B-1A. Miscommunications between the OAS and DAS were one of the major problems experienced by the B-1B in early operational service.

Unlike most previous systems, the DAS architecture allowed the integration of receiving and jamming functions into a single system. The DAS was designed to receive and record these signals, then compare them with a known threat library, positively identify each one and assign it a priority, and, finally, jam the highest priority threats. One of the perceived advantages of having the receiving function completely integrated with the jamming function was that it allows the receiving system to detect new signals and continue to monitor old signals while jamming in the same frequency band. The ALQ-161A allows this to be accomplished by monitoring the output of the jamming transmitters and adjusting the receivers continuously. All main computers on the B-1B, including the one in the ALQ-161A, communicate over a time-multiplexing Mil-Std-1553B serial data bus. Via this bus, the ALQ-161A communicates with the ASQ-164 to coordinate transmissions between the OAS and DAS (so the radar and ECM system do not conflict with one another), and also presents information to the DSO in the cockpit.

It should be noted, in all fairness, that modern ECM systems have traditionally been troublesome to develop and introduce into operation. This is partly because, by their nature, they are developed without a full understanding of the threats they are expected to counter (the Soviets hardly released data on their radars to AIL). It is also a constantly changing world, and the threats change frequently. The B-1B was not the only aircraft of its era to suffer problems with its ECM system—the McDonnell Douglas F-15E Strike Eagle went into combat during Operation Desert Storm with a marginally operational AN/ALQ-135B ECM system after almost 10 years of development, a fact that might have contributed to the loss of two aircraft.

In order to meet the 1986 IOC date, the DAS was put into production before development and testing were complete, an accepted practice known as "concurrent development." This was to prove a costly mistake. Constant changes during production led to a variety of configurations (it has been stated, sarcastically, that no two B-1Bs had the same DAS installations), none of which proved terribly effective. The major problem was that the ALQ-161A frequently interpreted its own jamming transmissions, or the transmissions from the aircraft's offensive avionics, as hostile threats and attempted to jam them.

The General Accounting Office (GAO) issued a report in the mid-1980s severely criticizing the ALQ-161A, and the media quickly began touting the "self-jamming bomber" as an example of the waste of tax dollars on expensive and unworkable systems. But the criticism ignored other shortcomings of the system. Limited by the amount of computer power available in the original AP-101C computers, the system was easily overloaded by multiple threats. Although it proved to be fairly successful at detecting 1970s-era threat signals, newer, higher-frequency or pulse rate threats went largely undetected. The interface between the offensive avionics and defensive avionics proved to be marginally effective, resulting in conflicting signals that largely destroyed the effectiveness of both systems. An early switch to more modern IBM AP-101F computers has helped somewhat.

During 1986–1987, the Air Force embarked on an extensive upgrade so the DAS could, at least, meet the original specifications, even though this meant the system would still be incapable of defending the aircraft against the most current threats. A three-stage "core" program was developed (called Mod 0, 1, and 2) to be completed by the end of 1992.

The first phase, Mod 0, consisted of bringing all aircraft up to the same standard, generally similar to that delivered on the last few aircraft. This phase was projected to take several years, during which time Mod 1 and Mod 2 would be developed and tested. After looking at the schedules, the Air Force decided that Mod 2 would probably be ready before the last 18 aircraft could be upgraded to the Mod 0 standard. It was decided, therefore, to allow these 18 aircraft to skip Mod 0 and Mod 1 and proceed directly to Mod 2 when it was available. This was done primarily as a cost-saving measure.

Mod 1 would introduce several new features, including additional manual control options, and would include a range of hardware and software modifications designed to increase performance and reliability. The initial Mod 1 installation was flight tested in

March–June 1988, and it was soon apparent that there were still significant problems. Although the Mod 1 system had "good capabilities to identify and counter the top 10 airborne threats," it was unable to process a large number of radar signals simultaneously. The projected threat environment over the Soviet Union included an unprecedented number of different radars, and this had been part of the original B-1B specifications. The root cause lay in the basic architecture of the DAS, a problem that everyone feared might prove impossible to overcome. Not only were the individual processors dangerously overloaded, but the sophisticated data buses connecting the distributed processors were becoming overloaded.

The 1987 plan had been to design and test Mod 2 in 1988–1989, and to complete installation on the fleet by 1992. By 1988 it was clear that this objective was not achievable, and Mod 2 was put on hold. By this time funding limitations prevented the Mod 1 hardware improvements from reaching the fleet, but much of the updated software was installed on the Mod 0 hardware already on operational aircraft. Ten years later, the B-1B fleet is still at essentially the Mod 0 hardware configuration, although the software has been continually improved.

The DAS was still not performing to a level the Air Force found acceptable, although this was largely because the necessary funding had never been made available to implement the changes already identified by AIL. Nevertheless, evaluations were made for replacing the ALQ-161A with equipment already in the inventory, and eventually a plan was drawn up that included using the best available ECM equipment from a variety of sources, including the Navy. In January 1995, the USD/A&T approved the Defensive System Upgrade Program (DSUP) at the same time that approval for the CMUP Block D upgrade was granted.

As an interim measure, a pair of AN/ALE-50 towed decoys are being added to the sides of the aft fuselage. When deployed, these decoys trail the B-1B by several hundred feet and present a radar target slightly more inviting than the B-1B itself, hopefully luring missiles away from the bomber. These towed decoys do, however, have limitations, especially when the bomber is maneuvering.

As currently envisioned, the DSUP will eventually replace all of the existing DAS except the TWF. Since this subsystem has been functioning well for several years, it will be retained and integrated with the new ECM equipment. The remaining ALQ-161A and ASQ-184 defensive functions will be replaced by a Loral/Litton AN/ALR-56M, similar to that used by late-model F-16Cs, and a Navy-developed Sanders Integrated Defensive Electronic Countermeasures (IDECM) system originally designed for the F/A-18E/F. But AIL has not totally given up, and has developed an alternative it believes will be more cost effective and provide a more capable system. Only time will tell.

The Air Force and GAO Battle It Out

Although all current heavy bombers were initially designed and procured primarily to meet nuclear war-fighting requirements, since the end of the Cold War the DoD has placed increased emphasis on the role of bombers in future conventional conflicts. The end of the Cold War also permitted the Air Force to reduce the number of operational bombers from a total of 360 aircraft in 1989 to 208 in 1998. Since 1990, the Air Force has conducted four major studies of heavy bomber requirements that have helped shape the current bomber force—the Nuclear Posture Review, the Bottom-Up Review, the Bomber Roadmap, and the congressionally mandated Heavy Bomber Force Study.

During 1992, the Air Force determined that the conventional capabilities of its bombers were not sufficient to destroy critical ground targets during the initial stages of a major regional conflict. Therefore, the Air Force developed a plan to provide the bomber force with the capability to drop additional unguided gravity weapons and precision-guided munitions. The Air Force plan included configuring the B-2 and B-52H for both conventional or nuclear missions, while the B-1B would be reconfigured for a conventional role only. As part of a general realignment of forces within the Air Force, some B-1Bs and B-52Hs would be placed in the Air National Guard and the Air Force Reserves.

According to the Air Force, only 66 B-52Hs and 20 B-2As would be needed for the nuclear role. The decision to keep 209 bombers in the force reflected the DoD's view that long-range bombers were needed primarily to supplement the conventional capabilities of other ground-attack assets such as Air Force and Navy tactical fighters and cruise missiles. The 1993 Bottom-Up Review had concluded that 100 bombers were needed to fight a major regional conflict and up to 184 bombers should be maintained in the inventory. The Air Force's Bomber Roadmap established a requirement for 210 bombers. The Heavy Bomber Force Study, completed in May 1995, concluded that as few as 100 bombers could meet the anticipated requirements.

Despite any internal squabbling between the DoD, Air Force, and Congress, there was a very real shortage of funds for the massive upgrades the Air Force wanted to accomplish on the B-1B. One part of the solution, formalized by the Air Force in 1993, became known as the "attrition reserve." The attrition reserve concept became possible when the U.S. embraced the assumption that the 1990s would be a fairly low-risk period for a large-scale conventional or nuclear war. That risk assessment allowed the Air Force "to remove from the books" a portion of the bomber force. Although it would still physically exist, it would not be counted as part of the combat inventory. No pilots or crew chiefs were assigned to these aircraft, and spare parts were not purchased for them (leading to yet more shortages of spare parts).

"They were put in caretaker status," Major J. C. Valle, a B-1B pilot and ACC's chief of tactics development for the aircraft, said. "We'd fly them. . . . You couldn't tell a regular 'Bone' from an 'attrition reserve' one, but we didn't budget" for the costs of operating or maintaining them. Spare parts were available for a certain number of the aircraft, said Valle, which were "cycled in and out of the flying inventory by tail number," so that the fleet aged at the same rate in terms of hours flown, hours between overhauls, etc.

At the end of 1993, the Air Force had 96 B-1Bs on strength, of which 74 were "operational" and 22 were allocated to training, test, and depot maintenance. The number of operational aircraft was reduced to 53 by placing 21 B-1Bs into the attrition reserve. (A similar reduction effort covered the B-52H.) In time, 18 of the 53 operational B-1Bs were assigned to the Air National Guard. Savings on personnel, spare parts, fuel, and other operating costs flowed into the Conventional Munitions Upgrade Program. Converting the B-1B to a conventional role has been a gradual process, beginning in 1993 and culminating in October 1997, when the 7th BW at Dyess stood the last nuclear alert with the B-1B.

In 1996, Congress requested that the GAO evaluate possible methods to save money on the bomber fleet. The resulting study estimated that retiring the entire B-1B fleet would save $5900 million between FY97-01. Retiring the 27 B-1Bs that were in attrition reserve would save about $450 million over the same five years. Placing 24 additional B-1Bs in the Air National Guard would save approximately $15 million per year because these units have fewer full-time personnel and are less costly to operate.

An endemic problem identified by the GAO (which has very gradually eased) has been shortage of spare parts, caused almost entirely by inadequate funding. Throughout 1987, the first two B-1B bases were able to keep flying only by cannibalization (removing parts from one aircraft to keep another mission capable). At Dyess the mission-capable rate from June 1987 through June 1988 varied between 28.2 and 45.9 percent, completely unacceptable levels.

The GAO believed that although the Air Force demonstrated that one squadron of B-1Bs could exceed the required 75 percent mission-capable rate if properly funded (i.e., the

ORA), it had not demonstrated that the overall B-1B force could achieve and sustain this rate. The Air Force embarked on a program to improve the overall B-1B MC rate and expects to achieve a fleetwide 75 percent rate by the year 2001.

During the last five years, the employment concept for the B-1B and its training syllabus have changed radically, according to Colonel Glenn Spears, 28th Operations Group commander at Ellsworth AFB. The training emphasis has changed to emphasize operations "within a composite force," Spears said. "We're more fluid . . . more flexible." In the days of the nuclear role, B-1B crews trained on very long, fairly static missions, "single ship, practicing threat reactions," Spears noted. Today, the B-1B sortie is typically a two-ship formation, "working a bombing range and dealing with all sorts of surprises."

"If we simulate that a threat has come up . . . we practice evading the threat and altering the route," with the prime objective of getting to and away from the target safely. Because the B-1B is so valuable an asset, the mission commander is charged with ensuring that it returns, even if it means passing up the target until conditions are more favorable. If there's no way to "safely get my package out," the B-1B pilot will forgo the target and "I'll survive to fight another day," Spears said.

In past planning for nuclear missions, the bombers would have only enough fuel for a one-way trip along a carefully prescribed course. In the conventional role, with mission length shorter and tankers available, there's a good deal more flexibility to try things a different way, Spears added.

He explained that crew training emphasizes "defensive maneuvers and advanced handling of the aircraft," which does not necessarily mean low-level flight. The B-1B, with its variable geometry wings and powerful engines, can perform the type of violent maneuvers one would not expect of such a large aircraft. "The B-1B Wings train our crews to use the full safe envelope of the aircraft's capabilities," Spears noted. "There's no doubt that it's a bomber, but it's a very maneuverable bomber." Part of the training involves maneuvering to avoid surface-to-air and air-to-air missiles. Pilots are also now equipped with night vision goggles (NVG) and the cockpit has been modified to accommodate the NVG devices.

The DoD's FY97 Future Years Defense Program included $17 billion to operate and maintain the Air Force bomber force for the next five years. This included $6.3 billion (37 percent) for modernization and $10.7 billion (63 percent) for operations and support. The B-1B fleet will account for the largest portion of future bomber operations and support costs. However, the B-2 will be the most costly to operate on a per aircraft basis, costing more than three times as much as the B-1B and more than four times as much as the B-52H.

Conventional Mission Upgrade Program

The B-1B was the only operational Air Force warplane that did not participate in Operation Desert Storm during 1991, a fact its critics held up as proof that the Air Force had bought a lemon it was afraid to send into combat. What the critics never mentioned was that, at the time, the B-1B was doing its job—standing nuclear alert. There were other reasons, of course. The DAS still did not work very well, making the Air Force reluctant to send the B-1B into combat, and there was a general shortage of B-1B crews with experience dropping conventional ordnance. Besides, the B-52 had proven itself very adept at conventional warfare, and was readily available for Operation Desert Storm.

The decision to shift the manned bomber's role came shortly after the Gulf War. That conflict proved, among other things, that the lines between strategic and tactical targets had become permanently blurred. The formation of Air Combat Command—unifying the forces and personnel of SAC and TAC—put this into organizational practice. After the Air Force decided in 1992 to realign its heavy bomber force to provide additional conventional weapons capabilities, the B-1B was selected as a dedicated conventional bomber. This left only the 94 remaining B-52Hs and 21 B-2As to fulfill the manned bomber portion of the nuclear triad.

To accomplish this, the Air Force initiated the Conventional Mission Upgrade Program (CMUP). As originally envisioned, the CMUP program had three major phases. Phase I consisted of hardware and software modifications to allow the delivery of cluster bombs. Phase II included the addition of a Mil-Std-1760 data bus and weapons carriage modifications for delivery of the GBU-32 Joint Direct Attack Munition (JDAM). This phase also included software and additional avionics modifications for new secure-voice radios, a Global Positioning System (GPS) receiver, and computer improvements. Phase III included the capability to use the AGM-154 Joint Stand-Off Weapon (JSOW) and the AGM-158 Joint Air-to-Surface Standoff Missile (JASSM). Although most of the capabilities remained the same, the nomenclature and order of inclusion would subsequently change.

Operational Readiness Assessment

Prior to full approval of the CMUP, Congress sought assurances that the B-1B was sufficiently reliable and supportable to meet its planned mission-capable (MC)

High-speed, low-level flight is still the main defensive tactic of the B-1B, although unlike the B-1A the aircraft cannot sustain supersonic speeds at low level. *(Boeing North American)*

rate. As a result, the FY94 National Defense Authorization Act directed the Air Force to conduct an evaluation of B-1B sustainability. The B-1B operational readiness assessment (ORA) concentrated spares and other logistics support for the B-1B at a single Wing, and focused on the ability of the B-1B to achieve the planned MC rate. The test also included a period of deployed operations, simulating combat missions from a base that did not normally support B-1Bs. The objective was to establish whether the completion of planned procurements of B-1B spares would provide a robust capability for sustained offensive conventional operations.

The B-1B ORA began on 1 June 1994 with a five-month reliability, maintainability, and availability assessment of the 28th BW at Ellsworth AFB. The second phase of the ORA took place during the first two weeks of November 1994 at Roswell Industrial Air Center, New Mexico, where nine B-1Bs deployed and conducted intensive operations, simulating a deployment to a combat theater. To ensure that the B-1Bs were adequately supported, spare parts, equipment, and personnel were brought in from the 7th BW and 384th BW.

AFOTEC monitored the ORA by conducting periodic on-site monitoring visits at Ellsworth and by having on-site observers present throughout the two-week deployment to Roswell. AFOTEC also evaluated the logistics performance reported by the Air Force during the test, and gathered additional data to characterize the operational demands of the flying schedule. In addition, AFOTEC monitored the flying program to ensure that the simulated missions were as realistic as possible and that B-1Bs were being flown as if they were in a combat role, particularly during the deployment phase.

The B-1B ORA was successful, exceeding the test requirement and ACC's future goal of a 75 percent MC rate. Overall, the ORA consisted of 1251 sorties and 5670 flight hours, averaging a 84.3 percent MC rate (on a daily basis it fluctuated between 82.8 and 85.6 percent). During the deployment to Roswell, the MC rate of the nine aircraft was 84.4 percent. While deployed, the Wing flew 109 mission sorties with an average sortie duration of 6 hours, for a total of 657 flight hours. All deployed sorties were representative of combat operations

Prior to authorizing funding for the CMUP program, the Air Force was directed to conduct an operation readiness assessment of the B-1B. This included a sustained period of operations from an "austere" site that did not normally support the B-1B. The location chosen was the Roswell Air Industrial Center in New Mexico, shown here. *(U.S. Air Force/DVIC DF-ST-97-00965)*

from a forward operating base, and included simulated threat penetrations and 247 live or practice weapon deliveries.

The MC rates achieved during the ORA were not, however, indicative of the overall B-1B readiness rate. It only proved that a single Wing, equipped with almost all of the Air Force's supply of spare parts and supported by nearly all the available trained personnel, could achieve a satisfactory MC rate. It should have demonstrated to Congress and the DoD that at least part of the problem with modern combat aircraft's dismal MC rates was due to a lack of sufficient spares and training. But as with many lessons, it was not learned, and the B-1B, like most Air Force combat aircraft, would continue to suffer from a severe shortage of spare parts. Analysis of the ORA test results was completed, and in March 1995 AFOTEC submitted a report to Congress containing the results of the ORA. Congress was apparently satisfied and released the first increment of CMUP funding.

All B-1Bs were designated as Block A models when the CMUP began. A modest Block B upgrade included improvements to the synthetic aperture radar, and some minor changes to the DAS to improve maintainability and "reduce the false alarm rate." The Block B upgrade reached the field in 1995.

Block C

The Block C program added an improved conventional weapons capability to the B-1B and improved overall system reliability and maintainability. New conventional munitions added included the CBU-87 Combined Effect Munition (CEM), CBU-89 Gator, and CBU-97 Sensor-Fused Weapon (SFW).

All three cluster bombs use the Tactical Munitions Dispenser (TMD) shell. The CBU-87 contains 202 BLU-97/B combined effects bomblets, each consisting of a shaped charge, scored steel casing, and zirconium ring for antiarmor, fragmentation, and incendiary capability. The CBU-89 contains 72 magnetic sensing BLU-91/B antitank mines and 22 trip-wire-activated BLU-92/B antipersonnel mines. The CBU-97 contains 10 BLU-108/B

The first new conventional weapons certified for use on the B-1B as part of the CMUP program were three different cluster bombs. These weapons used the existing conventional weapons modules, and were fairly easy to incorporate into the bomber's software. *(U.S. Air Force via the Tony Landis Collection)*

submunitions, each containing four skeet designed to provide a multiple kills per pass capability against tanks and other vehicles.

The CBU-97 was qualified on the B-1B following a May 1998 test when a B-1B flew 1300 miles nonstop from Ellsworth to Eglin, dropped a single SFW at low altitude, and returned to Ellsworth. The weapon achieved 13 hits on four targets in an armored vehicle convoy.

Block C software upgrades included the addition of a "modifiable ballistics" capability that allowed new weapon characteristics to be added to the weapons computers without having the manufacturer reprogram them. Once the modifiable ballistics software was certified on the B-1B, new unguided conventional munitions could be added via a process developed by the Air Force SEEK EAGLE Office (AFSEO). This involved confirming that the munitions could be safely dropped from the aircraft (safe separation testing) and determining the ballistic characteristics of the munitions (ballistic accuracy verification). The weapon ballistics coefficients could then be loaded directly into the avionics flight software.

Hardware modifications included adapting 50 of the original 28-station conventional weapons modules (CWM) to carry ten 1250-pound class weapons. It should be noted that the 50 modified CWMs are sufficient to equip only 25 aircraft (assuming two CWMs per aircraft, with a fuel tank in the third weapons bay). This was accomplished by adding a new internal module structure and strengthening the module shell. The modified CWM allows other weapons to be carried as long as their center of gravity (cg) and dimensions are similar to the TMD/CBU, and they are compatible with the standard 14-inch ejector racks. At the same time, the CWM was modified with provisions for mounting Mil-Std-1760 cables and connectors, although the data bus itself would not come until later. Due to limitations in the weapons computers, the CBU-certified aircraft had to carry identical weapons in all

After falling a safe distance from the aircraft, the cluster bombs release submunitions. These submunitions may be mines or "smart" antitank rounds, depending upon the type of cluster bomb. The weapons proved to be very effective during Operation Desert Storm, although the B-1B was not involved in that campaign. *(U.S. Air Force via the Tony Landis Collection)*

three weapons bays. It would have to wait until after the computer upgrade accomplished as part of Block E until the B-1B was able to carry different weapons in each bay. (It should be noted that before the CMUP, the CWM was usually referred to as the "nonnuclear weapons module.")

Another concern is how to maintain a high sortie rate with conventional bombs from austere sites. The CWM was designed to be loaded with weapons outside the aircraft, then moved into the weapons bay using an MHU-196/M trailer. It takes a C-5 or C-17 to carry the 40,000-pound MHU-196 needed move a loaded CWM. Without this piece of ground support equipment, the CWM must be serviced while it is still in the aircraft. Fifty-six spent impulse cartridges must be removed from each CWM, the area scrubbed to remove carbon, and fresh cartridges installed. Loading the first bomb takes up to 40 minutes, and every subsequent bomb takes approximately 5 minutes, so loading each CWM takes 3 hours for 28 bombs, or 1.5 hours for 10 CBUs.

One of the drawbacks encountered during Block C was the inability to use precision-guided weapons on the B-1B due to a lack of a Mil-Std-1760 interface that allows the aircraft to download information to the weapons. Concurrently with this phase of the CMUP, Rockwell International initiated a project to show the feasibility of rebroadcasting GPS signals within the B-1B weapons bay to a modified Mk 82 bomb with a GPS guided tail kit. This "Bomber Virtual Umbilical Program" was intended to show how a semi-precision-guided weapon could be added to the B-1B without requiring a Mil-Std-1760 interface. The Air Force permitted Rockwell to flight test the concept in conjunction with the Block C flight testing on a "no cost to the government, noninterference" basis. Although the basic concept proved feasible, the Air Force elected not to pursue the capability since the Mil-Std-1760 interface was much more versatile and was already scheduled to be added in a later CMUP block.

At the end of Block C, the B-1B had the capability to carry 10 CBUs per weapons bay, for a total of 30 CBUs per bomber, in addition to its original capability to carry up to 84 Mk 82 bombs per aircraft. The first operational aircraft was delivered to the ACC in September 1996, and the last CBU-certified B-1B was redelivered one year later.

Block D

In January 1995, the USD/A&T approved Block D to equip the B-1B fleet with the 2000-pound GBU-32 JDAM, a GPS navigation capability, and various communications upgrades. The DSUP effort to provide a truly workable ECM system for the B-1B was approved at the same time.

Block D also incorporated a Mil-Std-1760 interface into the B-1B. Structural provisions for this interface had been included in the CWMs that were modified as part of Block C. The Mil-Std-1760 bus is a standard "smart" weapons interface that allows the aircraft to communicate with the JDAM, and will make it easier (cheaper) to add weapons such as the WCMD, JSOW, and JASSM in the future.

One of the new weapons being integrated onto the B-1B is the Joint Direct Attack Munition (JDAM). This is a GPS kit that attaches to a Mk 80-series iron bomb to create a semiprecision weapon. This is an artist's concept. *(U.S. Air Force)*

An operational assessment (OA) of the antijam radios and GPS upgrades for Block D was conducted from October 1996 to May 1997. One of the existing Magnavox AN/ARC-164(V) radios was maintained, but the control head was replaced by a modern digital FMS-900 display in the cockpit. In addition, new Collins AN/ARC-210 UHF/VHF/HQ-II/Voice SAT-COM radios were installed with KY-100 encryption units. The existing KY-58 encryption unit was left in place to serve the ARC-164 radio.

The GBU-32 uses a low-cost guidance kit produced by Boeing to convert existing Mk 84 (general purpose) and BLU-109 (penetrator) 2000-pound bombs into near-precision "smart" weapons. JDAMs can be dropped from more than 15 miles from the target, with updates from GPS satellites guiding the bombs to their target. The JDAMs, like all 2000-pound class conventional weapons, are carried on modified versions of the 180-inch multipurpose rotary launcher (MPRL).

The first JDAM deployment from a B-1B occurred on 11 February 1998 over the Chine Lake test range. Dropped from 24,000 feet at Mach 0.85, the JDAM impacted within 22 feet of the center of the target aircraft revetment, demonstrating an accuracy better than the test requirement. By July 1998 15 JDAMs had been successfully released from the B-1B. As part of the testing, a crew from Ellsworth was deployed to Edwards to demonstrate that 24 JDAMs could be loaded into a B-1B within 6 hours. The operational crew accomplished the task in 3.5 hours.

On 29 October 1998, the first Block D aircraft (85-0091) arrived at Ellsworth, and the formal acceptance ceremony was held on 3 December 1998, although the seventh modi-

A trio of GBU-32 2000-pound JDAMs is dropped over the Edwards AFB test range while an F-16 chase aircraft looks on. The JDAM uses a strap-on GPS receiver, computer, and movable tail fins to turn a "dumb" Mk 80-series general purpose bomb into a semiprecision guided weapon. *(U.S. Air Force)*

Modifications began quickly on the first B-1B to arrive at the Oklahoma City Air Logistics Center (OC-ALC) at Tinker AFB for the Global Positioning System (GPS) installation and communications upgrade. Surprisingly, work continued around the clock on the first few aircraft in order to speed their reintroduction into the fleet. Note the portable flood lights and mass of tool boxes surrounding the aircraft. *(Tinker AFB photo by Margo Wright)*

Aircraft electrician John Alexander reaches for an electrical plug in a B-1B (85-0077) during the GPS and communications upgrade at OC-ALC. Noteworthy are the size and shapes of the holes for the various instruments and controls. All four ejection seats were removed for maintenance at the same time the upgraded avionics were installed. *(Tinker AFB photo by Margo Wright)*

Mike McClarin, a B-1B avionics technician, removes components from within the electronics bay as part of the GPS and communications upgrade. This one bay contains most of the B-1B avionics boxes and is located directly behind the cockpit. Panels on the outside of the fuselage can be removed to access the back side of many components. The bay is quite large, as shown in this photo. *(Tinker AFB photo by Margo Wright)*

A fairly constant stream of B-1Bs flies into and out of Tinker AFB. The OC-ALC provides heavy maintenance in addition to being the primary facility performing CMUP modifications. *(Tinker AFB photo by Margo Wright)*

Paul Fluitt holds a control assembly-pitch stabilization (STAPAC) normally hidden under the ACES II ejection seat. The device is part of the seat's stabilization system. Notice the two ejection seats in the background. *(Tinker AFB photo by Margo Wright)*

fied aircraft was not delivered to the ACC until mid-February 1999. All B-1Bs will be modified to the Block D configuration by early 2001. To demonstrate the new capability, on 4 December 1998 General Richard Hawley, commander of the ACC, personally flew a mission from Ellsworth using one of the three Block D aircraft delivered so far. The General dropped a live GBU-32 JDAM over a bombing range in Utah, scoring a direct hit.

A major improvement in premission support was also included in Block D. The B-1B Mission Planning System consists of the Air Force's Mission Support System (AFMSS) hardware and core software and a B-1B specific aircraft/weapon/electronic (A/W/E) module. AFMSS consists of computer-based tools to help air crews conduct effective and timely premission planning, materials preparation, and postmission review for air training, exercise, and combat operations. The B-1B A/W/E module enables the user to plan and validate missions and produce mission materials for the B-1B. AFMSS was developed by Sanders (a Lockheed Martin company), and the B-1B A/W/E was developed by Logicon (a Northrop Grumman company). The system became operational in late 1998.

Block E

As with other older weapons systems, by the mid-1990s the 1975-vintage computer systems in the B-1B were operating near capacity and could not support additional weapons or capabilities. In addition, because the software used in the B-1B was complex and poorly documented and had been extensively modified over the years, it was difficult and expensive to maintain.

Steve Cox (left) and Mike Meyer will replace 477 individual lines of the B-1B energy transfer system during the aircraft overhaul. The system connects the four ejection seats, and enables the pilot or copilot to initiate the ejection of all crewmembers. This is the rear bulkhead of the OSO position. *(Tinker AFB photo by Margo Wright)*

The Air Force recognized that in order to support additional B-1B capabilities, the computer systems had to be modernized. During 1995, the Air Force identified several preliminary computer upgrade options, ranging from a simple memory upgrade to installing all new computer processors and Ada software. Ada is a modern computer language that offers advantages in design, coding, and documentation, and cost-effective software maintenance and support. Initially, because of a desire to maximize weapons upgrades, the Air Force only allocated $412 million of the $2700 million CMUP for the computer upgrade. As a result, the only affordable option was a simple memory upgrade.

There were, however, concerns that the memory upgrade would not support the conventional weapons and related capabilities that the Air Force wanted to add to the B-1B and could, therefore, jeopardize the entire CMUP effort. Further analysis showed that the memory upgrade, which only doubled the memory of the existing processors and did not increase throughput, was clearly inadequate to support the JSOW and JASSM.

The Air Force subsequently increased funding to $510 million to upgrade the B-1B by replacing the existing computers with new 32-bit processors and converting most of the outdated software to Ada. In addition to allowing additional capabilities, the upgrade

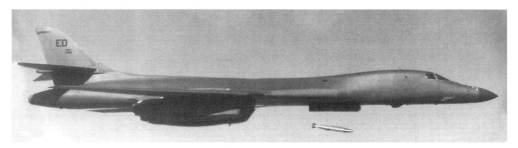

Up to eight 2000-pound JDAMs may be carried in each weapons bay, for a total of 24 per aircraft. This gives the B-1B a powerful new tool to destroy targets without causing the collateral damage normally associated with "dumb" bombs. *(U.S. Air Force)*

could potentially save over $800 million in software maintenance and support costs over the expected 20-plus year life of the upgraded aircraft.

In Block E, the B-1B's seven AP-101C computers will be replaced by four much more capable AP-101F units, and the aircraft will be equipped to carry 24 AGM-154 JSOWs, 24 AGM-158 JASSMs, or 30 Wind-Corrected Munitions Dispensers (WCMDs). Up to eight AGM-154 or AGM-158s are carried on each modified 180-inch MPRL, while the WCMD are carried 10 per CWM. Although the modified CWM was always capable of carrying WCMDs, the lack of a Mil-Std-1760 interface meant that correction data could not be downloaded in real-time. Since Block D finally added a Mil-Std-1760 interface into the weapons bay, it became a relatively easy change to incorporate the WCMD. Block E may be fielded as soon as late 2001. Block E also is procuring additional CWMs, with deliveries scheduled for March–September 2000. The non-computer-related portions of Block E are valued at $179 million.

A rotary launcher armed with Raytheon AGM-154 JSOWs is loaded into the aft weapons bay of a B-1B. The JSOW uses GPS for midcourse guidance and imaging infrared (IIR) for terminal guidance. *(U.S. Air Force)*

The AGM-154 JSOW has a range of over 17 miles when delivered from low altitude, and can be extended to 46 miles if dropped at high altitudes. A set of wings is seen folded back along the top of the missile. At a preset speed these wings deploy to provide additional lift for the missile. *(U.S. Air Force)*

An AGM-154 JSOW is loaded into a B-1B. A special cradle was developed that allows the missile to be loaded using the standard loading truck. Note the four fins on the aft end of the missile that help to stabilize it after launch until the wings deploy. *(U.S. Air Force)*

An AGM-158 JASSM can barely be seen in the aft bay of this B-1B over Edwards AFB. This aircraft also has the ALE-50 towed decoy launcher on the bottom of the aft fuselage. *(U.S. Air Force)*

Block F

The latest CMUP phase to be approved is Block F and is largely related to the DSUP effort that is being undertaken separately. Block F Integrates the Navy-developed AN/ALE-50 Towed Decoy System (TDS) to provide an interim improvement in the survivability of the B-1B until the DSUP is complete. The major components of the ALE-50 are a launcher, controller, display unit, and the decoy. This modification will require the addition of two fairings to the tail section of the B-1B to house the launcher and decoys. Each fairing carries four decoys, which have proven effective against certain types of radar threats but are not considered to be general purpose. The first modified aircraft entered flight test in mid-1998, and operational aircraft will be fielded during 1999. The cost of the ALE-50 upgrade is estimated at $227 million.

The Block F upgrades are being installed in many aircraft at the same time as the Block D upgrades, leading to a certain amount of confusion about which upgrades are contained in each block. The towed decoy installation is slated to be completed in 2003.

Defensive Systems Upgrade Program

The Defensive Systems Upgrade Program (DSUP) is a major modification to provide improved threat warning to the air crew and enhance the survivability of the B-1B in a hostile environment. DSUP will replace the current DAS with the Loral/Litton AN/ALR-56M radar-warning receiver and the Navy-developed Sanders Integrated Defensive Electronic Countermeasures (IDECM) jamming system, which includes a fiber optic towed decoy (FOTD). The ALR-56M detects, identifies, and displays the relative location of enemy radars. The IDECM uses a combination of onboard transmitters and the FOTD to deceive enemy radars and missile systems. The existing ALQ-161A TWF will be retained in the new configuration.

Operation Desert Fox in December 1998 would provide the first combat experience for the B-1B. Here a conventional weapons module is readied for installation in a 28th BW B-1B prior to deploying to Southwest Asia. *(U.S. Air Force/7th BW Public Affairs)*

This modification will reduce the number of defensive system "black boxes" from 120 to 34 and will reduce the weight of the B-1B by approximately 4000 pounds. The first modified aircraft will be operational in 2002, and full-scale production will begin in 2003. The entire B-1B fleet will be modified by the end of 2009, 24 years after becoming operational. The total cost of the DSUP is estimated at $1260 million in FY98 dollars.

Summary

General Richard E. Hawley, head of Air Combat Command, noted, "When the B-1B force is fully matured, with all these modifications incorporated, and fully equipped with all these families of precision and near-precision weapons, it will be 10 times more capable—as measured by the number of targets that we can destroy—than the bomber force that we started with."

Weapons: Nuclear and Conventional Armament

The B-1B is equipped with three internal weapons bays consisting of a 31.25-foot section forward of the wing carry-through structure, and a single 15-foot bay aft of the main landing gear wells. The forward bay is equipped with a movable bulkhead that can be positioned to provide two 15-foot bays, one 22-foot bay plus an 8-foot forward bay, or left out entirely to provide one 31-foot bay. The forward bay has 2 two-piece doors and the aft section of the forward door can be merged with the intermediate doors when the moveable bulkhead is in the long (22-foot) intermediate bay configuration. The intermediate and aft weapons bays each have two single-piece doors. All of the composite doors are hydraulically actuated. Most conventional weapons are released with the doors fully open; air-launched missiles and nuclear weapons are released with the doors only partially open. All three bays are equipped with retractable spoilers at the forward end of the bay to reduce acoustic loads on the doors and allow clean separation of weapons from the bay. For aerodynamic reasons, some weapons (e.g., SRAMs) in the aft bay are released with the spoilers only partially deployed.

The B-1B also has provisions for six dual-pylon hardpoints and two single-pylon hardpoints beneath the fuselage that can be used to accommodate additional weapons or external fuel tanks.

The B-1B differs from most of its heavy bomber predecessors in that all weapons are mounted on removable launchers, not directly to the aircraft. Each launcher (rotary or conventional) is equipped with the necessary interfaces to allow the weapons to be armed and launched/dropped. All commands and communications to and from the weapons/weapon release system, including the actual release command, occur across a serial data bus. As a result, in order for the B-1B to release/launch a weapon, a program for the weapon must be contained in the avionics system software that includes the physical characteristics of the weapon, the weight of the weapon (to be used by FCGMS for management of the aircraft cg), the weapon's ballistics, and any targeting or navigation data that must be transmitted to the weapon prior to release.

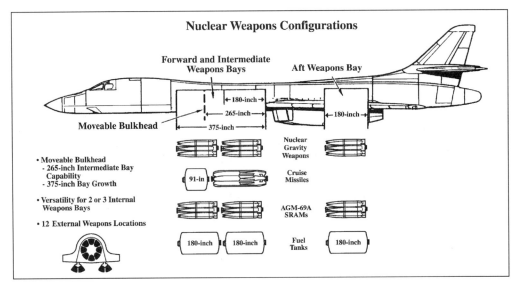

As designed and delivered, the B-1B was a nuclear bomber. It could carry a wide variety of nuclear gravity bombs, cruise missiles, SRAMs, and fuel tanks. External pylons were also available to carry additional cruise missiles. SALT/START treaty restrictions were imposed that eliminated the capability to carry cruise missiles, but all other nuclear weapon types are still available to the B-1B with some reconfiguration. *(U.S. Air Force)*

Nuclear Rotary Launchers

Three different types of rotary launchers are provided for the carriage and release/launch of nuclear weapons.

The 180-inch multipurpose rotary launcher (MPRL) is configured to carry nuclear gravity bombs. It can physically accommodate eight B28, B61, or B83 weapons, plus BDU-38

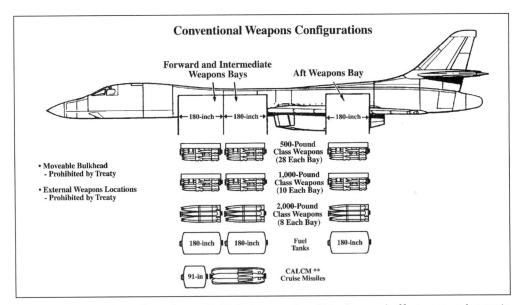

The B-1B is currently configured as a dedicated conventional bomber, and efforts are underway to certify various conventional and precision-guided munitions for use on the aircraft. It is technically possible for the B-1B to carry conventionally armed cruise missiles, but the SALT/START treaties do not differentiate between these and nuclear cruise missiles, so the B-1B is procedurally prohibited from carrying these weapons. *(U.S. Air Force)*

WEAPONS LAUNCHERS

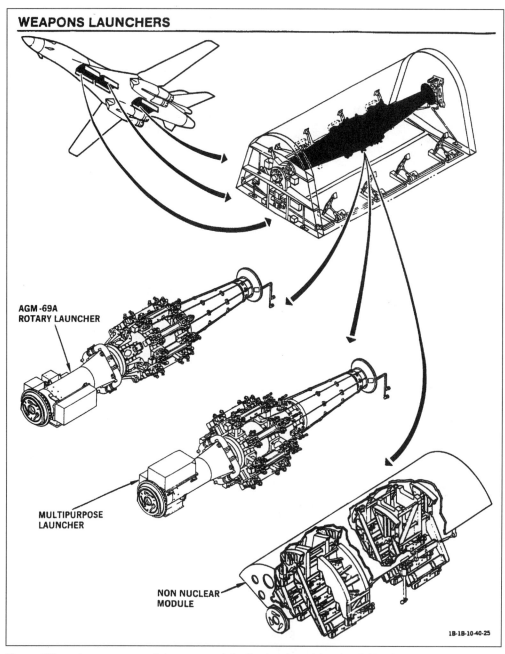

AGM-69A
ROTARY LAUNCHER

MULTIPURPOSE
LAUNCHER

NON NUCLEAR
MODULE

1B-1B-10-40-25

Three different weapons modules were originally developed for the B-1B. One was dedicated to SRAMs; one a multipurpose launcher for nuclear missiles and free-fall weapons; and the last for conventional munitions, which initially meant the Mk 82 iron bomb and its AIR derivative. A fourth launcher has since been added, a variation of the rotary launcher, to carry heavier conventional munitions. *(U.S. Air Force)*

and BDU-46 practice bombs. With the use of the PBAR adapter, it can also carry BDU-33 practice bombs. A single MPRL may be carried in each of the three weapons bays.

The 180-inch SRAM rotary launcher can accommodate up to eight AGM-69 missiles on individual ejector racks. This launcher is almost identical to the MPRL except for ancillary equipment such as power supplies and missile interface units. A single SRAM rotary launcher may be carried in each of the three weapons bays.

The 256-inch cruise missile launcher (CRM) was developed using the B-52G/H common strategic rotary launcher (CSRL) as a baseline. This is the only internal launcher that can

The movable bulkhead in a B-1B in its normal position, giving two equal-length weapons bays. Note all the wiring in the bays. The forward weapons bays doors can be divided in the middle to allow the bay to be reconfigured. *(U.S. Air Force/DVIC DF-SC-90-10076)*

Only the Nos. 9 and 28 aircraft have ever been reconfigured with the long intermediate weapons bay to carry cruise missiles. The bay was outlined in white during the test program to enhance photo coverage. *(Don Logan via the Mick Roth Collection)*

accommodate air-launched cruise missiles (ALCM or CALCM). Due to its size, it can only be accommodated in the 22-foot intermediate weapons bay. The B-52 CSRL will also fit in the 22-foot intermediate weapons bay, and limited testing was accomplished using the launcher in the B-1B. The START treaty prohibits the B-1B from carrying either of these launchers.

Initially, due to software limitations, each launcher had to be loaded with weapons of the same type. B61 bombs and B83 bombs could not be loaded on the same launcher, nor could gravity bombs and missiles be loaded on the same launcher. This has been rectified by the computer enhancements accomplished as part of CMUP.

Normally, the launchers are loaded with weapons before installation in the aircraft. During a mission, the launchers are rotated, using a hydraulic drive unit mounted on the forward bulkhead of the bay, to place the weapon scheduled for release in the down (6 o'clock) position. After the weapon has been released, the launcher rotates to place the next weapon in the down position. Rotation of the launcher takes approximately 5 seconds for each weapon position.

Conventional Weapon Modules

Unlike the nuclear launchers, the conventional weapons module (CWM) does not rotate. It is made up of a rigid frame mounted to the same locations in the weapons bays as the rotary launchers. This frame carries four swing arms, A/A2 at the front and B1/B2 at the rear, and two fixed supports (A3/B3). These arms vary in length and each carries between three and six standard 14-inch ejector racks. The Mk 82 AIR is slightly too long to be carried in tandem nose-to-tail on these racks, so the noses of the "B" bombs are interleaved between the tails of the "A" bombs. The software controls the release in a predetermined timed sequence beginning with A11 (the lowest bomb on the A1 arm) and continuing to A13 (the upper bomb on the A1 arm). The A1 arm then swings vertical, out of the way, permitting the release of the bombs in the B1 arm. Next come the bombs on the A2 arm, then the bombs on the B2 arm. Last come the bombs on the two fixed supports. A complex series of software and mechanical controls prevent the release of any bomb out of sequence. The CWM is usually placed into the weapons bays already loaded with up to 28 bombs.

The 10-carry module is a version of the CWM that permits the carriage of up to ten 1250-pound class weapons such as CBUs and WCMDs. These launchers are equipped with a Mil-Std-1760 interface, permitting targeting and other information to be downloaded from the aircraft to the weapon before release.

There is also a modified version of the 180-inch MPRL that is configured to carry conventional weapons. It can physically accommodate eight Mk 84 or GBU-32 bombs, or eight AGM-154 JASSM missiles. In reality, most of the modified rotary launchers began life as 180-inch SRAM launchers, which were no longer needed since the SRAM had been retired.

External Pylons

The bottom of the fuselage has hardpoints with provisions for installation of six dual pylons and two single pylons. The only weapons tested for external carriage have been AGM-86B and AGM-129A missiles, although external fuel tanks were designed to be carried on some of the stations. The only time a B-1B has used the pylons was during cruise missile integration when two aircraft (84-0049 and 85-0069) were temporarily equipped with them. In order to use these stations, additional weapons interface units and pylon control units must be installed on the aircraft, and these are prohibited under the START treaty.

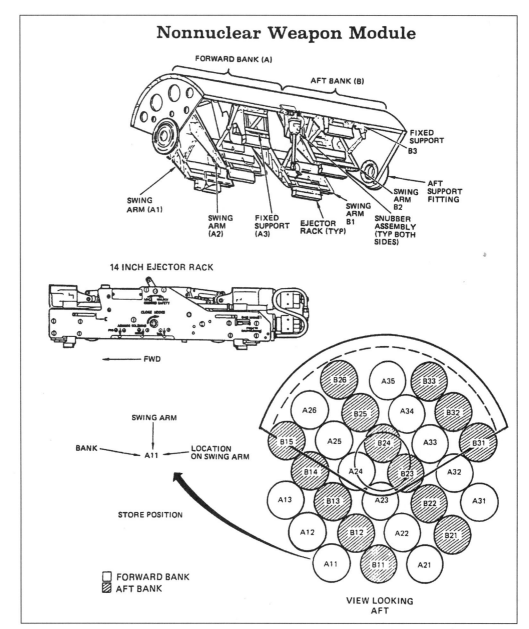

Originally, the conventional weapons module was called the nonnuclear weapons module—either name is accurate. Unlike earlier strategic bombers that used vertical bomb racks, the B-1B uses a complex series of swing arms to carry the bombs, maximizing the number that could be carried in the limited space available. *(U.S. Air Force)*

Nuclear Weapons

Nuclear-compatibility testing was accomplished to determine if specific existing weapons could be carried and deployed from the B-1B. The testing was performed by the B-1 CTF at Edwards from March 1983 until June 1990. Compatibility testing was accomplished for the B61-1, B61-7, and B83 gravity nuclear bombs and AGM-69A, AGM-86B, and AGM-129A nuclear missiles. Once a weapon has been determined to be compatible with an aircraft type, it must then be certified for carriage by that aircraft. Certification testing confirms that all equipment and procedures are in place to ensure the safe handling and delivery of the weapon. Certification of nuclear weapons is more stringent than for conventional weapons. Nuclear certification of the B61, B83, and AGM-69A was accomplished as part of compatibility testing. Compatibility testing of the AGM-86B and AGM-129A was completed, but nuclear certification on the B-1B was not completed.

During the summer of 1995, a Russian Federation delegation inspected every B-1B to ensure that the nuclear arming and fuzing equipment had been removed and that the weapons bay bulkhead was installed in such a manner (i.e., in its normal position) that precluded the ability to carry ALCMs. In reality, the decision had been made in 1991 to limit the B-1B to a conventional role, and most aircraft had lost their nuclear capability by 1992.

B28 Nuclear Bomb

The B28 (mod 0 and 1) was a thermonuclear weapon with a yield of between 70 kilotons and 1.45 megatons. The bomb was first introduced in 1958, and over 1200 were manufactured in various versions. The bomb had four low aspect-ratio fins, and most versions were equipped with a parachute retarder that allowed additional time for the attacking aircraft to egress the area. The B28 was approximately 14 feet long (it varied slightly by version) and 20 inches in diameter and weighed between 2027 and 2540 pounds. Due to the size and configuration of the bomb, only four could be loaded per MPRL in each of the three weapons bays. All B28 weapons had been retired from the inventory by 1984, and most were disassembled shortly thereafter in compliance with the SALT II treaty.

The swing arms of a conventional weapons module. Like the rotary launchers, the CWM can be preloaded with weapons and then loaded into the weapons bay, or each bomb can be loaded individually. There are currently not enough CWMs to fully equip the B-1B fleet, although more are being procured as part of the CMUP program. *(Thomas A. Schoene)*

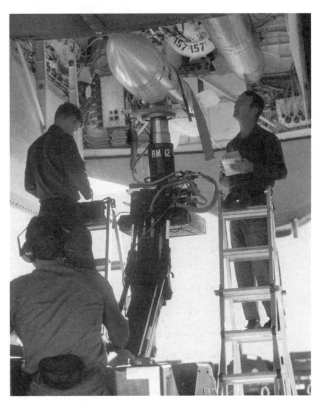

An MJ-1 weapons loader is used by members of the 28th Munitions Maintenance Squadron to load a BDU-38 practice bomb onto a B-1B during the 1988 Proud Shield competition. The BDU-38 is the practice equivalent of the B61 nuclear bomb. *(U.S. Air Force/DVIC DF-ST-91-02491)*

B61 Nuclear Bomb

The B61 (mod 1 and 7) is a thermonuclear weapon with a yield of 10 to 500 kilotons. Up to eight B61s could be carried on a MPRL in each of the three weapons bays. The B61-1 is 11.8 feet long and 13 inches in diameter and weighs 740 pounds. It is configured with four tail fins in an "X" configuration and uses either spin rockets or a parachute for stabilization. Of approximately 3000 operational B61s delivered, only a few hundred mod 1 and mod 7 versions remain in service. The mod 7 is the most advanced version and uses a new electronic safety system and insensitive trigger explosive.

Flight tests to certify the B61 for carriage and release from the B-1B were conducted as part of the FSD program. Static drops, mechanical fit, and electrical function tests were conducted to verify the physical and functional interfaces in preparation for the first in-flight release. Static ejection tests were conducted using the third B-1A (74-0160) and a standard production MPRL. The use of one of the nonflyable B-1As permitted less disruption to the tight B-1B flight test schedule. Mechanical fit and electrical function tests were also conducted on the first B-1B (82-0001) using a B61 CTU. Additional ground tests using the CSRL instead of the MPRL were also conducted.

After the completion of ground testing, flight tests were performed that demonstrated that the B-1B could carry, prearm, and release the bomb. Vibration tests demonstrating the B61 carriage environment during eight flights were completed between June 1983 and February 1984 using an MPRL installed on the second B-1A (74-0159). Five additional vibration test flights were completed on the first B-1B. These were followed by 19 releases during the FSD program. Seven releases were made from No. 2 B-1A using the MPRL (two from the forward weapons bay and five from the aft weapons bay), and five releases were made from No. 1 B-1B using the MPRL (one from the forward weapons bay, two from the intermediate weapons bay, and two from the aft weapons bay). Seven releases were also made from the CSRL installed in the long intermediate weapons bay of No. 9 B-1B (84-0049). All release trajectories were flat and stable, and the program completed successfully.

B83 Nuclear Bomb

The B83 is a thermonuclear gravity weapon with a yield of 1 or 2 megatons developed as a replacement for the B28. Up to eight B83s could be carried on a MPRL in each of the three weapons bays. On the B-1B, three tail fins in a "Y" configuration are used instead of the four fin "X" configuration used on the B-52 and F-111. The B83 can be dropped using a lay-down delivery at speeds up to 660 knots from an altitude of 200 feet, or free-fall delivery from up to 50,000 feet. Delivery options include free-fall air burst, free-fall ground burst, retarded air burst, and lay-down. The B83 is 12 feet long and 18.5 inches in diameter and weighs 2456 pounds.

The certification program for the B83 nuclear bomb was generally similar to that performed for the B61. Mechanical fit, electrical function tests, and static drops were conducted on the first B-1B using B83 CTU or BDU-46E practice bombs and an MPRL. The prearm, safe, and air/ground options were checked out using two weapons bays, loaded with up to eight CTU/BDUs in each bay. Additional ground tests using the CSRL instead of the MPRL were also conducted.

Of the 25 releases conducted during the FSD program, 14 were made from the second B-1A using an MPRL (two from the forward weapons bay, six from the intermediate weapons bay, and six from the aft weapons bay), and eight were made from an MPRL using the first B-1B (two from the forward weapons bay, three from the intermediate weapons bay, and three from the aft weapons bay). Three releases were also made from an CSRL installed in the long intermediate weapons bay of No. 9 B-1B. All release trajectories were flat and stable, and the program completed successfully.

A single BDU-46/E practice bomb (simulating a B83 nuclear store) is dropped from a B-1B over the Edwards AFB range. The drogue chute has already pulled the main chute out, although it is not fully reefed yet. The chute slows the bomb's descent sufficiently to allow the bomber to escape. *(U.S. Air Force via the Tony Landis Collection)*

AGM-69A SRAM

The Boeing AGM-69A Short Range Attack Missile (SRAM, later called the SRAM A) was originally developed for carriage and launch from B-52G/H aircraft and was also carried by the FB-111A. The SRAM was 14 feet long and 17.5 inches in diameter and weighed approximately 2230 pounds. Armed with a 170-kiloton W69 nuclear warhead and equipped with a simple inertial guidance system, the SRAM was propelled by a solid-propellant rocket motor to a range of 60 to 115 miles. The missile could fly a low-level, terrain-contour-following trajectory at high supersonic speeds or a semiballistic trajectory from the launch point to the target. The B-1B was designed to carry up to 24 SRAMs on three 180-inch SRAM rotary launchers, each equipped with eight SRAMs. No external capability for SRAM existed on the B-1B.

Flight tests to demonstrate the compatibility of the AGM-69A were conducted as part of the B-1B FSD program. Even though the SRAM had been launched from the B-1A, the major changes to the B-1B avionics and stores management system required additional ground and flight tests. The first live SRAM launch from a B-1B occurred on 16 January 1987 over the Tonopah Test Range using the first B-1B. The missile was launched from position No. 5 in the intermediate weapons bay, and flight performance was outstanding, resulting in a direct hit on the target.

All AGM-69A missiles have been retired from active service, although some are still in storage. It is, however, very unlikely they will ever be used again since most of the missiles have developed cracks in the solid-propellant grains of their rocket motors and are considered a safety hazard.

SRAMs could be loaded one at a time onto a rotary launcher in the weapons bay, or they could be preloaded on the launcher and the entire launcher loaded into the bay as a unit. Here members of the 96th Munitions Maintenance Squadron prepare to load an inert SRAM at Dyess AFB. *(U.S. Air Force/DVIC DF-ST-88-03500)*

An inert AGM-69A SRAM on a trailer is readied to be loaded in the forward weapons bay of a B-1B at Edwards AFB. Note the B-52H (60-0050) in the background. Live SRAMs were launched by the B-1A and B-1B, and some were even carried by nuclear alert aircraft early in the B-1B's career. *(Mark McLauchlin)*

Technicians install the last SRAM on an eight-position rotary launcher. Note the lack of clearance around the sides of the weapons bay when all the missiles are installed. *(U.S. Air Force)*

The third B-1A launches an AGM-69A SRAM from the forward weapons bay. Note the weapons bay doors are only partially open—most nuclear weapons were dropped with the doors in this configuration. *(Tony Landis Collection)*

A live SRAM is launched by a B-1B over the test range at Edwards AFB. Note the F-111 safety chase aircraft. *(Tony Landis Collection)*

AGM-131A SRAM II

The Boeing AGM-131A Short Range Attack Missile II (SRAM II) was developed for use on the B-1B and B-2A. Up to eight SRAM IIs could be loaded on a 180-inch SRAM rotary launcher, and no external capability was planned for the B-1B. The missile was to carry a 150-kiloton W89 warhead. The missile could fly from the launch point to the target following either a low-level trajectory using its altitude position sensor or a ballistic trajectory.

Testing of the AGM-131A began in June 1990, and was terminated immediately following cancellation of the program by President George Bush on 27 September 1991 as part of the President's unilateral cutback of the U.S. nuclear forces. Missile carriage, jettison, captive-carriage and missile/aircraft software integration tests had been completed by July 1991 using B-1B No. 9, but no live launches were accomplished during the test program.

Nuclear Weapons Locations

The list below is completely unofficial, and is probably open to debate. However, it provides at least a glimpse into the number of nuclear weapons maintained by the United States that are directly applicable to the B-1B. The list comes from the Internet version of

An AGM-131A (formerly called the AGM-69B) SRAM II shape in the forward weapons bay of a B-1B at Edwards AFB. Note the unique folding fins around the aft end of the missile. The SRAM II program was cancelled before any live launches were made from a B-1B. *(Mark McLauchlin)*

the Natural Resources Defense Council report *Taking Stock: Worldwide Nuclear Deployments, 1997* (weapons not related to the B-1B have been deleted).

Approximately 11,000 nuclear warheads have been retired by the United States since the end of the Cold War. The reductions in Europe are especially dramatic, with more than 6000 warheads of almost a dozen types deployed in 1985 and only some 150 B61 weapons in 1997. The locations of nuclear weapons remains an official secret despite the fact that nuclear security requirements and other indicators generally make their presence obvious. According to the Natural Resources Defense Council, nuclear weapons directly related to the B-1B include:

B61-7 bomb: 50 at Ellsworth AFB, South Dakota

B83 bomb: 120 at Ellsworth AFB, South Dakota

ALCM/W80-1: 365 at Kirtland AFB, New Mexico (storage)

SRAM/W69: 950 at Kirtland AFB, New Mexico; 50 at the Pantex Plant, near Amarillo, Texas

Since the B-1B has become a dedicated conventional bomber, the Air Force no longer openly discusses its nuclear capability. However, there is no reason to believe that the B-1B has lost its ability to carry nuclear weapons if the need ever arose.

Cruise Missile Testing

Two B-1Bs were used for cruise missile integration testing by the B-1 CTF at Edwards. These are the only B-1Bs to have had their intermediate weapons bay configured to the 22-foot

Early in the test program both AGM-86B and AGM-129A cruise missiles were carried on external pylons, and the intermediate weapons bay was reconfigured to carry internal cruise missiles. Both of these capabilities are specifically prohibited by the SALT/START treaties, and only two aircraft have ever been so configured. *(U.S. Air Force via Steve Pace)*

The forward AGM-129A external pylon on the No. 28 B-1B during testing. Note the foam rubber taped to the pointed front end of the pylon—some ground crewmember undoubtedly got tired of bumping the sharp edge. Photographers would not be allowed anywhere near the aircraft when the stealth advanced cruise missiles (ACM) were installed since even their exterior shape was considered classified. Missions were generally launched before dawn to help hide the missiles from prying eyes. *(Craig Kaston via the Mick Roth Collection)*

length, and also the only ones with their external weapons pylons activated. Due to SALT II treaty restrictions, which limited the cruise missile carrier aircraft to 12 external missiles, the two single pylon stations were not tested. The ninth aircraft (84-0049) was primarily used for AGM-86B ALCM tests, while No. 28 (85-0068) was used for AGM-129A ACM tests.

The SALT II treaty also required all cruise missile carriers be distinguishable by an external obvious difference (EOD). For the B-1B, the EOD is a white, nonfunctional ALT-32H ECM antenna placed on top of the aircraft at the approximate midfuselage point. (The EOD on B-52G cruise missile carriers was the "strakelet" fairing mounted at the leading edge of both wings at the root; on B-52H aircraft the EOD is a functional ALT-32H antenna mounted horizontally on both sides of the fuselage aft of the aft main landing gear.) Following completion of cruise missile testing, both B-1Bs were converted back to the standard three weapons bay (non-cruise-missile) configuration, the external pylons were deactivated, and the EOD antenna was removed.

AGM-86B ALCM

The ALCM development program began in June 1974 and six AGM-86A short-range ALCM missiles were test-flown in 1976. These were specifically designed to fit inside the 15-foot B-1A weapons bays, but their 850-mile range was considered less than ideal. When the B-1A production program was cancelled, the Air Force decided to revisit the ALCM concept in the hopes of obtaining a longer-range weapon for use on the B-52G/H.

In 1977, the longer range Boeing AGM-86B began a competitive flyoff with the General Dynamics AGM-109 Tomahawk. In March 1980, Boeing was declared the winner and received production awards for 225 missiles (FY80), 480 missiles (FY81), 440 missiles (FY82), 330 missiles (FY83), and 240 missiles (FY84). The last of 1715 production missiles was delivered on 26 September 1986. Each missile, exclusive of its nuclear warhead, cost approximately $1 million.

A single Williams Research Corp. F-107-WR-10 turbofan engine produces 600 pounds-thrust to allow the AGM-86B to cruise at speeds up to approximately 550 mph (Mach 0.73) over a 1500-mile range. The missile is 20.75 feet long and 24.5 inches in diameter and weighs 3150 pounds. When the wings are extended, it has a wingspan of 12 feet. A 200-kiloton W80-1 nuclear warhead is fitted. The Litton inertial navigation element with terrain contour matching allows the missile to fly complicated routes to a target through use of maps of the planned flight route stored in onboard computers. Eight AGM-86Bs can be carried internally in the long intermediate weapons bay on the CRM rotary launcher, and 12 ALCMs can be carried externally on the six dual-missile pylons.

The first ALCM launch from a B-1B (84-0049) occurred on 24 November 1987 against a target on the Utah Test and Training Range. After a flight of more than 4 hours, the missile scored a direct hit on the target. On 7 April 1989, the No. 28 aircraft made the second, and last, live launch, which also scored a direct hit on the target.

AGM-129A ACM

The General Dynamics AGM-129A Advanced Cruise Missile (ACM) is a low-observable ("stealth") strategic missile. Armed with a 200-kiloton W80-1 nuclear warhead, the 2750-pound jet-powered missile has a range of 2000 miles. Procurement of the AGM-129 was halted at 460 missiles in lieu of the 1460 originally planned. The missiles are operational on the B-52H and B-2A.

The B-1B can carry four AGM-129As in the 22-foot intermediate weapons bay on the CRM rotary launcher. Twelve AGM-129As could also be carried externally on the six dual missile pylons. Five live launches from the CSRL and external pylons were scheduled, but no actual launches of an ACM from the B-1B were ever accomplished; the actual flight testing was conducted from the B-52H instead.

Even the exterior shape of the Boeing AGM-129A Advanced Cruise Missile (ACM) was highly classified for years. Some initial testing was accomplished on the B-1B, but the missile is currently only used by the B-2A and the B-52H. Note the flush "NACA duct" intake, and the sculpting on the nose and aft fuselage, all efforts to lower the missile's radar cross-section. *(Via Mark McLauchlin)*

Conventional Bombs

Compatibility testing for the Mk 82 AIR and Mk 36 AIR conventional gravity bombs was also completed at Edwards, and conventional certification was completed by the 28th BW at Ellsworth AFB. The CMUP program significantly expanded the B-1B's conventional weapons capability, which currently includes the CBU-87, CBU-89, CBU-97, JDAM, JSOW, and WCMD.

The Mk 80 series of "dumb" bombs was developed during the 1950s and is currently the Air Force's standard general-purpose bomb. All Mk 80-series bombs are similar in construction, cylindrical in shape, and equipped with conical fins or retarders for external high-speed carriage. The bombs are usually equipped with mechanical M904 (nose) and M905 (tail) fuzes, or radar-proximity FMU-113 air-burst fuzes. The addition of a BSU-49/B ballute converts any Mk 80-series into an air inflatable retard (AIR) bomb. The BSU-49/B ballute has two modes, low drag and high drag, which are in-flight selectable by the OSO using the offensive avionics system. In the low-drag mode, the bomb is stabilized by the metal fins on the stabilizer canister. In the high-drag mode, the AIR inflates a ballute using ram air flowing into inlets on the side of the ballute. The ballute deploys shortly after the bomb is dropped, stabilizing and slowing its descent.

Mk 82 AIR Bombs

Until 1995, the only nonnuclear weapon certified for use on the B-1B was the Mk 82, the Mk 82 AIR, and their Mk 36 counterparts. Up to twenty-eight Mk 82 bombs can be loaded on a CWM in each weapons bay for a maximum internal bomb load of 84 bombs. The 500-pound Mk 82 bomb is 86.75 inches long and 10.75 inches in diameter and carries 192 pounds of Tritonal, Minol II, or H-6 explosives.

Testing has been accomplished with laser-guided bombs, although the B-1B does not have any target designating capability itself. In combat it would be up to ground troops, Army helicopters, or another aircraft to designate the target for the B-1B, greatly limiting its effectiveness. The weapons bays doors are completely open to drop this 2000-pound class laser-guided bomb. Note the rearward facing camera and the EOD on top of the fuselage. *Thunder from the Sky* (84-0049) was used for many of the weapons tests. *(U.S. Air Force via the Tony Landis Collection)*

The configuration of the MK 82 AIR carried on the B-1B differs from the configuration for other aircraft in that it does not use the arming wires and Fahnestock clips for deployment of the BSU-49 after release. Due to the proximity of the forward and intermediate weapons bays to the engine intakes, a DTU-31/B timer actuator and frangible link are used instead of wires and clips. This timer-and-link installation prevents foreign object damage (FOD) to the engines that might occur if wires and clips were ingested. As the bomb leaves the rack, the frangible link pulls the actuating lanyard before the link breaks. The lanyard starts the timer, which, when it expires, pulls the BSU-49 actuating lanyard and deploys the ballute.

Mk 82 AIR release certification was accomplished by the 28th BW at Ellsworth AFB using aircraft No. 51 (85-0091) and No. 59 (86-0099). Nonnuclear safety certification occurred in February 1989 and full weapons certification was granted on 21 July 1989.

Mk 84 Bomb

The Mk 84 is the 2000-pound version of the Mk 80 general-purpose bomb. An AIR kit is also available for this weapon. The capability to carry Mk 84s was planned for the B-1B even before the CMUP program was approved. Up to eight Mk 84s may be carried in each weapons bay on a modified 180-inch MPRL. The 2000-pound Mk 84 bomb is 151.5 inches long and 18 inches in diameter and carries 945 pounds of explosives. The BLU-109 hard target penetrator and BDU-56 practice bomb versions of the Mk 84 may also be carried.

Mk 36 AIR Bombs

The Mk 36 AIR is an MK 82 AIR bomb fitted with a Mk 75 arming kit, which converts the bomb into a land or water mine. The Mk 75 arming kit consists of Mk 32 nose fuze and a Mk 42 tail fuze. The Mk 36 AIR weapon, released in high drag mode only, also uses the DTU-31/B timer actuator and frangible link. Up to 28 Mk 36 AIR bombs can be carried on a CWM in each weapons bay.

GBU-32 Joint Direct Attack Munition

The Joint Direct Attack Munition (JDAM) is a high-accuracy all-weather conventional bomb. JDAM is intended to upgrade the existing inventory of Mk 80-series general purpose bombs and the BLU-109 2000-pound hard target penetrator by integrating a GPS/INS guidance kit. No changes to the bomb casing, explosive fill, or fuzing mechanism are required. The tail kit may be fitted to any Mk 80 series bomb: the 250-pound (Mk 81) and 500-pound (Mk 82) bombs are designated GBU-29 and GBU-30, respectively, while the 1,000-pound (Mk 83) and 2000-pound (Mk 84/BLU-109) versions are designated GBU-31 and GBU-32, respectively. Currently, only the 2000-pound GBU-32 is being integrated on the B-1B, although there is no reason the other variants could not be carried if necessary.

The JDAM position information is continuously updated by aircraft avionics prior to release via the Mil-Std-1760 interface. Once released, the bomb's GPS/INS guides the bomb to its target with a delivery accuracy of approximately 45 feet when GPS is available and less than 100 feet when GPS is absent or jammed. Up to eight GBU-32s may be carried on each modified version of the 180-inch MPRL.

Eighty-four 500-pound Mk 82 bombs are released from a B-1B during testing—28 from each weapons bay. This is the weapon the B-1B used during Operation Desert Fox in December 1998. Unlike nuclear weapons, conventional bombs are dropped with the weapons bay doors completely open. Noteworthy are the aft-looking camera on the crew entry door, and the "external obvious difference" device (white) on the top of the fuselage. *(U.S. Air Force via the Tony Landis Collection)*

A1C Shannon McLean drives a MJ-40 weapons loader, preparing to load an Mk 82 bomb onto a 28th BW B-1B in support of Operation Desert Fox. Four different B-1Bs flew sorties during Desert Fox. *(U.S. Air Force Photo by Staff Sgt. Krista M. Foeller via 7th BW Public Affairs)*

SrA Brent Raney guides a Mk 82 bomb onto a 28th BS B-1B in support of Operation Desert Fox. The B-1Bs were part of a joint-service strike package that attacked Republican Guard barracks in Iraq during December 1998. *(U.S. Air Force photo by Staff Sgt. Krista M. Foeller via 7th BW Public Affairs)*

In October 1995, Boeing (formerly McDonnell Douglas) was awarded a contract for the first 4635 JDAM kits at an average unit cost of $18,000, less than half the original $40,000 estimate. The FY00 procurement of JDAM will total 6195, and the JDAM production rate is expected to exceed 1000 kits per month during the planned procurement of 87,496 JDAMs. JDAM will be carried on virtually all Air Force fighters and bombers, including the B-1B, B-2A, B-52H, F-15E, F-16C/D, F-22A, F-117A, and the Navy's F/A-18E/F.

CBU-87 Cluster Bomb Unit

The CBU-87 combined effects munition (CEM) consists of a SUU-65 tactical munitions dispenser (TMD) with an optional FZU-39/B proximity sensor. A total of 202 BLU-97/B combined effects bomblets (CEB) are loaded in each dispenser, enabling an attack with wide area coverage. The bomblet case is made of scored steel designed to break into approximately 300 preformed fragments for defeating light armor and personnel. There are 10 different height-of-burst selections that can be made before the weapon is dropped. The weapon is spin-stabilized during descent, with six different spin settings selectable before release. The weapon is 92 inches long and 15.6 inches in diameter and weighs 950 pounds. During FY90, the CBU-87 acquisition cost was $13,941 per weapon. Up to 10 CBU-87s can be carried on a CWM in each weapons bay.

The last bomb in the bay is attached and connected in preparation for sorties during Operation Desert Fox. *(U.S. Air Force/7th BW Public Affairs)*

A1C Todd Sturz prepares a Mk 82 general purpose bomb for loading into a B-1B during Operation Desert Fox. *(DoD photo by TSgt Paul G. Laughhunn via 7th BW Public Affairs)*

CBU-89 Cluster Bomb Unit

The CBU-89 Gator Mine is a 1000-pound cluster munition consisting of a SUU-64/B TMD with 72 BLU-91/B antitank mines, 22 BLU-92/B antipersonnel mines, and an optional FZU-39/B proximity sensor. The BLU-91/B antitank mine contains microelectronics that can detect armored vehicles and detonate the mine when the target reaches the most vulnerable approach point. A Misznay-Schardin explosive charge defeats the belly armor of most vehicles. The BLU-92/B antipersonnel mines serve to discourage minefield clearing. Upon activation, the BLU-92/B explosion sends high-velocity fragments in a horizontal plane over a wide area.

Both mines have a programmable self-destruct feature that permits the battlefield commander to control the timing of a counterattack or defensive maneuver. The self-destruct time is set just prior to aircraft takeoff using a simple selector switch on the dispenser and permits a high degree of tactical flexibility during combat operations. After dispenser opening, the mines are self-dispersed using aerodynamic forces. The mine pattern on the ground is directly proportional to opening altitude, which is controlled by either the dispenser electromechanical fuze or an optional proximity sensor. Up to 10 CBU-89s can be carried on a CWM in each weapons bay.

CBU-97 Cluster Bomb Unit

The CBU-97 Sensor-Fuzed Weapon (SFW) consists of the SUU-66/B TMD which opens and dispenses 10 parachute-stabilized BLU-108/B submunitions. Each of the 10 submunitions contains four 5-inch-diameter armor-penetrating "Skeet" projectiles with infrared sensors to detect armored targets. The SFW is the production derivative of the Skeet weapon developed for the original DARPA Assault Breaker program. At a preset altitude sensed by a radar altimeter, a rocket motor fires to spin the submunition and initiate an ascent. The submunition then releases its four projectiles, which are lofted over the target area. When the Skeet detects a heat source such as a tank engine, it fires an explosively formed penetrator

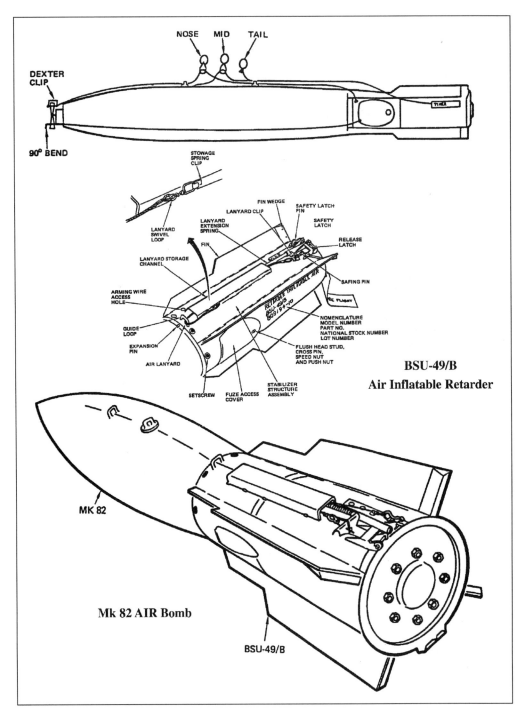

The addition of a BSU-49/A air inflatable retarder allows the B-1B to drop the Mk 82 iron bomb from lower altitudes than would be possible otherwise. The AIR slows the descent of the bomb, allowing the bomber to escape collateral damage as the bombs explode. *(U.S. Air Force)*

slug downward through the top of the target vehicle. Each Skeet scans 29,000 square feet; the 40 Skeets in each CBU-97 search a total of approximately 650,000 square feet. If no target is detected after a period of time, the projectile fires automatically after a preset time interval.

The weapon was designed to be employed from altitudes between 200 and 20,000 feet at speeds between 250 to 650 knots. The CBU-97 is 92 inches long and 16 inches in diameter and weighs 927 pounds. The baseline cost in FY90 was $360,000 per CBU, although this has subsequently been reduced to $260,000. As of January 1998, there were 500 weapons in the Air Force inventory, with a planned procurement of 5000. Up to 10 CBU-89 SFWs can be carried on a CWM in each weapons bay.

Wind Corrected Munitions Dispenser

While low-altitude, high-speed laydown deliveries are consistent with tactics used against heavily defended targets such as the Warsaw Pact threat envisioned in Central Europe during the 1980s, low-altitude tactics were not the preferred option during Operation Desert Storm, in which the Air Force used medium-to-high altitude weapons delivery to provide aircraft a measure of safety against short-range surface-to-air missiles and antiaircraft artillery fire. Unfortunately, winds aloft affected the accuracy of weapons such as cluster bombs when released from high altitudes.

The Wind Compensated Munitions Dispenser (WCMD; pronounced "Wick-Mid") is a GPS-guided tail kit for the TMD-bodied CBU-87/89/97. The tail kit is equipped with movable tail fins to counteract the wind drift and allow accurate employment of CBUs from high altitudes. The add-on tail kit and counter ballast increase the CBU's weight by approximately 250 pounds. WCMD-equipped weapons are planned for use on the B-1B, B-52H, F-15E, F-16C/D, and F-117A. The Air Force plans to modify 40,000 tactical munitions dispensers over the next 10 years. Up to 10 WCMDs can be carried on a CWM in each weapons bay.

AGM-154 Joint Standoff Weapon

The Raytheon (formerly Texas Instruments) AGM-154 Joint Standoff Weapon (JSOW) is designed to replace Vietnam-era glide bombs such as the Walleye. The missile uses a GPS/INS system for midcourse navigation and imaging infrared (IIR) for terminal homing. The JSOW is just over 13 feet long and weighs between 1000 and 1500 pounds. The JSOW will be employed on the F-14A/B/D, F/A-18E/F, AV-8B, F-15E, F-16C/D, F-117A, B-1B, and B-52H.

The JSOW provides a standoff range of 17 miles for a low-level release and 46 miles for a high-altitude release. The weapon can turn through 180° to engage off-boresite targets. Once programmed, as long as it is released at such an altitude and range to be able to aerodynamically reach its target, it will autonomously calculate the flight path and profile to hit its target. If released at high speeds, JSOW will delay wing deployment to avoid penalizing its range by drag. The weapon can also be programmed to attack a target from a specific heading and to fly between multiple programmed waypoints. A typical profile is to glide in at an altitude of 200 feet, pop up close to the target and dive in to dispense its payload from several hundred feet.

The AGM-154A (Baseline JSOW) is intended for use against soft targets such as parked aircraft, vehicles, SAM sites, and mobile command posts. It carries 145 BLU-97A/B CEBs, which are deployed as the JSOW dives from medium altitudes. These are the same CEBs that are used on the CBU-87 cluster bomb. Each CEB has a conically shaped charge that can penetrate 5 to 7 inches of armor, a main charge that produces about 300 high-velocity fragments, and a Zirconium sponge incendiary element.

The AGM-154B is a specialized antiarmor weapon that carries six BLU-108/B SFW submunitions. These are the same SFWs that are used in the CBU-97 cluster bomb. Planned Air Force improvements to the SFW submunition will include a better IR sensor and a warhead that will produce a slug and a shrapnel pattern.

The AGM-154C variant is intended specifically to replace the Walleye glide bomb. The Navy-only AGM-154C will use a combination of an IIR terminal seeker and a two-way data

A large flash accompanies the release of submunitions from a cluster bomb after being dropped from a B-1B over the test range at Edwards AFB. *(U.S. Air Force via Steve Pace)*

link to achieve point target accuracy through aimpoint refinement and man-in-the-loop guidance. This version will not be carried by the B-1B.

The Navy began Operational Evaluation (OPEVAL) testing of the JSOW in February 1997, and the Air Force began DT&E flight testing of JSOW on the F-16 at Eglin AFB in March 1996, although this was initially hindered by less than desired progress in the area of F-16/JSOW integration. The JSOW testing included five live weapon launches by a Navy aircraft against representative real-world threat targets parked in an area of San Clemente Island, California. The targets consisted of an unrevetted MiG-23 aircraft, two ZSU-23-4 antiaircraft gun platforms, two Russian trucks, and a surrogate of a surface-to-air missile system.

The development cost for the AGM-154A version was $417.9 million, with a further $227.8 million being expended on the AGM-154B version and $452.4 million more on the AGM-154C. The unit costs of the three versions are $282,000, $484,167, and $719,012, respectively and total acquisition costs are $3327.6, $2033.5, and $5608.3 million, respectively. The Air Force is currently programmed to acquire 3000 each of the AGM-154A and AGM-154B models, and has ordered 193 in FY00.

AGM-137 Tri-Service Standoff Attack Missile

In 1986 the Air Force began developing the AGM-137 Tri-Service Standoff Attack Missile (TSSAM) to provide a low-observable conventional cruise missile. All variants used a GPS/INS for early course guidance. The Navy and Air Force unitary-warhead variants used an IIR terminal sensor for autonomous recognition and homing on fixed land targets and sea targets. The other Air Force variant used BLU-97A/B CEB submunitions to attack land targets. The weapon was intended to be carried by the B-52H, B-1B, B-2A, F-16C/D, and the Navy's F/A-18C/D.

The missile had significant development problems, and estimates of the unit cost increased from an estimated $728,000 in 1986 to $2 million in 1993. The missile was subsequently cancelled. Following a comprehensive reassessment of requirements, the Air Force and Navy agreed they urgently needed an affordable missile with most of TSSAM's characteristics, and on 20 September 1995 the USD/A&T approved the initiation of the AGM-158 program.

AGM-158 Joint Air-to-Surface Standoff Missile

The AGM-158 Joint Air to Surface Standoff Missile (JASSM) program was begun following cancellation of the TSSAM. The JASSM is a low observable air-launched cruise missile that will provide a conventional "launch-and-leave" precision-guided weapon capable of operating in adverse weather. It will have a range of 115+ miles and carry a 1000-pound-class unitary warhead. JASSM's midcourse guidance is provided by a GPS/INS protected by a new antijam GPS null steering antenna system. In the terminal phase, JASSM is guided by an IIR seeker and a pattern matching-autonomous target recognition system. The first aircraft to carry JASSM will be the B-52H, F-16C/D, and F/A-18E/F. Future integration is planned for the B-1B, B-2A, F-15E, F-117A, F/A-18C/D, P-3, S-3, and the Joint Strike Fighter. Up to eight AGM-158s may be carried on each modified version of the 180-inch MPRL, for a possible total of 24 JASSMs per B-1B.

In early 1998, Lockheed Martin was selected as the JASSM production contractor and began delivering preproduction units for continued testing. The first 87 missiles were ordered in FY00, and the total production for the Air Force is expected to be 2400 missiles; the total for the Navy is yet to be determined. The total program is valued at approximately $3000 million. The program is emerging as a model for acquisition reform, and the program office's objective is to keep the unit cost below $400,000 in FY95 dollars, with the threshold being $700,000. Estimates are currently at $300,000 per missile.

Mines

The Mk 62 Quick Strike mine is an aircraft-laid bottom mine for use against submarines and surface targets. The Mk 62 is a conversion of 500-pound Mk 82 general-purpose bomb. Up to 28 Mk 62 mines can be carried on a CWM in each of the three weapons bays.

The Mk 65 is a 2000-pound weapon, employing a thin-walled, mine-type case, as opposed to the thick-walled bomb-type case of the Mk 62. Other differences in the Mk 65 include a special arming device, a nose fairing, and a tail section adaptable to a parachute option. Up to eight Mk 65 mines can be carried on a modified 180-inch MPRL in each of the three weapons bays.

Practice Bombs

The BDU-38/B is a full-size practice bomb that simulates the B61 nuclear weapon. It has the same dimensions, weight, and release modes as the actual B61 weapon. The offensive avionics system uses B61 software for prearming, ranging, and release. The BDU-38 can be carried on the same weapons stations as the B61.

The BDU-46/E is a full-size practice bomb that simulates the B83 nuclear weapon. It has the same dimensions, weight, and release modes as the actual B83 weapon. The offensive avionics system uses B83 software for prearming, ranging, and release. The BDU-46 can be carried on the same weapons stations as the B83.

In May 1988, SAC headquarters determined a need for the development of a low-cost practice bomb to simulate nuclear free-fall bombs. Prior to this, the only practice bombs which the B-1B could carry and release were full-size (and expensive) inert examples of the actual bombs. The 28th BW was tasked with finding a new practice bomb, and initiated the development of the practice bomb adapter rack (PBAR), which is designed to attach to the MPRL. A single practice bomb can be attached to each PBAR. An SMU-105 electronic relay box provides the proper nuclear weapon indications to the cockpit controls and displays.

The BDU-33C/B high-drag, BDU-33D/B low-drag, BDU-48, and Mk-106 practice bombs were tested. All are less than 2 feet long and weigh less than 25 pounds. The weapon release cameras originally carried by the first B-1B (82-0001) were installed on B-1B No. 51 (85-0091) for a series of release tests to determine separation and ballistic data. The BDU-48 and Mk 106 demonstrated stability problems on release, but the two BDU-33 variants worked well.

The BDU-33C/B is a practice bomb that simulates low-drag bombs. It has a cast metal body with a conical fin assembly attached. It also contains a spotting charge, which provides a visual flash and white smoke on impact. The BDU-33C/B weighs 24 pounds and is 23 inches long. It can be carried on a PBAR at any MPRL station.

The BDU-33D/B is a practice bomb that simulates high-drag bombs. It has a cast metal body with a conical fin assembly with a flat circular metal plate (high-drag device) attached to the aft end of the fin assembly, perpendicular to the air flow. It also contains a spotting charge, which provides a visual flash and white smoke on impact. The BDU33D/B weighs 25 pounds and is 23 inches long. It can be carried on a PBAR at any MPRL station.

The BDU-50 AIR is a practice bomb that simulates the 500-pound Mk 82 AIR bomb. It has the same dimensions, weight, and release modes as the actual Mk 82 AIR bomb, but has no fuzing or explosives loaded. The BDU-50 AIR can be carried on the same weapons stations as the Mk 82 AIR.

The BDU-56 is a practice bomb which simulates the 2000-pound Mk 84 bomb. It has the same dimensions, weight, and release modes as the actual Mk 84 bomb, but has no fuzing or explosives loaded. The BDU-56 can be carried on the same weapons stations as the Mk 84, and may also be fitted with a JDAM GPS guidance kit to create a JDAM practice bomb.

Weapons Bay Auxiliary Fuel Tank

A 2950-gallon, 15-foot auxiliary fuel tank can be installed in each of the three weapons bays. The tank is mounted to the rotary launcher attachment hardware on the forward and aft weapons bay bulkheads. It is loaded empty using an MJ-40 lift truck and is filled using the single-point refueling connections on the bottom of the right engine nacelle or when the aircraft is in-flight using the air refueling system. The fuel can be dumped through the normal aircraft dump system. Alternately, a 7.5-foot, 1285-gallon tank can be installed in the "short" forward weapons bay.

AGM-86C CALCM

In June 1986, the Air Force awarded a then-classified contract (F34601-91-C-1156) to Boeing to modify a number of nuclear-armed AGM-86B ALCM missiles to the conventionally armed AGM-86C configuration. Boeing delivered the last unit on the initial CALCM contract (Block 0) in June 1993. A Block I contract (F34601-95-C-0478) was awarded in June 1995 for conversion of an additional 100 missiles (Lot 1), and in March 1996, Boeing received an extension for 100 additional Block I conversions (Lot 2). Boeing received a $53 million contract in FY00 to covert 92 additional ALCMs to the Block I CALCM configuration.

This modification replaced the AGM-86B ALCM's terrain contour-matching guidance system with an integrated GPS/INS. The CALCM became operational in January 1991 at the onset of Operation Desert Storm. Seven B-52Hs carrying a total of 39 CALCMs flew nonstop from Barksdale AFB, Louisiana, to the Persian Gulf where 35 missiles were launched against high-priority targets in Iraq. These missions marked the beginning of the air campaign for Kuwait's liberation and are the longest known combat sorties in history (more than 14,000 miles and 35 flight hours).

A single 600-pounds-thrust Williams F-107-WR-101 turbofan engine powers the AGM-86C, which is 20.75 feet long and 24.5 inches in diameter and weighs 3250 pounds. When the wings are fully extended, they span 12 feet. The Air Force will acknowledge a range of over 600 miles, but the specific figure is classified. The Air Force will not discuss the top speed of the missile, but it can be assumed to be similar to the nuclear-armed version, or approximately 550 mph. A Litton Inertial Navigation Element integrated with an onboard GPS receiver provides more accurate guidance than the terrain-matching feature of the earlier nuclear versions of the missile. Each missile is equipped with either an AFX-760 blast fragmentation warhead (Block 0 missiles) or a PBXN-111 blast fragmentation warhead (Block I). Each missile cost roughly $150,000 to convert from the AGM-86B configuration. The first Block 0 missile was declared operational in January 1991, while the Block I missile reached IOC in September 1996. A further 200 ALCMs were converted to CALCMs in mid-1999 after stocks were depleted during Operation Allied Force.

The AGM-86D (Block II) incorporates a penetrating warhead and an updated GPS guidance unit. To maximize the warhead's effectiveness against hardened targets, the AGM-86D will perform a near-vertical dive onto its target. The updated guidance system will increase the systems lethality by obtaining a less-than-15-foot CEP.

Under mutually agreed upon arms-control counting rules, the CALCMs are still regarded as nuclear weapons and are subject to the START treaty limitations. Because of these rules,

Although all three weapons bays are plumbed for fuel tanks, generally only the first bay is used because of center of gravity considerations. The other two bays are generally reserved for weapons. *(Don Logan via the Mick Roth Collection)*

CALCMs may not be stored at the same operating location as the B-1B since they cannot be externally differentiated from nuclear-armed ALCMs. The Air Force has begun to paint the CALCMs differently with a yellow stripe around the warhead area, but this may not be sufficient differentiation to satisfy arms-control monitors.

The B-1B can technically carry the CALCM if the intermediate weapons bay is reconfigured in the same manner as it would be to carry the nuclear-armed ALCM. However, at present this would violate various arms control treaties, leaving the B-52H as the only CALCM-capable aircraft in the U.S. inventory.

B-1A Serial Numbers

	Serial Number	First Flight	Number of Test Flights	Disposition
1	74-0158	23 December 1974	79 flights (405.3 hours)	At Rome Laboratory for antenna tests.
2	74-0159	14 June 1976	60 flights (282.5 hours)	Crashed on 29 August 1984; one fatality.
3	74-0160	1 April 1976	138 flights (829.4 hours)	On display at the Wings Over the Rockies Air and Space Museum, Denver, Colorado.
4	76-0174	14 February 1979	70 flights (378 hours)	On display at the U.S. Air Force Museum, Wright-Patterson AFB, Ohio.

B-1B Production Serial Numbers

	Serial Number	Delivery Date	Assigned as of June 1998	Aircraft Name(s)
1	82-0001	29 June 1985	Scrapped	*Leader Of The Fleet, Star Of Abilene* (for a week)
2	83-0065	17 June 1985	9 BS/7 BW	*Star Of Abilene, Star Of Palmdale*
3	83-0066	16 October 1985	28 BS/7 BW	*Ole' Puss*
4	83-0067	13 January 1986	9 BS/7 BW	*Texas Raiders*
5	83-0068	18 February 1986	28 BS/7 BW	*Spuds* (McKenzie; named after the Budweiser beer dog)
6	83-0069	13 March 1986	28 BS/7 BW	*Silent Penetrator* (note improper spelling), *Rebel*
7	83-0070	6 May 1986	28 BS/7 BW	*Shack Master, 7 Wishes*
8	83-0071	24 May 1986	9 BS/7 BW	*Grand Illusion, Spit Fire*
9	84-0049	6 June 1986	412 TW	*Thunder From The Sky*
10	84-0050	1 October 1986	28 BS/7 BW	*Surf Rat, Surprise Attack, Dawg B-ONE*
11	84-0051	30 July 1986	9 BS/7 BW	*Lucky Lady, Boss Hawg*
12	84-0052	11 July 1986	Crashed	Never named; crashed on 28 September 1987; three crewmembers perished, three survived
13	84-0053	10 July 1986	28 BS/7 BW	*Lucky 13*
14	84-0054	26 July 1986	28 BS/7 BW	*Silver Bullet, Tasmanian Terror, Aviators*
15	84-0055	22 August 1986	28 BS/7 BW	*Ridge Runner, Sunrise Surprise, Lethal Weapon*
16	84-0056	27 August 1986	28 BS/7 BW	*Sweet Sixteen*

17	84-0057	30 April 1987	Crashed	*Hellion;* crashed on 18 February 1998; all crewmembers survived
18	84-0058	26 March 1987	9 BS/7 BW	*Master of Disaster*
19	85-0059	26 September 1986	128 BS/116 BW	*Super Glider, Better Duck, Bad Dog*
20	85-0060	31 October 1986	127 BS/184 BW	*Night Hawk*, unnamed, *Rolling Thunder*
21	85-0061	18 March 1987	128 BS/116 BW	*Maverick, French Connection*, unnamed
22	85-0062	4 November 1986	9 BS/7 BW	*Sky Dancer, Uncaged*
23	85-0063	30 November 1986	Crashed	Never named; crashed on 8 November 1988; all four crewmembers survived
24	85-0064	3 November 1986	127 BS/184 BW	*Eliminator, Prairie Thunder*
25	85-0065	30 November 1986	128 BS/116 BW	*Trilogy Of Terror, Texas Armor*
26	85-0066	31 December 1986	37 BS/28 BW	*Special Delivery, Deadwood Express, Missouri Miss, Badlands Bomber*
27	85-0067	30 December 1986	28 BS/7 BW	*Wild Thang, Mis Behavin, Texas Raider, On Defense*
28	85-0068	16 November 1986	412 TW	*Spuds, Dragon's Fury*
29	85-0069	23 December 1986	127 BS/184 BW	*Silent Penetrator, Daisy Mae*
30	85-0070	7 January 1987	127 BS/184 BW	*Excalibur*
31	85-0071	4 February 1987	128 BS/116 BW	*Liberator*
32	85-0072	27 February 1987	9 BS/7 BW	*Polarized*
33	85-0073	13 January 1987	77 BS/28 BW	*Wings of Freedom, Cerberus*, unnamed
34	85-0074	18 February 1987	77 BS/28 BW	*Penetrator, Crewdawg*, unnamed
35	85-0075	21 March 1987	77 BS/28 BW	*Banshee, Dakota Demolition, Spirit of '76*, unnamed
36	85-0076	19 March 1987	Crashed	*Black Jack;* crashed on 17 November 1988; all four crewmembers survived
37	85-0077	13 February 1987	37 BS/28 BW	*Bones, Jap Happy, Hamton, Pride of South Dakota, Overnight Delivery*
38	85-0078	21 February 1987	Crashed	*Dakota Lightning, Heavy Metal;* crashed on 19 September 1997; all crewmembers perished
39	85-0079	13 March 1987	37 BS/28 BW	*Warriors Dream, Classy Lady, Deadwood Dealer*
40	85-0080	13 March 1987	127 BS/184 BW	*Lady Of The Nite, The Gate Keeper, Screamin' Demon*
41	85-0081	1 April 1987	127 BS/184 BW	*Equalizer*
42	85-0082	23 March 1987	9 BS/7 BW	*Gunsmoke, Global Power*
43	85-0083	30 March 1987	77 BS/28 BW	*Dark Star, Overnight Delivery*, unnamed
44	85-0084	17 April 1987	37 BS/28 BW	*Pandora's Box, Brute Force*
45	85-0085	4 May 1987	37 BS/28 BW	*America #1*
46	85-0086	22 April 1987	37 BS/28 BW	*My Mistress, Soaring with Eagles, Intimidator*

47	85-0087	1 May 1987	37 BS/28 BW	*Gremlin, Stars and Stripes*
48	85-0088	22 June 1987	127 BS/184 BW	*Phoenix, Loaded Dice*
49	85-0089	22 June 1987	128 BS/116 BW	*Midnight Prowler*
50	85-0090	14 May 1987	37 BS/28 BW	*Trail Blazer, Tiger Country*
51	85-0091	3 June 1987	77 BS/28 BW	*Thor, unnamed*
52	85-0092	17 June 1987	128 BS/116 BW	*Enforcer, The Uninvited*
53	86-0093	27 July 1987	37 BS/28 BW	*Ruthless Raven, Global Power*
54	86-0094	31 July 1987	37 BS/28 BW	*Night Hawk*
55	86-0095	2 June 1987	127 BS/184 BW	*Mystique, Undecided*
56	86-0096	2 July 1987	37 BS/28 BW	*Thunder Child, Wolf Pack*
57	86-0097	25 June 1987	77 BS/28 BW	*Iron Eagle, unnamed*
58	86-0098	15 July 1987	128 BS/116 BW	*Freedom I*
59	86-0099	3 August 1987	37 BS/28 BW	*Ghost Rider, Iron Eagle*
60	86-0100	20 July 1987	28 BS/7 BW	*Phantom, Night Hawk, Phoenix*
61	86-0101	21 August 1987	28 BS/7 BW	*Iron Butterfly, Low Level Devil, Rage*
62	86-0102	31 August 1987	37 BS/28 BW	*Lady Hawk, Black Hills Sentinel*
63	86-0103	8 September 1987	9 BS/7 BW	*Huntress, Lovely Lady, Reluctant Dragon*
64	86-0104	24 August 1987	77 BS/28 BW	*American Flyer, unnamed*
65	86-0105	24 September 1987	28 BS/7 BW	*Snake Eyes*
66	86-0106	5 September 1987	Crashed	*Lone Wolf; crashed on 30 November 1992*
67	86-0107	26 October 1987	128 BS/116 BW	*Vindicator, Valkyries, Bad to the B-one*
68	86-0108	30 November 1987	28 BS/7 BW	*HAWK, Alien with an Attitude*
69	86-0109	1 October 1987	28 BS/7 BW	*Spectre*
70	86-0110	19 September 1987	28 BS/7 BW	*Sunrise Surprise, Better Duck*
71	86-0111	16 October 1987	77 BS/28 BW	*Ace In The Hole, unnamed*
72	86-0112	28 October 1987	9 BS/7 BW	*Vanna, Black Widow*
73	86-0113	17 November 1987	37 BS/28 BW	*Charon, Viper, Dakota Reveille*
74	86-0114	9 December 1987	37 BS/28 BW	*Wolfhound, Dakota Drifter, Screamin' Eagle*
75	86-0115	5 November 1987	127 BS/184 BW	*Bump And Run, Top Secret*
76	86-0116	2 December 1987	34 BS/366 Wg	*Victress*
77	86-0117	4 December 1987	28 BS/7 BW	*Millennium Falcon, Pride Of North Dakota, Night Stalker*
78	86-0118	18 November 1987	34 BS/366 Wg	*Iron Mistress*
79	86-0119	2 December 1987	28 BS/7 BW	*Spud, Christine*
80	86-0120	22 December 1987	9 BS/7 BW	*Mad Dawg*
81	86-0121	5 January 1988	34 BS/366 Wg	*Exterminator, Terminator, Maiden American*

82	86-0122	12 January 1988	28 BS/7 BW	*Excalibur, No Antidote*
83	86-0123	8 January 1988	9 BS/7 BW	*Molester, Lester, High Noon*
84	86-0124	4 January 1988	128 BS/116 BW	*Penetrator, Winged Thunder*
85	86-0125	4 February 1988	34 BS/366 Wg	*Shack Attack*
86	86-0126	3 February 1988	28 BS/7 BW	*The Gun Fighter, Minotaur, Command Decision, Kansas Lancer*
87	86-0127	5 February 1988	127 BS/184 BW	*Freedom Bird, Ivan's Nightmare, Nightmare, Kansas Lancer*
88	86-0128	5 April 1988	37 BS/28 BW	*The HAWK* (acronym for holiday and weekend killer), *Mis Behavin, Boss, Pony Soldier, Dakota Fury*
89	86-0129	26 February 1988	37 BS/28 BW	*Pegasus, Mad Max*
90	86-0130	3 March 1988	28 BS/7 BW	*The Rose, Bad Company*
91	86-0131	16 March 1988	34 BS/366 Wg	*The 8th's Wonder, Ultimate Warrior*
92	86-0132	20 August 1988	28 BS/7 BW	*The Wizard, Oh! Hard Luck*
93	86-0133	14 April 1988	128 BS/116 BW	*Big Bird, The Outlaw*, unnamed, *Black Hills Bandit*
94	86-0134	24 March 1988	34 BS/366 Wg	*Green Hornet, Night Mission, Wild Ass Ride*
95	86-0135	28 April 1988	9 BS/7 BW	*Make My Day, Watchdog*
96	86-0136	15 April 1988	127 BS/184 BW	*Special Delivery*
97	86-0137	29 April 1988	28 BS/7 BW	*Wichita Express*
98	86-0138	24 April 1988	34 BS/366 Wg	*Easy Rider Too, Grand Illusion II*
99	86-0139	29 April 1988	34 BS/366 Wg	*Gallant Warrior*
100	86-0140	2 May 1988	9 BS/7 BW	*The Valda J* (for Major Valda J. Robbins who flew all 100 B-1B Air Force acceptance flights), *Peace Warrior*

Note: The aircraft names shown above are subject to change as new aircraft commanders are assigned to them. As of late 1998, many B-1Bs were not assigned names since several squadrons (beginning with the 77th BS) no longer wear nose art.

Chronology

13–21 MAY 1921   Bill Mitchell's MB-2 bombers sink a captured German warship, marking the beginning of strategic airpower.

6 AUGUST 1945   A B-29, *Enola Gay*, drops the first atomic bomb on Hiroshima, Japan, forever securing the bomber's position as a strategic weapon.

29 NOVEMBER 1952   The Boeing B-52 Stratofortress makes its first flight.

FEBRUARY 1955   The ARDC issues the WS-110A requirements that would evolve into the XB-70A.

1 MAY 1960   Francis Gary Powers's U-2 is shot down by a Soviet surface-to-air missile or SAM, prompting the United States to start thinking about the dangers of the high-speed, high-altitude bombardment mission.

26 OCTOBER 1962   The last B-52H is delivered to SAC.

21 SEPTEMBER 1964   The first North American XB-70A Valkyrie (62-0001) makes its first flight. The program had already been cancelled as a production bomber.

1961   The first of the post-B-70 design studies (SLAB) is completed.

1964   The first AMSA study results are delivered to the Air Force.

22 SEPTEMBER 1967   North American Aviation, Incorporated, and Rockwell Standard Corporation merged to form the North American Rockwell Corporation.

3 NOVEMBER 1969   The Air Force releases RFPs for the proposed AMSA to Boeing, General Dynamics, and North American Rockwell.

5 JUNE 1970   North American Rockwell receives the B-1A contract, and General Electric Aircraft Engines is contracted to develop the F101 engine.

18 JANUARY 1971   The first of several program reductions is made, reducing the number of flight test B-1As and F101 engines.

18–31 OCTOBER 1971   The full-scale B-1A engineering mock-up review is held.

15 MARCH 1972   Assembly of the first B-1A prototype begins at Palmdale, California.

16 FEBRUARY 1973   The North American Rockwell Corporation merges with the Rockwell Manufacturing Company, forming the Rockwell International Corporation.

4 OCTOBER 1973   Dr. Bisplinghoff delivers a report that both supported and criticized the B-1A program.

26 OCTOBER 1974   The first B-1A prototype (74-0158) rolls out at Palmdale.

23 DECEMBER 1974   The B-1A prototype makes its first flight from Palmdale to Edwards AFB.

1975   AIL is selected to develop the B-1A defensive avionics system.

15 APRIL 1975   The Joint Strategic Bomber Study is delivered to Congress.

16 JANUARY 1976   The third B-1A is rolled out at Palmdale; it will make its first flight on 26 March 1976.

11 MAY 1976   After serving as the structural test aircraft, the second B-1A is rolled out; it will make its first flight on 14 June 1976.

2 DECEMBER 1976   North American receives a production contract for three operational B-1As and long-lead items for eight additional aircraft.

28 JUNE 1977   An AGM-69A SRAM was launched from a B-1A for the first time.

30 JUNE 1977   President James E. "Jimmy" Carter, Jr., cancels the B-1A production program.

5 OCTOBER 1978   A B-1A (74-0159) makes the fastest flight of the program, achieving a speed of Mach 2.22.

30 SEPTEMBER 1979   Rockwell International submits a proposal for the B-1 "Core" aircraft concept.

17 DECEMBER 1978   The fourth B-1A is completed at Palmdale; its first flight is on 14 February 1979.

30 APRIL 1981   The last flight of the B-1A test program is made by the fourth B-1A; it is placed in flyable storage with the other three B-1As.

1 JUNE 1981   The Air Force recommends the B-1 LRCA instead of General Dynamics' proposed FB-111H as the new multirole bomber.

2 OCTOBER 1981   President Ronald Reagan announces his decision to build 100 B-1Bs under the Strategic Modernization Program.

23 MARCH 1983   The second B-1A makes its first flight as part of the B-1B test program.

21 DECEMBER 1983   President Reagan announces that Dyess AFB will be the first B-1B base.

30 JULY 1984   The fourth B-1A makes its first flight as part of the B-1B test program.

29 AUGUST 1984   The second B-1A crashes on a test flight; Doug Benefield is killed and two other crewmembers are injured when the escape capsule partially fails.

4 SEPTEMBER 1984   The first production B-1Bs is rolled out at Palmdale, five months ahead of schedule.

18 OCTOBER 1984   The B-1B makes its first flight from Palmdale.

29 JUNE 1985   The first B-1B is delivered to SAC.

31 OCTOBER 1985   The fourth B-1A makes its last flight and is turned over to the Air Force Museum.

JULY–AUGUST 1986   The B-1B undergoes climatic testing at Eglin AFB.

3 JUNE 1987   A 96th BW conducts the first launch of an AGM-69A SRAM by an operational B-1B squadron.

7 JULY 1987   The B-1B sets 12 world-class closed-circuit speed records.

17 SEPTEMBER 1987   The B-1B sets 18 additional world-class closed-circuit speed records.

28 SEPTEMBER 1987   The first operational B-1B loss results in the death of three crewmembers; three others survive.

29 OCTOBER 1987   The 96th BW passes its first operational readiness inspection (ORI) with the B-1B.

24 NOVEMBER 1987   A B-1B (85-0049) conducts the first test launch of an AGM-86B ALCM; it directly impacted its targeted area on the Utah Test and Training Range.

20 JANUARY 1988   The 100th and last B-1B is rolled out at Palmdale, on budget and ahead of schedule.

APRIL 1988   The combined DT&E and IOT&E test program concludes.

2 MAY 1988   The last B-1B is delivered to the 384th BW at McConnell AFB.

8 NOVEMBER 1988   A B-1B crashes immediately after taking off from Dyess AFB; the crew survives.

17 NOVEMBER 1988   Another B-1B crashes, this time while landing at Ellsworth; again the crew survives.

25 MARCH 1989   Four B-1Bs of the 96th BW deploy to Elmendorf AFB, Alaska, for Giant Warrior 99-3, marking the first B-1B deployment outside the contiguous United States.

15 MARCH 1990   The B-1B is officially named "Lancer"; the crews continue to call it "B-one."

17 JULY 1991   The nonnuclear weapon certification of the B-1B is completed following the successful release of 84 live 500-pound Mk 82 AIR bombs.

28–29 FEBRUARY 1992   The B-1B sets 11 world-class time-to-climb records; a 12th is set on 18 March 1992.

30 NOVEMBER 1992   A B-1B crashes on a low-level night flight near Van Horn, Texas; all four crewmembers are killed.

7 APRIL 1994   The B-1B sets three world-class closed-circuit speed records.

1 JUNE 1994   The B-1B begins an Operational Readiness Assessment (ORA) in preparation for the CMUP program.

1 JULY 1994   The 184th Bomb Wing of the Kansas ANG becomes the first ANG unit to operate a strategic bomber.

1995   The first B-1B is disassembled in accordance with the SALT/START treaties; portions of the airframe are used in JP-8 fire propagation tests.

SEPTEMBER 1996   The first B-1B modified under the CMUP Block C program is delivered to the ACC; all B-1Bs are modified within a year.

6 DECEMBER 1996   The North American Aircraft Operations Division of Rockwell International Corporation is purchased by The Boeing Company, forming Boeing North American.

21 APRIL 1997   B-1Bs drop Mk 62 mines for the first time in support of a Naval exercise.

19 SEPTEMBER 1997   A B-1B crashes in Montana; all four crewmembers are killed.

19 FEBRUARY 1998   A B-1B crashes in Montana; the crew survives.

OCTOBER 1998   The Air Force conducts Y2K testing of the B-1B—it passes.

29 OCTOBER 1998   The first CMUP Block D aircraft is delivered to the 28th BW at Ellsworth; all B-1Bs will be modified by 2001.

18 DECEMBER 1998   Two B-1Bs participate in Operation Desert Fox—marking the B-one's combat debut.

28 MARCH 1999   B-1Bs participate in Operation Allied Force over Serbia and Kosovo.

Acronyms and Abbreviations

A-X	Attack-Experimental (A-9/A-10)
A/W/E	aircraft/weapon/electronic
AAA	antiaircraft artillery
ACC	Air Combat Command
ACM	Advanced Cruise Missile (AGM-129)
ACUC	Avionics Control Unit Complex
AEDC	Arnold Engineering Development Center
AEF	Air Expeditionary Force
AFA	Air Force Anechoic Facility
AFB	Air Force Base
AFCS	automatic flight control system
AFMSS	Air Force Mission Support System
AFOTEC	Air Force Operational Test and Evaluation Center
AFS	avionics flight software
AFSEO	Air Force SEEK EAGLE Office
AI	avionics instructor
AIL	Airborne Instrument Laboratory (Eaton)
AIR	air inflatable retard
ALC	Air Logistics Center
ALCM	Air-Launched Cruise Missile
AMC	Air Mobility Command
AMPSS	Advanced Manned Precision Strike System (1964)
AMSA	Advanced Manned Strategic Aircraft (1967)
ANG	Air National Guard
APU	auxiliary power unit

ARDC	Air Research and Development Command
ARW	Air Refueling Wing
ASD	Aeronautical Systems Division
ATB	Advanced Technology Bomber (B-2)
BG	Bomb Group/Bombardment Group
BNA	Boeing North American
BPE	bomber penetration evaluation
BS	Bomb Squadron/Bombardment Squadron
BS(H)	Bombardment Squadron (Heavy)
BW	Bomb Wing/Bombardment Wing
BW(H)	Bombardment Wing (Heavy)
CALCM	Conventional Air-Launched Cruise Missile
CBU	cluster bomb unit
CCTS	Combat Crew Training Squadron
CEB	combined effects bomblet
CEM	combined effects munition
cg	center-of-gravity
CITS	central integrated test system
CLSS	Combat Logistics Support Squadron
CMUP	Conventional Munitions Upgrade Program
CPB	chemically powered bomber
CRM	cruise missile launcher
CRT	cathode ray tube
CSRL	common strategic rotary launcher
CTF	Combined Test Force
CWM	conventional weapons module
DAS	defensive avionics system
DoD	Department of Defense
DSARC	Defense Systems Acquisition Review Council
DSO	defensive systems operator
DSUP	Defensive System Upgrade Program
DT&E	development, test, and evaluation
DVIC	Defense Visual Information Center
ECM	electronic countermeasures
EMP	electromagnetic pulse
EMUX	electrical multiplex
EOD	external obvious difference
ERSA	Extended Range Strike Aircraft (1963)
EVS	Electro-Optical Viewing System
EXCM	Expendable Countermeasures System
FAI	Federation Aeronautique Internationale
FCGMS	Fuel Center-of-Gravity Management System
FLIR	forward-looking infrared

FLTS	Flight Test Squadron
FMS	Field Maintenance Squadron
FOD	foreign object damage
FOT&E	follow-on test and evaluation
FOTD	fiber optic towed decoy
FSD	full-scale development
FTE	flight test engineer
FY	fiscal year
GAO	General Accounting Office
GE	General Electric
GFE	government-furnished equipment
GHz	gigahertz
GPS	Global Positioning System (NavStar)
HAWK	holiday and weekend killer
HF	high frequency
IBM	International Business Machines
ICBM	intercontinental ballistic missile
IDECM	integrated defensive electric countermeasures
IFAST	Integrated Facility for Avionics System Testing
IIR	imaging infrared
INS	inertial navigation system
IOC	initial operational capability
IOT&E	initial operational test and evaluation
IP	instructor pilot
IR	infrared
JASSM	Joint Air-to-Surface Standoff Missile (AGM-158)
JDAM	Joint Direct Attack Munition (GBU-32)
JSOW	Joint Stand-Off Weapon (AGM-154)
kW	kilowatt
LAMP	Low-Altitude Manned Penetrator (1963)
LRCA	Long-Range Combat Aircraft (1979)
LRIP	low-rate initial production
LRU	line replaceable unit
LWF	Lightweight Fighter (F-16/F-17)
MC	mission capable (rate)
MHz	megahertz
MPRL	multipurpose rotary launcher
NAA	North American Aviation
NACA	National Advisory Committee on Aeronautics
NAR	North American Rockwell
NASA	National Aeronautics and Space Administration
NSBP	National Sonic Boom Program
NVG	night vision goggles

OA	operational assessment
OAS	offensive avionics system
OBOGS	onboard oxygen generating system
OC-ALC	Oklahoma City Air Logistics Center
ODF	Operation Desert Fox (December 1998)
OPEVAL	operational evaluation (Navy)
ORA	operational readiness assessment
ORI	operational readiness inspection
ORS	Offensive Radar System
OSO	offensive systems operator
OT&E	operational test and evaluation
P&W	Pratt & Whitney
PBAR	practice bomb adapter rack
RAAF	Royal Australian Air Force
RAM	radar-absorbing material
RCS	radar cross-section
RF	radio frequency
RFP	request for proposals
RFS/ECMS	Radio Frequency Surveillance/Electronic Countermeasures System
RWR	radar warning receiver
SAB	Scientific Advisory Board (Air Force)
SAC	Strategic Air Command
SALT	Strategic Arms Limitation Talks
SAR	synthetic aperture radar
SATCOM	satellite communications
SBTS	Strategic Bombardment Training Squadron
SCA	Shuttle Carrier Aircraft (NASA)
SFW	Sensor-Fuzed Weapon
SIOP	Single Integrated Operations Plan
SLAB	Subsonic Low Altitude Bomber (1961)
SLBM	submarine launched ballistic missile
SMCS	Structural Mode Control System
SPO	System Program Office
SRAM	Short-Range Attack Missile (AGM-69A)
SRAM II	Short-Range Attack Missile II (AGM-131A)
SST	supersonic transport
START	Strategic Arms Reduction Treaty
TAC	Tactical Air Command
TACAN	tactical air navigation
TDS	towed decoy system
TFR	terrain-following radar
TG	Test Group
TMD	Tactical Munitions Dispenser

TSSAM	Tri-Service Standoff Attack Missile (AGM-137)
TWF	Tail Warning Function (ALQ-161A)
UHF	ultrahigh frequency
UN	United Nations
USAF	United States Air Force
USD/A&T	Undersecretary of Defense for Acquisition and Technology
V/STOL	vertical/short takeoff and landing
VHF	very-high frequency
WCMD	Wind-Corrected Munitions Dispenser
WSO	weapons systems operator
Y2K	year 2000

World Records

The Fédération Aéronautique Internationale (FAI) is the world's air sports federation, and was founded in 1905. It is a nongovernmental and nonprofit international organization with the basic aim of furthering aeronautical and astronautical activities worldwide.

The FAI's new offices in the Olympic capital of Lausanne, Switzerland, were officially inaugurated on 21 January 1999 with a reception attended by IOC Senior Representatives and leading authorities from the Lausanne municipality and Swiss aviation circles.

FAI activities include the establishment of rules for the control and certification of world aeronautical and astronautical records. FAI establishes regulations for air sporting events that are organized by member countries throughout the world. FAI also promotes skill, proficiency and safety in aeronautics. FAI confers medals, diplomas, and other awards to those who have contributed to the achievement of these aims as well as for work done in the restoration of old aircraft. Further information on FAI activities, as well as information on most records, may be found on the Internet at http://www.fai.org.

The FAI has established a wide variety of categories for all types of aerial vehicles. The B-1B falls into the general category C—Aeroplanes, subcategory 1—Landplanes. The overall C-1 category includes all aircraft ("unlimited takeoff weight"), while numerous other weight classes also exist and are designated by a letter suffix (C-1.a is for aircraft with takeoff weights less than 300 kg, etc.). Each category is also broken into "groups" for piston-powered aircraft (group 1), turboprops (2), jets (3), and rockets (4). It should be noted that a single flight can set records in multiple categories (i.e., an aircraft weighing 190,000 kg can set records in C-1 and C-1.q at the same time), or an aircraft carrying a 30,000-kg payload can claim records for 5000-kg payload, 10,000-kg, etc.

The B-1B has set a total of 61 world records that have been recognized by the FAI. Of these, 43 still stood as of February 1999, and they are listed in the following charts. The other 17 records have subsequently been bettered, usually by the Russian Tu-160 Blackjack bomber.

World Closed-Circuit Speed Records

On 4 July 1987, a B-1B (86-0098—*Freedom I*) broke four previously established world records and set 14 new records during "Freedom Flight I." *Freedom I* took off from Palmdale and flew the record-breaking flight in restricted airspace along the Pacific coast off Vandenberg AFB, California. The B-1B flew 2000 km (1246 miles) with a payload of 30,000 kg (66,140 pounds), breaking records for 1000 km and 2000 km at a variety of payload weights. The record run was made during an acceptance test flight, and water contained in weapons bay auxiliary tanks was used as the payload. The crew consisted of pilots Lieutenant Colonel Robert Chamberlain and Captain Michael Waters, OSO Major Richard Fisher, and DSO Captain Nathan Gray.

Two of the records had been held since 1959 by a four-engine Soviet "103M" bomber. The other two existing records had been set in 1962 by a C-135. Four of the new records were bettered on 22 May 1990 by a Russian Tu-160 Blackjack.

On 17 September 1987, another B-1B (86-0110—*Sunrise Surprise*) broke nine previously established world records and set nine new records during "Freedom Flight II." *Sunrise Surprise* took off from Palmdale, entered the closed course for the record flight over Edwards AFB, and flew the record-breaking flight north along the Pacific coast to Washington State, then turned southeast to fly across Oregon, Idaho, Utah, and Colorado before it turned west back to Edwards. In setting the records, the B-1B traveled 5000 km (3116 miles) with a payload of 30,000 kg (66,140 pounds). The nine existing records were in class C-1.q, while the nine new records were in the unlimited weight class C-1.

Five of the nine existing records had been established by B-52 and KC-135 aircraft carrying payloads up to 10,000 kg (22,047 pounds) at speeds up to 596 mph. The remaining four existing records had been set by a Soviet IL-76 transport carrying payloads from 15,000 to 30,000 kg (33,071 to 66,140 pounds) at 507 mph. The crew on this flight consisted of pilots Lieutenant Colonel Robert Chamberlain and Major Brent Hedgpeth, OSO Captain Alexander F. J. Ivanchishin, and DSO Captain Daniel J. Novick. Both of the record-setting B-1Bs had just come off the production line and were not modified for the flights.

Sub-class C-1 (Unlimited Takeoff Weight), Group 3 (Jet Engines)

Type of Record	Date	Site/Course	Performance
Speed over a closed circuit of 5000 km without a payload	17 September 1987	Palmdale, Calif.	1054.21 km/h (655.1 mph)
Speed over a closed circuit of 5000 km with a 1000-kg payload	17 September 1987	Palmdale, Calif.	1054.21 km/h (655.1 mph)
Speed over a closed circuit of 5000 km with a 2000-kg payload	17 September 1987	Palmdale, Calif.	1054.21 km/h (655.1 mph)
Speed over a closed circuit of 5000 km with a 5000-kg payload	17 September 1987	Palmdale, Calif.	1054.21 km/h (655.1 mph)
Speed over a closed circuit of 5000 km with a 10,000-kg payload	17 September 1987	Palmdale, Calif.	1054.21 km/h (655.1 mph)
Speed over a closed circuit of 5000 km with a 15,000-kg payload	17 September 1987	Palmdale, Calif.	1054.21 km/h (655.1 mph)
Speed over a closed circuit of 5000 km with a 20,000-kg payload	17 September 1987	Palmdale, Calif.	1054.21 km/h (655.1 mph)
Speed over a closed circuit of 5000 km with a 25,000-kg payload	17 September 1987	Palmdale, Calif.	1054.21 km/h (655.1 mph)
Speed over a closed circuit of 5000 km with a 30,000-kg payload	17 September 1987	Palmdale, Calif.	1054.21 km/h (655.1 mph)

Sub-class C-1.q (Takeoff Weight 150,000 to Less than 200,000 kg), Group 3 (Jet Engines)

Type of Record	Date	Site/Course	Performance
Speed over a closed circuit of 1000 km with a 5000-kg payload	4 July 1987	Palmdale, Calif.	1089.36 km/h (676.9 mph)
Speed over a closed circuit of 1000 km with a 10,000-kg payload	4 July 1987	Palmdale, Calif.	1089.36 km/h (676.9 mph)
Speed over a closed circuit of 1000 km with a 15,000-kg payload	4 July 1987	Palmdale, Calif.	1089.36 km/h (676.9 mph)
Speed over a closed circuit of 1000 km with a 20,000-kg payload	4 July 1987	Palmdale, Calif.	1089.36 km/h (676.9 mph)
Speed over a closed circuit of 1000 km with a 25,000-kg payload	4 July 1987	Palmdale, Calif.	1089.36 km/h (676.9 mph)
Speed over a closed circuit of 1000 km with a 30,000-kg payload	4 July 1987	Palmdale, Calif.	1089.36 km/h (676.9 mph)
Speed over a closed circuit of 2000 km with a 5000-kg payload	4 July 1987	Palmdale, Calif.	1078.20 km/h (670.0 mph)
Speed over a closed circuit of 2000 km with a 10,000-kg payload	4 July 1987	Palmdale, Calif.	1078.20 km/h (670.0 mph)
Speed over a closed circuit of 2000 km with a 15,000-kg payload	4 July 1987	Palmdale, Calif.	1078.20 km/h (670.0 mph)
Speed over a closed circuit of 2000 km with a 20,000-kg payload	4 July 1987	Palmdale, Calif.	1078.20 km/h (670.0 mph)
Speed over a closed circuit of 2000 km with a 25,000-kg payload	4 July 1987	Palmdale, Calif.	1078.20 km/h (670.0 mph)
Speed over a closed circuit of 2000 km with a 30,000-kg payload	4 July 1987	Palmdale, Calif.	1078.20 km/h (670.0 mph)
Speed over a closed circuit of 5000 km without a payload	17 September 1987	Palmdale, Calif.	1054.21 km/h (655.1 mph)
Speed over a closed circuit of 5000 km with a 1000-kg payload	17 September 1987	Palmdale, Calif.	1054.21 km/h (655.1 mph)
Speed over a closed circuit of 5000 km with a 2000-kg payload	17 September 1987	Palmdale, Calif.	1054.21 km/h (655.1 mph)
Speed over a closed circuit of 5000 km with a 5000-kg payload	17 September 1987	Palmdale, Calif.	1054.21 km/h (655.1 mph)
Speed over a closed circuit of 5000 km with a 10,000-kg payload	17 September 1987	Palmdale, Calif.	1054.21 km/h (655.1 mph)
Speed over a closed circuit of 5000 km with a 15,000-kg payload	17 September 1987	Palmdale, Calif.	1054.21 km/h (655.1 mph)
Speed over a closed circuit of 5000 km with a 20,000-kg payload	17 September 1987	Palmdale, Calif.	1054.21 km/h (655.1 mph)
Speed over a closed circuit of 5000 km with a 25,000-kg payload	17 September 1987	Palmdale, Calif.	1054.21 km/h (655.1 mph)
Speed over a closed circuit of 5000 km with a 30,000-kg payload	17 September 1987	Palmdale, Calif.	1054.21 km/h (655.1 mph)

In August 1988, the Air Force Chief of Staff, General Larry Welch, presented the 1988 MacKay Trophy to representatives of the Air Force Contract Management Division Detachment 15 (the Air Force Plant 42 Representative Office, which oversaw Rockwell's B-1B operations), and to the B-1 SPO in recognition of the two B-1B world record-setting flights. This prestigious trophy, which dates back to 1912 with the Army Air Corps, is presented each year to an Air Force individual or group for carrying out "the most meritorious flight or flights of the year." Past recipients include such notable figures as Hap Arnold, Jimmy Doolittle, and Chuck Yeager. For the 1988 award, General Welch selected the Air Force team responsible for the B-1B flights that captured 36 world records for distance and payload on 4 July 1987 and 17 September 1987.

On 7 April 1994, a pair of B-1Bs from the 46th BS captured two world closed-course speed records that had been held by a B-52D since 1958. These records recorded the time necessary to complete a 10,000-km (6214-mile) course. Nine other records were also captured during the flights. The flight for the 150,000–200,000-kg class was accomplished in 10

Sub-class C-1 (Unlimited Takeoff Weight), Group 3 (Jet Engines)

Type of Record	Date	Site/Course	Performance
Speed over a recognized course	7 April 1994	Grand Forks, N.D. to Monroeville, Ala.	1008.37 km/h (626.5 mph)
Speed over a recognized course	7 April 1994	Monroeville, Ala. to Grand Forks, N.D.	956.42 km/h (594.2 mph)
Speed over a recognized course	7 April 1994	Monroeville, Ala. to Mullan, Ind.	920.72 km/h (572.0 mph)
Speed over a recognized course	7 April 1994	Mullan, Ind. to Monroeville, Ala.	993.93 km/h (617.5 mph)
Speed over a closed circuit of 10,000 km without a payload	7 April 1994	Grand Forks, N.D. to Monroeville, Ala. to Mullan, Ind.	956.93 km/h (594.6 mph)

Sub-class C-1.q (Takeoff Weight 150,000 to Less than 200,000 kg), Group 3 (Jet Engines)

Type of Record	Date	Site/Course	Performance
Speed over a recognized course	7 April 1994	Mullan, Ind. to Monroeville, Ala.	976.48 km/h (606.7 mph)
Speed over a recognized course	7 April 1994	Grand Forks, N.D. to Monroeville, Ala.	1010.46 km/h (627.8 mph)
Speed over a closed circuit of 10,000 km without a payload	7 April 1994	Grand Forks, N.D. to Monroeville, Ala. to Mullan, Ind.	956.93 km/h (594.6 mph)

Sub-class C-1.r (Takeoff Weight 200,000 to Less than 250,000 kg), Group 3 (Jet Engines)

Type of Record	Date	Site/Course	Performance
Speed over a recognized course	7 April 1994	Monroeville, Ala. to Grand Forks, N.D.	948.32 km/h (589.2 mph)
Speed over a recognized course	7 April 1994	Monroeville, Ala. to Mullan, Ind.	920.72 km/h (572.0 mph)
Speed over a closed circuit of 10,000 km without a payload	7 April 1994	Grand Forks, N.D. to Monroeville, Ala. to Mullan, Ind.	956.93 km/h (594.6 mph)

hours, 27 minutes, 34 seconds. The unlimited class (no weight limits) flight lasted 10 hours, 22 minutes, 20 seconds.

Time-to-Climb Records

On 28–29 February 1992, two B-1Bs (86-0111—*Ace in the Hole* and 86-0121—*Terminator*) flying out of Grand Forks AFB set 11 world-class time-to-climb records. A 12th record was set on 18 March. All four of the class C-1.o and three of the class C-1.p records had been previously set by a KC-135R of the 384th Wing from McConnell AFB. The fourth class C-1.p record was set by a Douglas DC-10 commercial transport. All four of the class C-1.q records had not previously been attempted.

Three crews, made up of an aircraft commander, copilot, and an OSO, from the 319th Wing were used to set the records. The DSO position was occupied on all 12 flights by an official of the National Aeronautic Association who was on board to certify the record. The first crew was made up of pilots Lieutenant Colonel Bill Moran (46th BS Commander and former B-1 CTF test pilot) and Captain Mark Eby and OSO Captain Rich Nehls. The second crew was made up of pilots Lieutenant Colonel Jim Robinson and Captain Scott Neumann and OSO Captain Jerry Murphy. The third crew was made up of pilots Captain Jeff Smith and Captain Tracy Sharp and OSO Captain Bryan Ferguson.

The profiles for the flights all started from a static takeoff. The wheel brakes were held while all four engines were accelerated to minimum afterburner. Once the engines had stabilized, the brakes were released and the throttles advanced to maximum afterburner. The engines were left in maximum afterburner throughout the climb.

Sub-class C-1.o (Takeoff Weight 80,000 to Less than 91,000 kg), Group 3 (Jet Engines)

Type of Record	Date	Site/Course	Performance
Time-to-climb to 3,000 m	28 February 1992	Grand Forks AFB, N.D.	1 minute, 13 seconds
Time-to-climb to 6,000 m	28 February 1992	Grand Forks AFB, N.D.	1 minute, 42 seconds
Time-to-climb to 9,000 m	28 February 1992	Grand Forks AFB, N.D.	2 minutes, 11 seconds
Time-to-climb to 12,000 m	28 February 1992	Grand Forks AFB, N.D.	5 minutes, 2 seconds

Sub-class C-1.p (Takeoff Weight 100,000 to Less than 150,000 kg), Group 3 (Jet Engines)

Type of Record	Date	Site/Course	Performance
Time-to-climb to 3000 m	28 February 1992	Grand Forks AFB, N.D.	1 minute, 19 seconds
Time-to-climb to 6000 m	28 February 1992	Grand Forks AFB, N.D.	1 minute, 55 seconds
Time-to-climb to 9000 m	28 February 1992	Grand Forks AFB, N.D.	2 minutes, 23 seconds
Time-to-climb to 12,000 m	28 February 1992	Grand Forks AFB, N.D.	6 minutes, 9 seconds

Sub-class C-1.q (Takeoff Weight 150,000 to Less than 200,000 kg), Group 3 (Jet Engines)

Type of Record	Date	Site/Course	Performance
Time-to-climb to 3000 m	29 February 1992	Grand Forks AFB, N.D.	2 minutes, 0 seconds
Time-to-climb to 6000 m	29 February 1992	Grand Forks AFB, N.D.	2 minutes, 39 seconds
Time-to-climb to 9000 m	29 February 1992	Grand Forks AFB, N.D.	3 minutes, 48 seconds
Time-to-climb to 12,000 m	18 March 1992	Grand Forks AFB, N.D.	9 minutes, 42 seconds

For the climbs to 3000 m (9843 feet) in all three classes, the wings were left at 25° during the climb. After the aircraft accelerated and the flaps and slats were retracted, the aircraft was pulled up to a pitch angle of 35° and zoomed to the altitude. After passing the 3000-m altitude, the aircraft was rolled 120° and recovered to level flight.

For the climbs to 6000 m (19,686 feet) and 9000 m (29,529 feet) in all three weight classes, the wings were swept to 55° after the flaps and slats were retracted. The aircraft was then zoomed with 20° pitch to Mach 0.9 after which it was pulled up to 30° pitch, holding approximately 1.2-g during the climb to altitude. The recovery technique was the same as used for 3000 m.

For the climbs to 12,000 m (39,372 feet) in all three weight classes, the wings were swept to 67.5° after the flaps and slats were retracted. The aircraft was then accelerated with 5° pitch to Mach 0.9 at 25,000 feet, then pitched down 7° until it reached Mach 1.2. A climb was initiated holding Mach 1.2 to 38,000 feet, then pitched up to zoom through the 12,000-m altitude. The climb to 12,000 m at the high gross weight was postponed until 18 March 1992 due to unseasonably high temperatures at altitude in the Grand Forks area on 28–29 February.

Coronet Bat

Two B-1Bs (84-0057—*Hellion* and 85-0082—*Global Power*) completed a nonstop around-the-world flight on 3 June 1995 during "Exercise Coronet Bat." The flight originated at Dyess AFB was routed over the North Atlantic Ocean, through the Straits of Gibraltar, across the Mediterranean Sea to the Indian Ocean, then north over the Pacific Ocean to the Aleutian Islands, and back to Dyess. The aircraft conducted successful bombing practice missions over Italy, the Western Pacific, and the Utah Test and Training Range. The aircraft covered 22,866 miles during the 36 hour, 13 minute flight. Both aircraft required only minor routine maintenance after landing.

Sub-class C-1 (Unlimited Takeoff Weight), Group 3 (Jet Engines)

Type of Record	Date	Site/Course	Performance
Speed around the world, eastbound, with refueling in flight	3 June 1995	Abilene, Tex., and return	1015.76 km/h (631.9 mph)

Sub-class C-1.q (Takeoff Weight 150,000 to Less than 200,000 kg), Group 3 (Jet Engines)

Type of Record	Date	Site/Course	Performance
Speed around the world, eastbound, with refueling in flight	3 June 1995	Abilene, Tex., and return	1015.76 km/h (631.9 mph)

ACC (*see* Air Combat Command)

ACES II (*see* Ejection seat)

Advanced Cruise Missile (*see* AGM-129)

Advanced Manned Precision Strike System, 22, 37

Advanced Manned Strategic Aircraft, 22–24, 37

Advanced Technology Bomber (*see* B-2)

AEDC (*see* Arnold Engineering Development Center)

AFAF (*see* Air Force Anechoic Facility)

AFCS (*see* Automatic flight control system)

AFOTEC (*see* Air Force Operational Test and Evaluation Center)

AGM-69A, 44, 60, 83, 140–143, 148

AGM-69B (*see* AGM-131A)

AGM-86, 46, 59, 139–140, 148, 150, 160

AGM-109, 59, 150

AGM-129, 139–141, 150

AGM-131A, 146

AGM-137, 158

AGM-154, 121, 130, 139, 150, 157

AGM-158, 121, 130, 150, 159

AIL (*see* Airborne Instrument Laboratory)

AIR (*see* Mk 8x bomb)
  (*See also* Mk 36)

Air Combat Command, 85, 111, 120, 133

Air Expeditionary Force, 87

Air Force Anechoic Facility, 68

Air Force Operational Test and Evaluation Center, 67, 121–122

Air Force Plant 42, 42, 44
  Site 3, 15, 36, 65
  Site 9, 65–66

Air-Launched Cruise Missile, 44
  (*See also* AGM-86)

Air National Guard, 85, 119

Airborne Instrument Laboratory, 30, 32, 41, 61–63, 117

ALCM (*see* AGM-86)
  carrier (*see* Cruise missile launcher)

ALE-50, 90, 108, 118, 132

Allied Force (*see* Operation Allied Force)

ALQ-161, 41, 45, 52, 55, 61–63, 72, 75, 90, 105–107, 110, 116–118, 132

ALR-56, 107–108, 118, 132

AMPSS (*see* Advanced Manned Precision Strike System)

AMSA (*see* Advanced Manned Strategic Aircraft)

ANG (*see* Air National Guard)

AP-101, 104, 106, 117, 130

APQ-146, 51

APQ-164, 104

APU (*see* Auxiliary power unit)

Arnold Engineering Development Center, 28, 46

ASQ-156, 51

ASQ-184, 52, 103, 105, 116

ATB (*see* B-2)

Attrition reserve, 119

Automatic flight control system, 51, 103

Autonetics, 26, 30

Auxiliary fuel tank (*see* Weapons bay auxiliary fuel tank)

Auxiliary power unit, 48–49, 100

B-1 Combined Test Force, 42, 64, 75, 140, 148

B-1 SPO, 26, 28, 30, 35–36, 64, 70–71, 74

B-1A:
  contract award, 26–27, 36
  contract cancellation, 44–46, 55
  description, 26–40
  first flights, 42, 44–45, 63
  IOC, 30
  mock-up, 32
  static test airframe, 27, 30, 37

B-1B:
  contract award, 62, 65
  crashes, 68–69, 114–116
  differences from B-1A, 62–64, 72, 92, 97, 101, 110
  first flights, 63–64
  IOC, 59, 62, 116
  named Lancer, 67

B-2, 59–61, 119–120, 146, 150

B-52, 7–10, 15, 22, 24, 26–30, 38–40, 48, 59–60, 63, 119–120, 137, 143

B-58, 7, 10, 24

B-70 (*see* XB-70)

B28, 136, 140–141

B61, 60, 67, 136, 140–142

B83, 60, 67, 136, 140–142

BAC-111 (*see* Support aircraft)

BDU-xx (*see* Practice bombs)

Bisplinghoff, Raymond L., 37–38

Boeing, 11

Boeing 747 (*see* Cruise missile launcher)

Bomber penetration evaluation, 61

Bush, George H. W., 146

C-5 (*see* Cruise missile launcher)

CALCM (*see* AGM-86)

Carter, Jimmy, 44

CBU-87, 122, 151, 154

CBU-89, 122, 151, 155

CBU-97, 122–123, 151, 155–157
CEM (*see* CBU-87)
Central Integrated Test System, 48, 51, 103, 113
Chemically powered bomber, 11–13
CITS (*see* Central Integrated Test System)
Climatic Laboratory (*see* McKinley Climatic Laboratory)
Cluster bomb unit (*see* CBU entries)
CMUP (*see* Conventional Munitions Upgrade Program)
Combined effects munition (*see* CBU-87)
Combined Test Force (*see* B-1 Combined Test Force)
Common strategic rotary launcher, 137, 150
Conventional Air-Launched Cruise Missile (*see* AGM-86)
Conventional bombs (*see* Mk 8x bomb)
Conventional Munitions Upgrade Program, 118–122, 139
Conventional weapons module, 123–124, 130, 139, 150–157
Core aircraft concept, 57
CPB (*see* Chemically powered bomber)
Crosseye (*see* Kuras Alterman Crosseye)
Cruise missile launcher, 38–39, 58–59, 137
CSRL (*see* Common strategic rotary launcher)
CTF (*see* B-1 Combined Test Force)
Curtiss-Wright, 11, 24
CWM (*see* Conventional weapons module)

DAS (*see* ALQ-161)
Defense Systems Acquisition Review Council, 28, 44
Defensive avionics system (*see* ALQ-161)
Defensive System Upgrade Program, 107, 118, 132
Defensive systems operator, 50, 84, 93, 104, 107, 110, 117
Desert Fox (*see* Operation Desert Fox)
Desert Storm (*see* Operation Desert Storm)
Development, test, and evaluation, 28, 67
Distance records (*see* Fédération Aéronautique Internationale)
DSARC (*see* Defense Systems Acquisition Review Council)

DSO (*see* Defensive systems operator) (*See also* Weapons systems operator)
DSUP (*see* Defensive System Upgrade Program)
DT&E (*see* Development, test, and evaluation)

Ejection seat:
B-1A, 45, 50
B-1B, 93
change from escape capsule, 35, 45, 51
Electro-Optical Viewing System, 51
Electromagnetic pulse (EMP), 22, 69–70
EOD (*see* External obvious difference)
ERSA (*see* Extended Range Strike Aircraft)
Escape capsule, 35, 38, 45, 50
change to ejection seat, 35, 45, 51
EVS (*see* Electro-Optical Viewing System)
Expendable Countermeasures System (EXCM), 109–110
Extended Range Strike Aircraft, 21
External obvious difference, 150, 152
External pylons, 51, 92, 135, 139, 149–150

F-4 (*see* Support aircraft)
F-106 (*see* Support aircraft)
F-111 (*see* Support aircraft) (*See also* FB-111)
F101, 48, 72, 99, 116
contract award, 27, 36, 62
FAI (*see* Fédération Aéronautique Internationale)
FB-111, 10, 24, 26, 29–30, 35, 38–40, 48, 59–61, 143
Fédération Aéronautique Internationale, 179
speed records, 180–183
time-to-climb records, 183–184
Fiber optic towed decoy (*see* ALE-50)
Flight test engineer, 50
FLIR (*see* Forward-looking infrared)
Follow-on test and evaluation, 67
Forward-looking infrared, 51
FOT&E (*see* Follow-on test and evaluation)
FOTD (*see* ALE-50)
FTE (*see* Flight test engineer)

GAO (*see* General Accounting Office)
GBU-32, 75, 121, 125, 139, 153
GE (*see* General Electric) (*See also* F101)

General Accounting Office, 40, 117–119
General Electric, 11, 13, 14, 24, 26, 27, 37
Global Positioning System (GPS), 74, 121, 124, 153
Griffiss AFB (*see* Rome Laboratory)

Hughes, 24

IBM (*see* International Business Machines)
ICBM (*see* Intercontinental ballistic missile)
IDECM (*see* Integrated defensive electric countermeasures)
IFAST (*see* Integrated Facility for Avionics System Testing)
Initial operational test and evaluation, 28, 44, 67
Integrated defensive electric countermeasures, 108–109, 118, 132
Integrated Facility for Avionics System Testing, 62
Intercontinental ballistic missile, 11–14, 21, 44
International Business Machines, 14, 24, 26, 30
IOC:
B-1A, 30
B-1B, 59, 62, 116
IOT&E (*see* Initial operational test and evaluation)

JASSM (*see* AGM-158)
JDAM (*see* GBU-32)
Johnson, Lyndon B., 23
Joint Air-to-Surface Standoff Missile (*see* AGM-158)
Joint Direct Attack Munition (*see* GBU-32)
Joint Stand-Off Weapon (*see* AGM-154)
Joint Strategic Bomber Study, 38–40, 59
JSOW (*see* AGM-154)
Junior Crown (*see* Project Junior Crown)

Kennedy, John F., 14
Kirtland AFB, EMP facility, 69–70
Kuras Alterman Crosseye, 46, 55

Laird, Melvin R., 26
LAMP (*see* Low-Altitude Manned Penetrator)
Lancer, origins of name (*see* B-1B, named Lancer)

LeMay, Gen. Curtis E., 4, 7, 10, 23, 82–83
Long-Range Combat Aircraft, 59, 61
Low-Altitude Manned Penetrator, 21–22
LRCA (*see* Long-Range Combat Aircraft)

MC [*see* Mission capable (rate)]
McKinley Climatic Laboratory, 67
McLucas, John L., 36, 38
McNamara, Robert S., 14, 22–27, 44
Mine (*see* Mk 62)
Mission capable (rate), 119, 121–122
Mitchell, Gen. William Lendrum "Billy," 1–4
Mk 36, 151–152
Mk 62, 86, 159
Mk 8x bomb, 67, 89, 124–125, 139, 151
Multipurpose rotary launcher (MPRL), 130, 136, 139, 142, 153, 159–160

NAVSTAR (*see* Global Positioning System)
Night vision goggles, 120
Nixon, Richard M., 26, 44
North American Rockwell, creation of, 26
Nuclear bombs (*see* B61)
  (*See also* B28; B83)
NVG (*see* Night vision goggles)

OA (*see* Operational assessment)
OAS (*see* ASQ-156)
OBOGS (*see* Onboard oxygen generating system)
Offensive avionics system (*see* ASQ-156)
Offensive Radar System (*see* APQ-164)
Offensive systems operator, 50, 93, 104
Onboard oxygen generating system, 48
Operation Allied Force, 90
Operation Desert Fox, 87–89, 133
Operation Desert Storm, 117, 120
Operational assessment, 125
Operational readiness assessment, 121
Operational readiness inspection, 83
Operational test and evaluation, 67
ORA (*see* Operational readiness assessment)
ORI (*see* Operational readiness inspection)
OSO (*see* Offensive systems operator)
  (*See also* Weapons systems operator)
OT&E (*see* Operational test and evaluation)

P&W (*see* Pratt & Whitney)
Packard, David, 26, 28
Paint schemes, 109–110
PBAR (*see* Practice bomb adapter rack)
Plant 42 (*see* Air Force Plant 42)
Power, Gen. Thomas S., 21
Practice bomb adapter rack, 160
Practice bombs, 137, 142, 159
Pratt & Whitney, 11, 24, 26
Production tools, 66
Project focus, 28–29, 36
Project forecast, 22
Project Junior Crown, 30

Quickstrike mine (*see* Mk 62)

Radar-absorbing material, 60, 69, 100
Radar cross-section, 32, 39, 40, 48, 60, 62
Radar warning receiver (*see* ALQ-161) (*See also* ALR-56)
RAM (*see* Radar-absorbing material)
RCS (*see* Radar cross-section)
RFS/ECMS (*see* ALQ-161)
Rockwell International, creation of, 36
Rolls-Royce (engines), 11
Rome Laboratory, 70–75
RS-70 (*see* XB-70)

SALT (*see* Strategic Arms Limitation Talks)
Seamans, Robert C., Jr., 26, 28–29, 36
Sensor-Fuzed Weapon (SFW) (*see* CBU-97)
747 (*see* Cruise missile launcher)
Short-Range Attack Missile (*see* AGM-69A)
Single Integrated Operations Plan (SIOP), 82, 85
Site 3 (*see* Air Force Plant 42, Site 3)
Site 9 (*see* Air Force Plant 42, Site 9)
SLAB (*see* Subsonic Low Altitude Bomber)
SMCS (*see* Structural Mode Control System)
Speed records (*see* Fédération Aéronautique Internationale)
SPO (*see* B-1 SPO)
SRAM (*see* AGM-69A)
SRAM II (*see* AGM-131A)
SRAM-B (*see* AGM-131A)
SRAM rotary launcher, 137
SST (*see* Supersonic transport)
START (*see* Strategic Arms Reduction Treaty)

Strategic Arms Limitation Talks, 136, 141, 150
Strategic Arms Reduction Treaty, 65, 136, 139, 161
Structural Mode Control System, 48, 98
Subsonic Low Altitude Bomber, 21
Supersonic transport, 12, 15, 17, 19
Support aircraft, 63, 75, 82
SUU-65, 154–155
System Program Office (*see* B-1 SPO)

Tactical Munitions Dispenser (*see* SUU-65)
Tail Warning Function (*see* ALQ-161)
TDS (*see* ALE-50)
Terrain-following radar (TFR) (*see* APQ-146)
Time-to-climb records (*see* Fédération Aéronautique Internationale)
TMD (*see* SUU-65)
Tomahawk (*see* AGM-109) (*See also* AGM-86)
Towed decoy system (*see* ALE-50)
Trestle (*see* Kirtland AFB, EMP facility)
Tri-Service Standoff Attack Missile (TSSAM) (*see* AGM-137)
TWF (*see* ALQ-161)

Undersecretary of Defense for Acquisition and Technology (USD/A&T), 67, 118, 125, 159

Valkyrie (*see* XB-70)

WCMD (*see* Wind-Corrected Munitions Dispenser)
Weapons bay auxiliary fuel tank, 101, 160
Weapons systems operator, 93, 107 (*See also* Defensive systems operator; Offensive systems operator)
Wind-Corrected Munitions Dispenser, 130, 150, 157
World records (*see* Fédération Aéronautique Internationale)
WS-110A (*see* XB-70)
WSO (*see* Weapons systems operator)

XB-70, 10–19, 21

YC-141A (*see* Support aircraft)
Year 2000, 74
YF101 (*see* F101)
Y2K (*see* Year 2000)

Dennis R. Jenkins has been a senior engineer/manager in the aerospace industry for more than 20 years. For corporations such as Lockheed Martin, he has worked on projects that included the Space Shuttle, the Ballistic Missile Early Warning System, X-33/VentureStar™, and the National Airspace System (FAA). The author of several books on air- and spacecraft, he has degrees in both computer engineering and R&D systems management.